Eddie Cicotte

ALSO BY DAVID L. FLEITZ
AND FROM MCFARLAND

Rowdy Patsy Tebeau and the Cleveland Spiders: Fighting to the Bottom of Baseball, 1887–1899 (2017)

Napoleon Lajoie: King of Ballplayers (2013)

Silver Bats and Automobiles: The Hotly Competitive, Sometimes Ignoble Pursuit of the Major League Batting Championship (2011)

The Irish in Baseball: An Early History (2009)

More Ghosts in the Gallery: Another Sixteen Little-Known Greats at Cooperstown (2007)

Cap Anson: The Grand Old Man of Baseball (2005)

Ghosts in the Gallery at Cooperstown: Sixteen Little-Known Members of the Hall of Fame (2004)

Louis Sockalexis: The First Cleveland Indian (2002)

Shoeless: The Life and Times of Joe Jackson (2001)

Eddie Cicotte
The Life and Career of the Banned Black Sox Pitcher

DAVID L. FLEITZ

McFarland & Company, Inc., Publishers
Jefferson, North Carolina

LIBRARY OF CONGRESS CATALOGUING-IN-PUBLICATION DATA

Names: Fleitz, David L., 1955– author.
Title: Eddie Cicotte : the life and career of the banned black sox pitcher / David L. Fleitz.
Description: Jefferson, North Carolina : McFarland & Company, Inc., Publishers, 2020. | Includes bibliographical references and index.
Identifiers: LCCN 2020035365 | ISBN 9781476680194 (paperback : acid free paper) ∞
ISBN 9781476640037 (ebook)
Subjects: LCSH: Cicotte, Edward (Edward V.) | Chicago White Sox (Baseball team) | Pitchers (Baseball)—United States—Biography.
Classification: LCC GV865.C4363 F54 2020 | DDC 796.357092 [B]—dc23
LC record available at https://lccn.loc.gov/2020035365

BRITISH LIBRARY CATALOGUING DATA ARE AVAILABLE

ISBN (print) 978-1-4766-8019-4
ISBN (ebook) 978-1-4766-4003-7

© 2020 David L. Fleitz. All rights reserved

No part of this book may be reproduced or transmitted in any form or by any means, electronic or mechanical, including photocopying or recording, or by any information storage and retrieval system, without permission in writing from the publisher.

Front cover: Chicago White Sox pitcher Eddie Cicotte in 1917 (Library of Congress)

Printed in the United States of America

*McFarland & Company, Inc., Publishers
Box 611, Jefferson, North Carolina 28640
www.mcfarlandpub.com*

Acknowledgments

I would like to thank a few people and organizations that helped make this book possible.

Research on the Black Sox Scandal has boomed in recent years, thanks in large part to the Chicago History Museum and its Black Sox collection. This collection holds copies of original court documents and correspondence from Black Sox–related legal proceedings, as well as player contracts, detective reports, depositions, and the like. Outstanding researchers such as Jacob Pomrenke, Bob Hoie, Gene Carney, William F. Lamb, and many others in the Society for American Baseball Research (SABR) have used this collection to expand our knowledge of the scandal and the people involved, including Eddie Cicotte. This biography would not be possible without their efforts, and I have credited them in the text and footnotes of my book.

Eliot Asinof wrote the best-selling novelization of the scandal, titled *Eight Men Out*, in 1963. Asinof was the man who brought attention to the Black Sox and made a household name of Shoeless Joe Jackson. I had the privilege of talking to Asinof on the phone in February of 2000. We now know that many of his assumptions and assertions about the scandal, and about Eddie Cicotte, were not correct, but he did not have access to the treasure trove of material that we have now. Nonetheless, Asinof was the man who told the story of the 1919 World Series fix, and later writers have built upon his work.

A terrific website called Baseball Reference (http://www.baseball-reference.com) provides player game logs, box scores, and play-by-play descriptions. Sean Forman and his team deserve a great deal of credit for developing this constantly expanding resource, and this book would have been much more difficult to write without it.

Another website, Project Retrosheet was founded in 1989 for the purpose of providing computerized play-by-play data for as many games as possible. It has blossomed into a site filled with useful information and is highly recommended as well. The statistics in this book come from Project Retrosheet, which in return asks only that the user include this statement: *The information used here was obtained free of charge from and is copy-*

righted by Retrosheet. Interested parties may contact Retrosheet at www.retrosheet.org.

Other helpful web sites include Newspapers.com, with digitized and searchable images of long-ago newspapers, and Paper of Record, which features images of *The Sporting News* beginning with its inaugural issue in 1886. The Brooklyn Public Library has digitized the *Brooklyn Eagle* from the years 1841 to 1902, and the LA84 Foundation, endowed with funds left over from the 1984 Olympic Games in Los Angeles, maintains a digital archive of *Sporting Life* and *Baseball Magazine* for the 1885 to 1920 period. Also, the Library of Congress has a collection called "American Memory" (at http://www.loc.gov) that shows images of baseball cards issued between 1887 and 1914, and those images are valuable as well.

Another good source of information is Google Books (http://www.google.com). This archive is free and extremely useful to any sports researcher. SABR maintains a site called BioProject (http://bioproj.sabr.org), to which I have contributed several articles. BioProject has posted several thousand biographies of major league players of the past and the present, and the information found there has been highly useful as well. Also, SABR's Black Sox Scandal Committee newsletter features the latest research by the best writers and historians, and appears twice a year.

Finally, I would like to thank my brother Bob, the family genealogist. Eddie Cicotte and I are both descended from French Canadians who settled in Michigan during the 1700s, and Bob informs me that I am, in fact, Eddie Cicotte's third cousin three times removed.

Table of Contents

Acknowledgments   v
Introduction   1

1. The Beginning   3
2. Boston   14
3. Chicago   27
4. Career Rejuvenation   39
5. The Championship Season   51
6. War and Turmoil   68
7. The 1919 Season   79
8. The 1919 World Series   96
9. The 1920 Season   109
10. The Walls Close In   122
11. The Trial   140
12. Outlaw Ball   155
13. Later Life   166

Epilogue   178
Appendix A: Indictment   183
Appendix B: Eddie Cicotte's Statistics   185
Chapter Notes   189
Bibliography   197
Index   201

Introduction

Eddie Cicotte, who pitched for three American League teams between 1905 and 1920, was one of the most popular players in baseball. Photographs usually showed him with a friendly look on his face and a big, gap-toothed smile. His teammates liked him, and opposing players respected him. A family man and a devout Catholic, Cicotte had ascended to stardom with nothing more than a mediocre fastball and an endless supply of guile and trick pitches. He won 29 games in 1919 and led the Chicago White Sox to the pennant, and though he pitched poorly in the World Series that October, the Chicago fans did not hold it against Eddie. A slump can happen to anybody.

Nearly 12 months later, in September of 1920, the paying public discovered the truth. Eddie's bad performance in the World Series was not a slump. Instead, by his own admission, Eddie Cicotte took a bribe to lose the Series. He and seven of his teammates were implicated in what became known as the Black Sox Scandal, the most disgraceful episode in the history of the sport.

Overnight, the popular pitcher became a pariah, and he would remain so for the rest of his life.

In 1963, Eliot Asinof wrote one of the most successful sports books in history. Titled *Eight Men Out*, Asinof's work turned the Black Sox Scandal into a detective novel, full of heroes and villains. He interviewed some of the living principals of the 1919 World Series and gained many of his insights from the men who lived through that painful episode and now, more than 40 years later, were willing to discuss the tragic events of 1919.

Eddie Cicotte, however, was not interested in revisiting the past. Cicotte turned down all of Asinof's entreaties; as the ex-pitcher told another reporter several years before, "I took my medicine and I've forgotten about it."[1] In 1969, as the 84-year-old Cicotte lay dying in a Detroit hospital, Asinof heard that Cicotte might be willing to talk. He hurried to Michigan, but he was too late. The old pitcher passed away before Asinof could reach him.

On October 7, 1920, *The Sporting News* displayed a collage of eight photos, one of each of the White Sox implicated in the scandal. The heading read, "Fix These Faces in Your Memory," and the text below, with the caption

"Eight Men Charged with Selling Out Baseball," fairly dripped with righteous scorn:

> These are the White Sox players who committed the astounding and contemptible crime of selling out the baseball world in the 1919 World Series.... Four of them are guilty by their own confessions, and the evidence against the other four is so conclusive that their denials only add to the contempt in which they are held.... Some of the eight have been great stars in their day, but they will be remembered from now on only for the depths of depravity to which they could sink.[2]

The man in the middle of the collage, the most prominently displayed of all, was Eddie Cicotte.
    This is his story.

1

The Beginning

> *Detroit's only Detroit-bred player is Eddie Cicotte, the most coltish of all the colts on the club, who, if he gets a regular place on the team, probably will be the youngest player in the American League.*—Detroit Free Press, March 28, 1905

Edward Victor Cicotte was born on June 19, 1884, in Springwells Township, Michigan, in the River Rouge area of southwest Detroit. He was the son of Ambrose Cicotte, whose ancestors had lived in and around Detroit for more than 150 years, and the former Archange Drouillard,[1] the daughter of French-Canadian immigrants from Montreal. The family last name has always been pronounced as "SEE-cot" in Detroit, though the future ballplayer heard his friends, teammates, fans, and sportswriters mangle his surname in many inventive ways all his life.

The Cicotte clan was one of the most prominent families of early Detroit and Wayne County, Michigan. The Cicottes descended from Jean Cicot (or Chicot), who left Rochelle, France, in 1650 and settled in New France, now called Canada, at Montreal. The family adopted the name Cicotte around 1700 and soon afterward, Jean's grandson, Zacharias Cicotte, moved to the fur-trading outpost of Fort Pontchartrain du Détroit, where the French government offered free land to those willing to settle there. After Detroit became part of the United States, Zacharias' descendant, Francis of Assisi Cicotte, was commissioned as a militia captain during the War of 1812 and led excursions against the local Indians at the direction of Michigan's territorial governor. When Francis died in 1859, he was praised as "a fine specimen of the early Frenchman, possessing that rare charm of manner which seemed a peculiar legacy to these descendants of the first pioneers."[2] His son, Francis Xavier Cicotte, held the offices of city clerk and treasurer of Detroit, and served as sheriff of Wayne County from 1865 to his death in 1867. He was succeeded by his brother, Edward V. Cicotte, the future ballplayer's namesake, who had held that post a decade before. Cicotte Street in Detroit, which exists today, was named to honor Edward V. Cicotte. The Cicottes also claimed descent from Antoine de la Mothe, sieur de Cadillac, the French explorer who founded Detroit in 1701.

Despite his impressive lineage, Ambrose Cicotte was a poor man with a large family. He and Archange had nine children, eight of whom lived to adulthood. Eddie was the youngest of the brood, coming into the world when his mother was 40 years old. Ambrose earned a meager living as a foreman and laborer on the railroad, and he was severely injured in 1893 when he tried to jump aboard a moving railroad car in Churubusco, Indiana. The accident crushed his right foot and injured his back, and he may not have worked after that.

Ambrose Cicotte died under mysterious circumstances in June of 1894. One evening around ten o'clock, he took ill on the street during a night of drinking whiskey. Two policemen allowed Ambrose's companions to take him home, where he told Archange that he felt sick to his stomach. Ambrose died the next morning. An autopsy was inconclusive, but it appears that Ambrose was killed when he drank poisoned or tainted alcohol.[3] This tragedy happened when his youngest son was ten years old, and it cost the family its main source of income. Archange went to work as a dressmaker, and Eddie dropped out of school and found employment in a box factory. People who knew the Cicottes said that Eddie was very protective of his widowed mother, who lived until 1909.

Eddie worked hard but found time for his favorite sport. He loved playing and watching baseball, and when the Detroit Tigers of the Western League built Bennett Park at the corner of Michigan and Trumbull avenues in 1896, the 12-year-old became a dedicated fan. Five years later, the Tigers joined the majors as one of eight clubs in the new American League. Eddie, a pitcher who played anywhere and anytime he could, was 17 by this time and dreamed of hurling in the major leagues.

Eddie, a right-hander, was small for an athlete, standing five feet, nine inches tall and weighing about 135 pounds as he entered adulthood. Handicapped by the lack of a blazing fastball, Eddie instead learned to change speeds and move the ball around the strike zone. He was always eager to learn new ways to throw (and doctor) the baseball, in an era in which the spitball and other now-banned deliveries were perfectly legal. He learned to throw the spitball, which became his out pitch. As his pitching skills developed, Eddie dominated the semipro and amateur scene in Detroit.

He spent the 1903 season pitching semipro ball in northern Michigan. His first professional engagement came in 1904, when the 20-year-old Eddie joined the Calumet (Michigan) club in the Northern Copper League. He transferred to Sault Ste. Marie (Ontario) in the same circuit later that year, and the *Detroit Free Press* reported that the "star slabbist of the Sault Ste. Marie team" won 38 games in 1904 while losing only four, with 11 shutouts.

1. The Beginning

This strong performance gained the notice of his hometown team, the Detroit Tigers, who offered Eddie a tryout. In the spring of 1905, Eddie traveled from Detroit to Augusta, Georgia, home of the Tigers' spring training camp.

At camp, Eddie impressed the Tigers with his curve and his spitball, if not his speed. He pitched in intrasquad games and in exhibitions against minor league clubs, and as a final test, Detroit manager Bill Armour gave Eddie a start at Bennett Park in Detroit against Brooklyn of the National League on March 29. The Superbas (they became the Dodgers later) had all their regulars in the lineup, and Eddie, facing a real major league team for the first time, was fairly shaking with nervousness. He walked the first batter in four of the first five innings and spent all day getting into and out of jams. The Superbas scored two runs in the first, one in the third, and three in the eighth, assisted by Eddie's five walks, a hit batter, and a damaging balk. Brooklyn won the game, 6–3, and the *Free Press* opined, "Cicotte plainly was beaten through stage fright."[4]

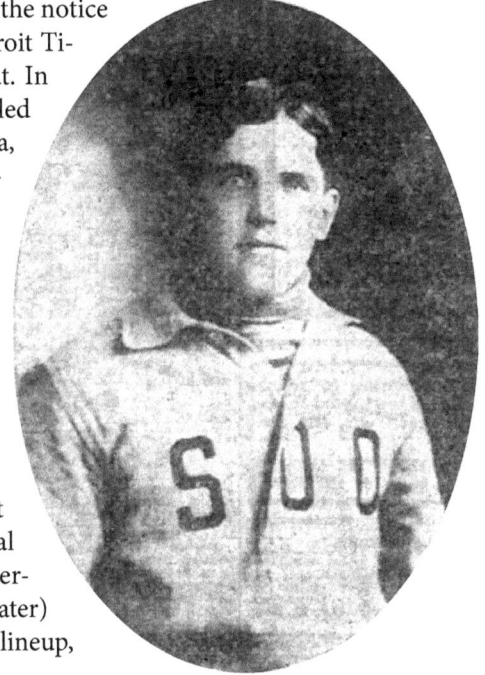

Eddie Cicotte with the Sault Ste. Marie club in 1904 (author's collection).

Armour, a veteran baseball man, liked what he saw in Eddie, though the Brooklyn game proved that the youngster was not yet ready to face a major league lineup. He signed the 21-year-old Cicotte to a contract, then assigned him to the nearby South Atlantic League team, the Augusta Travelers, with which the Tigers had connections. As the *Free Press* explained, "In Augusta … there is great hope that when Armour begins to pack up he may overlook Cicotte and leave him behind."[5] In exchange for Cicotte's services, the Travelers gave the Detroit club the right to buy one player from the Augusta roster at season's end.

Manager Andy Roth chose Eddie to pitch the Travelers' first game of the season at Savannah on April 16, and Eddie answered with a one-hit, 2–1 victory. The only hit was a scratch single, and the only run came in on an error by the third baseman. Eddie was so dominant that according to the *Free*

Press, he was "said to be the best pitcher ever seen on the local [Savannah] grounds."⁶ Five days later, at Augusta's home opener, he two-hit Charleston by a 2–1 count. He struck out ten batters and drove in the winning run himself in the bottom of the ninth. He won two more games in quick succession and ran his record to 5–0 with a two-hitter against Macon, the defending league champion, on May 8. While Augusta struggled to stay above the break-even mark—they were 9–7 after Eddie's win over Macon—the young Detroiter emerged as the star of the team.

The first problem Eddie faced in Augusta was homesickness. He had never traveled farther from Detroit than Michigan's Upper Peninsula, and Georgia, with its different climate, food, and accents, was an unfamiliar scene for him. Besides, Eddie missed his fiancée. He was engaged to Rose Ellen Freer, a 20-year-old from Jackson, Michigan, whose parents had emigrated from Quebec. Eddie and Rose planned to marry in the spring of 1905, but when he was assigned to Augusta, Eddie agreed to put off the wedding until fall. Still, team management could tell that he was unhappy, despite his success on the mound. Eddie asked for a leave of absence to return to Michigan to marry Rose in May, but with an important road trip coming up, the club turned him down.

In mid-May, the Detroit club proposed a compromise. Tigers management offered to pay for a round-trip train ticket for Rose from Detroit to Augusta. This would allow the couple to marry in Augusta before Eddie and his team left on their road trip. Eddie and Rose agreed, and they were married on May 18, 1905. A year and a half later, the Cicottes welcomed their first child, a daughter also named Rose, to the family. Eddie lost his first game after the wedding, his first defeat of the year after five wins, but on May 25 he won, 4–3, at Columbia, and two days later he shut out Columbia at home on four hits. He topped that performance on June 1, when he shut out Jacksonville on one hit. The only safety Eddie gave up that day was a bunt down the first base line.

The young pitcher's win-loss record suffered after his near no-hitter at Jacksonville left his mark at 8–1. Augusta had trouble scoring runs, and Eddie lost some games in June and July because of the Travelers' weak offense. As the team fell in the standings, manager Andy Roth resigned and was replaced by center fielder George Leidy. Still, Cicotte had proven himself in professional ball, and in early June the Detroit papers reported that the Tigers intended to call him up in August. Because several star spitball pitchers in the American League had either slumped or been injured in early 1905, *Free Press* writer Joe S. Jackson recommended that Eddie give up the wet pitch. "As Eddie is coming north to twirl for the Tigers," wrote Jackson, "he would do well to cut out this ball, heedless of the praise it is getting him. A glance at what has happened to Messrs. Chesbro, Dineen [*sic*], Patton, Mullin, and other spit ball slingers should be sufficient."⁷ Perhaps Jackson did not realize that Eddie's fastball was merely average at best and that the young pitcher needed some degree of trickery to succeed.

In Augusta, Eddie met a teenaged outfielder who would cross his path many times in the future. Tyrus Cobb, an 18-year-old from Royston, Georgia, had played for the Travelers the year before and was released for poor play, but redeemed himself by performing well for a club in Anniston, Alabama. Reinstated to the Augusta nine, Cobb, despite his youth, claimed the starting left field position for the Travelers.

Young Ty Cobb had not yet learned to take the sport seriously, and his nonchalant attitude led to a scrap with the club's new pitcher. Eddie entered the ninth inning of a game against Savannah with a 2–0 lead, but Cobb, for reasons known only to himself, took his spot in left field with his glove full of popcorn. He munched lazily on the popcorn until a fly ball came his way. Cobb dropped both the ball and the contents of his glove, allowing a run to score and spoiling Cicotte's bid for a shutout. The Travelers held on for the win, but Eddie accosted the outfielder so vehemently that the two men traded punches before their teammates broke it up.

Eddie had every right to be angry, and Cobb, who readily admitted that he was in the wrong, regarded the incident as a turning point in his career. The new manager, George Leidy, chewed him out for the gaffe, but impressed upon the young Cobb the importance of playing the game in a professional manner. "Right then and there," recalled Cobb in 1925, "I made up my mind to concentrate my whole thought on the game and, if possible, to make of myself as big a star as my natural ability would permit."[8] Leidy became Cobb's mentor, teaching him the fine points of bunting, base stealing, and defense, and Cobb always credited Leidy as the man who set him on the road to big league stardom.

Eddie Cicotte needed no such wake-up call. He was already a determined competitor, and despite his small stature, he was hailed as the top pitcher in the South Atlantic League. Though the Augusta club had talent in Cobb, Cicotte, and two other future major leaguers in pitcher George "Nap" Rucker and infielder Clyde Engle, the Travelers struggled to reach the .500 mark. Despite Eddie's fine 15–9 record in 32 games, the Travelers finished fourth in a six-team league. At season's end, Bill Armour summoned Eddie to Detroit for a trial against major league competition. The Tigers also selected Ty Cobb, the league batting champion, from the Augusta roster, paying the Travelers $750 for the outfielder's contract.

Cobb made his debut for the Tigers on August 30, 1905. Eddie Cicotte followed four days later, hurling three innings in relief on the road against St. Louis. Eddie entered the game in the eighth inning with the score tied 2–2. He retired the side in the eighth and ninth innings, but in the tenth, the Browns scored on a bunt single, a sacrifice, and an RBI single, handing Eddie the loss. On September 5, Eddie earned his first major league win in a 3–2 victory in Detroit over the Chicago White Sox. "For a youngster in his first big league game [actually his second], Cicotte made a fine showing," said the *Free Press*. "He was a little wild at the start of the game, and this cost him one run."[9] Eddie, nervous in his debut before his hometown fans, walked two in the first inning but kept the White Sox from scoring. He walked Frank Isbell to start the second, and Isbell scored on a sequence of bunts and sacrifices to give the White Sox an early lead. Eddie settled down after that and belted two hits of his own. The Tigers rallied for two runs in the seventh, and Eddie made it stand up for his first win.

Two other future stars appeared in that contest. Second-year pitcher Ed Walsh, like Eddie a spitballer, started the game for Chicago and took the loss. For Detroit, Ty Cobb had a terrible day. He was called out when a batted ball hit him on the basepaths, and in the ninth inning, with the game on the line, Cobb ran into left fielder Matty McIntyre and caused his teammate to drop a fly ball. The next batter singled, putting two men on base with two out, but Eddie retired Chicago's Danny Green to end the game.

Eddie pitched only one more American League game in 1905, a six-inning relief stint against Cleveland on September 13. Detroit starter Frank Kitson was tossed from the game in the third inning for disputing an umpire's call, and Bill Armour rushed Eddie into combat. Eddie gave up 12 hits in six and two-thirds innings as Cleveland won, 9–2, with Kitson taking the loss. This performance was a disappointment, but Eddie rallied with a three-hit shutout, with seven strikeouts, in an exhibition game against Homestead, a semipro club from the Pittsburgh area, on September 21. He also defeated Newark of the Eastern League in another exhibition on October 1. Eddie pitched creditably, if not brilliantly, in his late-season call-up, but the Tigers decided that he needed more seasoning. The club assigned him to the Indianapolis Indians of the American Association to begin the 1906 season.

Cicotte was touted as a "wonder" when he arrived in Indianapolis, and he performed well in spring practice. He pitched four strong innings against the Detroit parent club, allowing only one run, on April 10, and threw the final four innings of a shutout against Wabash College three days later. However, Eddie had already decided that he needed another pitch in his repertoire. His spitter was good enough, but his fastball was only average, and he needed more to succeed in the majors. Fortunately, his stay in Indiana brought him into contact with another pitcher who liked to experiment with trick pitches. His name was Ed Summers, called "Kickapoo Ed," and he worked with Cicotte on a totally new pitch. The pitch was the knuckleball, and it was Eddie Cicotte's ticket back to the major leagues.

The knuckleball, which is not necessarily delivered with the knuckles, leaves the pitcher's hand with as little spin as possible, or no spin at all. The raised stitches of the baseball react to air currents and make the ball sail, dive, or veer in unpredictable ways. As a Washington newspaper described it, "The ball shoots toward the plate in the same way that the spitter does, without twisting or turning in the least. You can count the seams in the ball as it comes toward you. Being pushed against the air without any revolving movement, it floats along with a jerky movement."[10] Eddie experimented with a number of grips until he found the one that worked for him. The *Washington Post* took notice of Eddie's success and stated that Cicotte gripped the knuckler by holding the ball "on the three fingers of a closed hand, with his thumb and forefinger to guide it, throwing it with an overhand motion, and sending it from his hand as one would snap a whip. The ball acts like a 'spitter,' but is a new-fangled thing."[11]

No one knows who discovered this trick pitch, though there is evidence that Cicotte learned it from Forrest "Frosty" Thomas, who pitched two games for Detroit in 1905 and showed it to both Cicotte and Nap Rucker in spring training at Augusta that year. Summers, years later, stated that Cicotte taught the pitch to him at Indianapolis. No matter who discovered it, both Summers and Cicotte worked hard to control it. In April, the Indianapolis club sent Summers to Grand Rapids of the Central League, leaving Eddie Cicotte to carry on with the knuckler.

The Indians got off to a bad start in 1906, and Eddie Cicotte posted a 1–4 record in 72 innings in April and May. Still, the knuckler was impressive, though the pitcher struggled to control it. As the *Indianapolis News* stated, "The youngster obtained from Detroit is said to have a new ball that is calculated to make catchers think they see double and to give batters attacks of blind staggers. It has a double shoot.... All catchers that have caught his delivery predict that he will be a major league pitcher next year. Cicotte is admirably built for hard work. He is cool and deliberate in the box and has fine style."[12] Eddie's best game for the Indians came on May 13, when he threw an 11-inning, three-hit shutout to defeat the St. Paul Saints, 1–0. Nine days later, he five-hit Columbus, though the Indians managed only three hits and failed to score in a 1–0 loss. With the Indians in last place and Eddie's command of the knuckler and the spitter lacking in consistency, team management made a series of roster changes after Memorial Day. After Eddie allowed 14 hits in a 7–2 loss to Louisville on June 3, Indianapolis sent him to Des Moines of the Western League.

One problem that Eddie faced in Indianapolis, according to Indians first baseman and manager Charlie Carr, was a lack of confidence. Eddie loved throwing the knuckleball, or "snake pitch" as some called it, but was not yet convinced that he could rely on it in a pinch. As Carr told an Indianapolis newspaper after Eddie returned to the major leagues, Eddie nearly failed to complete his 1–0 win over St. Paul. In the final inning, the Saints put runners on second and third with two out. Carr called Eddie over to discuss the matter.

"Use the snake shoot," said Carr.

"I can't," replied Eddie. "I'm liable to hit the grandstand."

"Use it anyway," said the manager. "We might as well lose in that way as any other."[13] Eddie did as he was told and struck out the last batter.

During his stay at Indianapolis, the club discovered that Eddie, who was packing more weight on his five-foot, nine-inch frame, disliked training. As the *Indianapolis News* described it:

> Cicotte apparently had everything a pitcher needs when with the Indians, except nerve and energy. He refused to train during the spring practice season, and was not at his best until the regular season was several weeks old. He showed flashed of great pitching for Manager Carr, but on the whole was erratic. He lost several games as the result of one bad inning, the real reason for which probably was lack of condition and confidence in himself.[14]

The Western League was one step below the American Association on the baseball ladder, and Des Moines, with a big lead in the pennant chase, was the perfect place for Eddie to work on his "snake ball." He pitched four strong innings in relief against Sioux City in his first appearance for Des Moines, and on June 15 he shut out the same team on six hits, with no walks.

Eddie's other main pitch was the spitball, which was all the rage in baseball at the time. A pitcher named Elmer Stricklett was the Pied Piper of the spitball; though Stricklett enjoyed little success in the majors himself, he taught the secret of the spitball to anyone who would listen. Ed Walsh, who won 40 games for the White Sox in 1908, and Jack Chesbro, who won 41 for New York in 1904, were students of Stricklett's, and their success made the wet pitch popular. Cicotte, who later said that he gained knowledge of the technique from an unnamed Stricklett disciple, learned to wet his fingers and snap his wrist sharply upon releasing the ball, causing the ball to shoot from his hand like a watermelon seed and break sharply downward upon reaching the plate. Walsh could reportedly make the ball break as much as two feet while batters swung helplessly. As Detroit slugger Sam Crawford complained, "I think the ball disintegrated on the way to the plate and the catcher put it back together again. I swear, when it went past the plate it was just the spit went by."[15] The knuckler was a fine complement to the spitter, and now Eddie could confuse the batters with two trick pitches and the occasional fastball and curve.

With Cicotte as its ace, throwing a knuckleball that few batters had seen and a spitter that few knew how to hit, Des Moines ran away with the pennant, finishing 23 games ahead of second-place Lincoln. Des Moines dominated the circuit so completely that only they and Lincoln finished above the .500 mark, and Lincoln did so by only one game. The other four teams ended up below the break-even line, and the pennant race was over early. Though Eddie did not join the team until early June, he finished the 1906 campaign with an 18–9 record in 30 starts.

Armed with the knuckleball, the spitball, and improved control, Eddie Cicotte was making progress. However, the Tigers did not call him up to Detroit in the fall of 1906. Some say that Frank Navin, the Detroit owner, preferred big pitchers, especially if they were right-handers. The Tigers already owned a trick-pitch specialist in Ed Summers, who was five inches taller than Eddie. Despite Eddie's fine pitching at Des Moines, the Detroit club sold his contract to Newark of the Eastern League in late 1906. As Ty Cobb explained many years later,

> Detroit finally discarded Cicotte. He weighed 135 pounds and Detroit considered that much too light for a pitcher. Few major league clubs ever cared for little fellows as pitchers.... He was too small. He would be of no help. Betters would not respect him. History proved Detroit wrong.[16]

The 22-year-old Detroiter, however, did not want to play in the East. He and his wife, Rose, made their home in Detroit, where they remained all their lives, and Newark was too far away. He told the Newark management that he would not report to the club the following spring and was perfectly happy to wait for a trade to his native Midwest. A standoff ensued, and Newark blinked first. The Lincoln club of the Western League, Des Moines' main rival, had seen Eddie pitch several times and lost to him more often than not. Lincoln put in a bid, and in March of 1907, Newark sold Eddie's contract to Lincoln.

The Lincoln Treeplanters were managed by James "Ducky" Holmes, a scrappy former Baltimore Oriole who had recently ended his stay in the majors with the Chicago White Sox. Holmes was determined to close the gap with Des Moines, and he installed Eddie as his number one starter. Eddie and his manager had known each other for several years; as the local Lincoln newspaper explained, Holmes played for the Detroit Tigers in 1900, a year before the new American League assumed major status, and Eddie, then a teenager, gained entry into Detroit's Bennett Park by carrying Holmes' equipment.[17] Holmes gave Eddie the Opening Day start on April 17, and Eddie responded with a four-hitter, a 4–1 win over Pueblo with 10 strikeouts on a near-freezing afternoon in Lincoln.

At age 23, Eddie's physique was filling out. He had weighed 135 pounds when he pitched for Detroit in 1905, but when Eddie returned to Des Moines with his new Lincoln team, the local paper called him "the short, chunky individual" and the "prodigal son ... who killed his own fatted calf and prepared his own celebration." The paper also remarked upon "the zeroes he passed out as souvenirs of the game"[18] in a 7–1 win over his former teammates. He had gained a noticeable amount of weight, and his conditioning would be a recurring issue during his career.

After a two-week layoff to nurse a twisted ankle followed by a series of close defeats, Eddie's record stood at 4–10 in late June, and the Lincoln paper called him "the unluckiest pitcher in the circuit."[19] Thereafter, he found a winning formula. He turned his season around with a 16-inning win over Omaha on July 1 and a three-hit shutout of Sioux City three days later. Eddie's one-hit, 2–1 win against Des Moines on July 20 boosted Lincoln into second place in the Western League standings.

He wasn't much of an umpire, though. On June 14, Eddie defeated Des Moines in the first game of a doubleheader. Because the umpire sat out the second game with an injury, both clubs agreed to allow Eddie to preside over the second contest. This proved disastrous when Ducky Holmes, Lincoln's playing manager, ran far out of a baseline to avoid being tagged and Eddie, understandably reluctant to anger the man who paid his salary, ruled him safe. This decision resulted in a fight between Holmes and one of the Des Moines players, and a general ruckus caused Eddie to call an end to the game in a 1–1 tie.

Eddie won 17 of his final 21 decisions to end the season with a 21–14 record, and though the Treeplanters finished second again, this time to Omaha, the knuckleball specialist was suddenly in demand. People were already calling him "Knuckles" Cicotte, and major league teams inquired as to his availability. The Boston Americans won the bidding, paying $2,500 for his contract in August of 1907. Eddie was assigned to stay with Lincoln until the Western League season ended and report to Boston in late September. "Manager Holmes and other critics predict that he will develop into a great major league pitcher," said the *Boston Globe*. "Cicotte is a youngster of splendid habits and temperament and should prove easy to manage. Although of short stature, he carries the muscle and weighs 180 pounds."[20]

Perhaps the Americans decided that Eddie had pitched enough for one season, after throwing over 300 innings in 35 starts for Lincoln, because they did not send for the young pitcher. Instead, they invited him to their 1908 spring training camp in Little Rock, Arkansas. After an absence of three years, Eddie Cicotte had made it back to the American League.

Cicotte returned to the major league scene with his secret weapon. No big league pitcher had yet made a living by throwing the knuckleball, and now both Eddie and Ed Summers, recently promoted to Detroit, prepared to throw the tricky pitch in American League play. Summers might have become baseball's first full-time knuckleballer the year before, but when the Tigers called him up in 1907, Kickapoo Ed declined the invitation. He did not believe that he was ready and preferred to end the 1907 campaign at Indianapolis while the Tigers battled for the pennant. The Detroit club won the flag without Summers, though they lost the World Series to the Chicago Cubs. Summers thus lost out on a check for $1,946, the loser's share of the World Series money.

Summers did not deploy his pitch as often as Cicotte; Tigers catcher Boss Schmidt reported that Summers threw "about fifty" of them in a game. Also, the pitch that Ed Summers threw was not the same as Cicotte's, because Summers did not use his knuckles. Interviewed during spring training in 1908, Summers explained, "I watched Eddie Cicotte, who first used it, and followed him. He rested the ball on his knuckles, but I couldn't see the value of that, because I couldn't control it, and one can put little speed on it.... I found by holding the ball with my finger tips and steadying it with my thumb alone I could get a peculiar break to it and send it to the batters with considerable speed and good control." Summers held the ball in place by digging into it with his fingernails, and for this reason, Summers didn't even call his new pitch a knuckleball. "It's—I don't know what," he said. "It's just this."[21] However, the Summers grip is the one used by most knuckleball pitchers today, and the term "knuckleball" is now used to describe any pitch that does not spin on its way to the plate.

Thus began the controversy over who invented the knuckleball. Summers insisted that Eddie Cicotte taught it to him, but in 1952 Eddie gave an interview in which he said, "They say I invented the knuckleball but Eddie "Kickapoo" Summers deserves a full share of the credit. We worked on it together and developed it at Indianapolis in 1906."[22] Another candidate for the title of "father of the knuckleball" is Nap Rucker, Eddie's teammate at Augusta in 1905, who threw it for Brooklyn of the National League in 1907, but only as a change of pace. (Rucker relied upon it more regularly later in his career.) A long-forgotten National Leaguer, Lew Moren, used his version of the pitch for the Philadelphia Phillies in this period as well, though he was not as successful as the others. Most baseball historians, however, agree that Eddie Cicotte and Ed Summers were the first to use the knuckler successfully as a main pitch.

Ed Summers employed his "dry spitter" to win 24 games for Detroit in 1908, his first major league season, but arm problems ended his career only four years later. Therefore, Eddie Cicotte was the first knuckleball pitcher to enjoy a long career. He may not have invented the pitch—Frosty Thomas appears to be the man who introduced it to Cicotte and Rucker in 1905—but Eddie was the one who proved its value. Later knuckleball pitchers, including Hall of Famers Hoyt Wilhelm and Phil Niekro, owed much to Eddie Cicotte.

2

Boston

> *Veteran Jim McGuire believes that E. Cicotte, the Boston Americans' pitcher, showed what will prove the latest wrinkle in freak curves today, when he uncovered the "knuckle curve." It is pitched with the fingers doubled and the thumb grasping the ball. The new curve breaks fast after floating to the plate in lazy fashion. Cicotte has been practicing it for two years, and, with assistance from McGuire, believes he has mastered it.—Chicago Tribune, March 7, 1908*

During the spring of 1908, Eddie Cicotte joined a new ballclub with a new nickname. Boston's entry in the American League didn't have an official nickname during its first seven years of play; some reporters referred to them every now and then as the Pilgrims or the Somersets, but most people simply called them the Boston Americans to distinguish them from the city's National League club. John I. Taylor, the president of the team, saw an opening when the Boston Nationals dropped the traditional red stockings that they had used since 1876. When the Nationals decided to wear white stockings in 1908, Taylor claimed the abandoned color for himself. He declared that the 1908 edition of his team would wear red stockings and be called the Boston Red Sox, a name that has lasted for more than a century.

John I. Taylor was one of the most controversial figures in Boston baseball history. His father, General Charles H. Taylor, publisher of the *Boston Globe*, bought the team in 1904 and turned it over to his son to manage. John I. was only 29 years old at the time and had a reputation as a spoiled rich kid. He had quit working for the *Globe* because he did not like the newspaper business. However, as his grandson later described him, John I. was "an absolute nut about baseball," so perhaps his father put him in charge of the team to teach him some responsibility. The younger Taylor was a mercurial team president, easy to get along with when the team was winning, but bitter and sarcastic when it lost.

The Boston club had hit rock bottom since their American League pennants in 1903 and 1904 and their victory in the first modern World Series in

1903 (there was no Series in 1904). The 1905 club, managed by third baseman Jimmy Collins and with most of the championship cast intact, began to age and dropped to fourth in the standings. Collins was reluctant to bench his favorites, many of whom were his friends, and in 1906 the bottom fell out. The Americans lost 20 games in a row in May and finished the season in last place with 105 losses. As the 1906 *Reach Guide* put it, "The poor tail enders of 1906 presented the most melancholy spectacle ever witnessed in major league ball. The cause of this awful slump was the decadence of the team's veterans, which had set in the year before."[1] To make matters worse, John I. Taylor did not take losing well and berated his players after losses. After Collins discouraged Taylor from entering the clubhouse, the team president set up a chair in the hall outside and made nasty remarks to his men as they walked by. It was a poisonous situation that lasted until Taylor fired Collins and put veteran outfielder Chick Stahl in charge.

Tragedy struck in 1907 when Stahl, beset by personal problems, killed himself with carbolic acid during spring training. Pitcher Cy Young opened the season as manager but soon gave way to George Huff, the football and baseball coach at the University of Illinois, who scouted for the Red Sox. Huff, after only a few games, went back to scouting and turned the job over to first baseman Bob Unglaub. In early June, Taylor acquired veteran catcher Jim "Deacon" McGuire on waivers from the New York Highlanders and installed him as manager. Despite the managerial merry-go-round, the Americans made a 15-game improvement over the previous year and landed in seventh place. Now, as the newly-named Boston Red Sox, there was nowhere to go but up. McGuire, who retained the post for 1908 and still played every now and then, owned a reputation as a good handler of pitchers.

To Taylor's credit, he had invested in the team's scouting effort, and his labors paid off. Eddie Cicotte was but one of the young, talented players acquired by the Red Sox as the wave of the future. George Huff, in his capacity as a scout, signed Tris Speaker, a 19-year-old outfielder from Hubbard, Texas. Speaker played in seven games in 1907 and battled for a starting slot in 1908. Later that season, another Huff discovery, an 18-year-old pitcher named Joe Wood, joined the club and showed his exceptional fastball. Wood could hit, too. Another future star was Bill Carrigan, a tough, no-nonsense catcher from Maine. The team still employed Cy Young, the ageless pitcher who had already won more than 450 major league games and looked as if he could last forever. The talent level on the Boston roster was rising, and for the first time in several seasons, the fans of the Hub showed some enthusiasm for their team.

During spring training, Eddie Cicotte was the talk of the Red Sox camp. The knuckleball was briefly a sensation, and Eddie's name and picture became familiar to readers in the nation's newspapers. One such picture compared

Cicotte's knuckleball and the "dry spitter" of Ed Summers, thrown with the fingertips. These two similar pitches brought to the game a new kind of delivery that acted like a spitball, but without the unsanitary—and to some, frankly disgusting—baggage of the spitter. Said veteran catcher Lou Criger, "The way Cicotte uses it, it's the best slow ball I ever caught. And it's also the hardest slow ball to handle that was ever sent up to me."[2]

On a personal level, Eddie was friendly and outgoing, popular with his teammates. He was something of a jester—he might pick up a piece of glass and say to Wood, "Hey, Joe, I found your arm"—and the other young stars-to-be on the Red Sox accepted him as one of their own. All during his career, Eddie found it easy to make friends, both on his own team and around the league. He was also an object of interest for the fans, as his "double-shoot" knuckleball was still rare enough to be regarded as exotic. People wanted to see this unusual pitch, and Eddie's delivery brought fans to the ballpark.

Eddie had his ups and downs but acquitted himself well during the 1908 season. After three appearances in relief, he earned his first win for the Red Sox with a shutout against the New York Highlanders on May 6. His control of the knuckleball was spotty, as he led the league with 14 wild pitches. Catchers Lou Criger and Bill Carrigan were as unfamiliar with the knuckler as American League batters were, and most of their 20 passed balls came with Eddie on the mound.

The young hurler also displayed a tendency to lose command in the late innings. Pitchers were expected to finish their games in that era, but Eddie had trouble doing so, probably due to his recent weight gain. He had put on some poundage since his three-game trial with Detroit three years earlier, and in early August, after Eddie hung on to defeat the Tigers despite allowing three runs in the seventh inning and one more in the eighth, the *Detroit Times* called him "the stubby little wet-goods retailer" and reported that "Eddie, as usual, let down after the sixth inning."[3] The Red Sox were far enough ahead that Cicotte was able to finish the contest, though Deacon McGuire had Cy Young warming up just in case.

The Detroit paper also commended McGuire for the progress of the Red Sox. "The Boston club is looking better every time it strikes town," said the *Times*. "The dash of the bunch is highly commendable and the crowd, by its frequent and unstinted applause, was plainly smitten with the looks of Deacon McGuire's fine young team."[4] John I. Taylor was not as impressed, as the Red Sox remained buried in sixth place for most of the season, and on August 27, after six losses in a row at home to the White Sox and Browns, Taylor fired McGuire and hired Fred Lake to manage the team. Lake, who briefly played the infield for Boston's National League club during the 1890s, was a minor league manager and promoter who also scouted for the Red Sox.

The Red Sox won 22 of 40 games with Lake at the helm, and the club nearly reached the .500 mark, finishing at 75–79 in fifth place. Eddie Cicotte ended his first full season with two complete-game wins against the Philadelphia A's, one at home and the other on the road, to lift his win–loss mark to 11–12. He completed 17 of his 24 starts, including his last five, and did not allow a home run all year. His performance was promising enough to virtually assure Eddie a roster spot in 1909.

Taylor was determined to make his Red Sox younger, and in November of 1908 he sold veteran catcher Lou Criger to the St. Louis Browns. This move was not unexpected, with the emergence of Bill Carrigan as Boston's backstop of the future, but in February of 1909, Taylor stunned all of New England with another player move. He traded Cy Young, the last remaining member of the 1903 World Series champions, to Cleveland for two pitchers and $12,500 in cash.

Young was still a valuable pitcher, having rebounded in 1908, his 19th major league season, with 21 wins, a 1.26 earned run average, and his third no-hitter. He had also served as a mentor and role model for Eddie Cicotte, Joe Wood, and other young Red Sox hurlers. Besides, new manager Fred Lake had dismissed the idea of trading the nearly 42-year-old Young mere weeks before. "We have no intentions of letting Cy go," said Lake, "and he will be with the Boston team as long as he lives if he cares to remain in baseball."[5] Perhaps Taylor recognized that the aging Young could not last forever and decided to deal him while his trade value was still high. Whatever the reason, the fans were surprised by the move. "News that Young had died could not have been a greater shock,"[6] said the *Boston Globe*.

Young's departure put a great deal of responsibility on the shoulders of Eddie Cicotte and the other young Boston hurlers. The young Detroiter had performed well enough in 1908 that his manager expected him to be "25 percent stronger" during the coming campaign. Lake also singled out Joe Wood as "a boy who I will bank heavily on" in 1909 and predicted that right-hander Frank Arellanes "should be a star in the American League this season."[7] All in all, Lake professed to be satisfied with his pitching staff.

Eddie's 1909 season was a mixture of highs and lows. Used in both starting and relief roles, Eddie won his first seven decisions as the youthful Red Sox jumped into pennant contention. His control was still a problem—he walked five men in his first win of the season at Washington on April 19, then walked seven in a 10–4 win against the Yankees on April 29—but the Boston offense supported him well, and he learned how to pitch out of jams. However, he twisted an ankle on May 11 at Cleveland and remained on the sidelines until the last day of the month, when he pitched a three-hitter against the Philadelphia A's for his fifth consecutive win. With Eddie making a solid contribution, the rising Red Sox jumped into the pennant race, buoyed by their young talent.

Eddie finally lost a decision, dropping to 7–1 in a shutout loss to Cleveland on June 12, and his season took a turn for the worse seven days later. He pitched six strong innings in relief of Charlie Chech in a win over the A's, but complained of a "lame arm" afterwards. The team sent him home to Detroit to rest his arm, and Eddie did not pitch again for nearly seven weeks, sitting out the rest of June and almost all of July. On July 31, he started against St. Louis but pitched only two innings before giving way to Larry Pape. Eddie left with a 7–0 lead and received credit for the win (per the rules of the time), but spent another two weeks on the shelf. By mid–August, Eddie

Eddie on a Ramly cigarette card, 1909 (author's collection).

was back to normal and resumed his regular workload, running his record to 12–1 against the Browns on August 23, striking out eight.

Eddie was not the only rising star on the club. Tris Speaker, now the regular center fielder, batted .309 and stole 35 bases, while right fielder Harry Hooper, catcher Bill Carrigan, shortstop Heinie Wagner, and first baseman Jake Stahl gave the Red Sox a solid starting core. Joe Wood, still only 19 years old, won 11 games, with Frank Arellanes leading the staff with a 16–12 record. Eddie Cicotte managed to avoid injuries in August and September, but he lost four of his last six decisions to finish the year at 14–5. The Red Sox finished 1909 in third place with a respectable 88–63 record, a 13-win improvement over 1908.

At season's end, the Red Sox challenged the National League's third-place club, the New York Giants, to a best-of-seven post-season matchup. The Giants won the first game in New York behind Christy Mathewson, but Eddie Cicotte won the second contest with a 15-hit complete game, 9–5. Boston breezed through the next three games and won the series, four games to one, before disappointing crowds, but the matchup proved to be a coming-out party for Tris Speaker. The Red Sox center fielder batted .600 (12-for-20), won the third game with a walk-off, inside-the-park homer, and stunned the National Leaguers with his play in center field. Afterward, Giants manager John McGraw proclaimed Speaker the best player in baseball.

2. Boston

Fred Lake had led the Red Sox into contention, but when he demanded a raise at season's end, John I. Taylor curtly informed him that he was not the reason for the team's success. Both Lake and Taylor refused to budge, and on November 1 Taylor released Lake and hired former Boston outfielder Patsy Donovan as his new field boss.

Eddie Cicotte, often called the "chunky pitcher" by the local papers in 1909, looked a bit thinner when he arrived at Hot Springs, Arkansas, for spring training in March of 1910. He impressed Patsy Donovan, who gave the knuckleball specialist a strong recommendation to the *Boston Globe*. "Eddie Cicotte is one of the cleverest boys in baseball today," said Donovan, "and will be particularly useful against the strong clubs of the league. I look for Cicotte to hold up his end this season from start to finish."[8]

Eddie pitched so well in spring training that Donovan made him the team's number one pitcher. The manager gave Eddie the honor of starting the season opener in New York on April 14, and Eddie pitched the first seven innings of a 14-inning marathon that ended in a 4–4 tie as darkness fell. Five days later, he took the mound for Boston's home opener at the Huntington Avenue Grounds. Eddie responded with a three-hitter for a 2–1 win over Washington in the first game of an Opening Day doubleheader.

One early highlight of the season was a visit to the White House to meet President William Howard Taft on April 28. A Boston congressman arranged for the team to meet the President while in Washington to play the Senators, and Taft, a baseball fan, was intrigued when Eddie was introduced to him as "the knuckleball pitcher." Taft inspected Eddie's hands and asked, "What is this knuckleball?"

"Oh, nothing much," replied the pitcher nervously.[9]

Eddie's season, and his career in Boston, went downhill from there. The Red Sox were expected to challenge for the 1910 pennant, but the Philadelphia A's grabbed the early league lead and pulled away from the pack in June and July. By mid-summer, the pennant race was over, and John I. Taylor fumed. The team president decided that some of his men were not dedicated enough to their work, and he focused his rage on the struggling Eddie Cicotte. In mid–June, with Eddie's record at 4–4 and the Sox buried in fourth place, Taylor asked for waivers on Eddie. Boston's Opening Day starter had landed on the waiver wire. Even the *Boston Globe*, published by Taylor's father, was surprised by this turn of events. "It seems strange that Boston should ask for waivers on Cicotte, for he appears to be one of the team's best pitchers," said the paper on July 4. Two days earlier, Eddie had raised his record to 7–5, beating the Senators despite issuing five walks. But on July 6, Eddie walked seven New York Highlanders and lost his command in the ninth inning, losing the game, 3–2, when Jack Quinn bunted the winning run home from third.

To be fair, Eddie made no secret of his disdain for training, and his lax approach to conditioning had concerned his managers since his minor league days; Charlie Carr, his field boss at Indianapolis, had remarked upon it four years earlier. Eddie had grown stocky during his time in Boston, and he developed a reputation as a pitcher who ran out of gas in the late innings. At bat, he often failed to run out ground balls that appeared to be easy outs, not wanting to expend his energy in a lost cause. This attitude infuriated Taylor, and when young Joe Wood showed signs of following Cicotte's lead, Taylor asked waivers on Wood also. Both men were immediately claimed by other American League teams, and Taylor withdrew both names, having made his point. But the waiver incident turned Taylor and Cicotte into enemies. "[Taylor] wouldn't like the way I was working, or perhaps the opposition had made one or two hits," Cicotte later said. "Taylor never liked me; I never liked him, and it was seldom that I went through a game without having him comment upon it."[10]

Eddie ended the 1910 season with a 15–11 record, leading the Red Sox in wins and innings pitched, but his position in Boston was shaky. The team president actively disliked him, and the Red Sox had come up with a raft of good young pitchers vying for spots on the roster. One was Joe Wood, who posted a 12–13 mark but sported a 1.69 earned run average as a reliever and part-time starter. Others, like Ray Collins and Charlie Hall, performed well in 1910 and expected to improve further in 1911. Eddie, at age 27, would have to work harder to keep up with his younger teammates. As John I. Taylor told the *Boston Globe*, "I hope Eddie will keep in shape next season to give the club his best work, for when on edge no one can ask for a finer assortment of benders that the

Eddie warms up for Boston in 1910 (author's collection).

Detroit boy can serve."[11] A later report said that Cicotte and Wood would "have to walk the straight and narrow" in 1911.

Taylor made ambitious plans for Boston's 1911 spring training. The Red Sox set up camp in Pasa Robles, California, a town on the Pacific Ocean halfway between Los Angeles and San Francisco. The small town (population 1,100) was known for its natural hot water spas and its many wineries. The Red Sox boarded a train on February 20 in Boston and rode cross-country, a trip that took seven days. Once there, the team played intrasquad training games for two weeks, then barnstormed their way back East, with two teams of Red Sox playing more than 60 games against minor league clubs and local semipro and amateur aggregations.

Rumor had it that Eddie Cicotte had gained a lot of weight in the off-season, but the pitcher denied it. He declared in a letter to Taylor that "the man who said I was hog fat was not telling you the truth. I am tipping the scales at 171, and working hard to keep in condition."[12] Taylor, however, wanted Eddie at 165.

Despite the grueling travel schedule and the many rainouts during the spring months, Eddie pitched very well in the pre-season. On March 26, Eddie's group of Red Sox (which included Tris Speaker) traveled to Yuma, Arizona, to play a ragtag team of locals. Though the Red Sox lent a few men to the Yuma club, Eddie won the game, 17–5, belted five hits of his own, and stole a base. Four days later, on Tris Speaker Day in Dallas, Eddie struck out eight and threw a two-hit shutout. "Eddie Cicotte looks fine," said Tim Murnane in the *Boston Globe*, "and if the boy can make up his mind to go the full distance and not attempt to lay up too many heats in July, the club will be in luck."[13] The next day, "The Sportsman" in the *Globe* stated that the first base play of 29-year-old rookie Rip Williams and the fine pitching of Joe Wood and Eddie Cicotte were "the most encouraging bits of news from the Red Sox tour."[14] Eddie did his best work in St. Joseph, Missouri, on April 7, when he shut out the local minor league club, 13–0, on three hits.

The Red Sox, who may have been worn out by the cross-country trip to spring training and the long exhibition tour that followed, started slowly in 1911. By May 2, the Boston club, at 7–8, stood seven games behind the streaking Detroit Tigers at 15–2. Eddie was inconsistent, losing his first game of the season at Washington on April 13 but beating the defending champion Athletics, 13–4, at home on April 21. Five days later, the Red Sox staked Eddie to an 8–1 lead over the Highlanders, but the knuckleballer failed once again in the later innings. He gave up four runs in the seventh inning and one in the eighth before Charlie Hall came in to relieve. Boston hung on to win, 11–8.

Eddie sat on the bench for nine days before he received his next starting assignment. This time, he lost on the road to New York, 6–3, blowing up in the third and giving up five runs. To make matters worse, the Highlanders ended the game with a triple play. Bill Carrigan, pinch-hitting for Cicotte, drove a liner to short with two men on. Shortstop Roxey Roach caught the ball and tossed to Earle Gardner at second; Gardner relayed to first baseman Hal Chase to complete the triple killing.

In the meantime, the war between Eddie and John I. Taylor continued. After the loss in New York, Taylor suspended Eddie without pay, as described in *Sporting Life*:

> Pitcher Eddie Cicotte, of the Boston Americans, left today to join his club at Cleveland. He has been under suspension for an unusual reason. President John I. Taylor cast him off the pay-roll because he refused to run out grounders to the infield, but would almost always loaf on his way down to first. When called for this laziness he said that there was no sense in his running his head off and getting winded when he was a sure out anyway. Not liking that kind of spirit and figuring that a pitcher must be in poor condition if he could not run 90 feet without blowing up in the next inning, Mr. Taylor suspended him without pay for several days.[15]

A reporter for the *Cincinnati Enquirer* registered his approval of Cicotte's punishment.

> Without knowing anything about the merits of this particular case, it looks as if Mr. Taylor has the right dope after all. It is a pretty poor athlete who cannot run to first base at top speed without losing his wind. A fine or suspension is about right for such loafers. Nothing is more disgusting in a ball game than to see some fellow quit as soon as he has hit a grounder and give up long before he reaches first base. A player who won't run out his hits, whether he is a pitcher or not, is not the right kind of a fellow to have on a winning club.[16]

In a conference with Taylor and manager Patsy Donovan, Eddie agreed to work harder on his conditioning. He was reinstated to the team, but he would be required to show up at the ballpark every morning for workouts. "There is nothing the matter with Cicotte," said the *Globe*, "except that he does not seem to be able to go the full distance, and is generally due to slow up after five or six innings, and sometimes sooner if he happens to have much running on the bases. This weakness, it is believed, can be eradicated by his engaging in plenty of work for a while."[17] The pitcher rejoined the team in Cleveland and threw one and two-thirds innings in relief against the Naps two days later, giving up three hits and three runs in a game the Red Sox won anyway. The next day, he gave up nine hits but beat the Indians, 6–2.

Eddie was on a short leash, and Taylor's animosity toward him never abated. He pitched poorly at Detroit on May 16, giving up seven hits and taking the loss in relief, but followed it up with a shutout against the last-place St. Louis Browns. Taylor was still not satisfied, and in June, when the Red Sox fell to fifth place in what appeared to be another lost season, the team president placed four Red Sox on waivers—Cicotte, pitcher Ray Collins, second baseman Heinie Wagner, and first baseman Clyde Engle.

Eddie drew the most attention from other American League teams, and though Taylor quickly withdrew his name from the waiver wire, several clubs made it known that they were interested in the knuckleball specialist. Connie Mack, manager and part-owner of the Philadelphia A's, reportedly offered to trade pitcher Harry Krause and one more hurler for Eddie, and the Tigers, White Sox, and Browns also expressed interest. In July, the New York Highlanders offered $3,500 in cash for Eddie; Taylor consented to the deal, but then changed his mind, demanding the inclusion of pitcher Ray Fisher. The Highlanders thought they had an agreement and took the dispute to baseball's ruling body, the National Commission.

It was a tough season for Eddie. On July 4, an intensely hot afternoon in Boston, Eddie started the first game of an Independence Day doubleheader but failed to make it through the third inning, giving up four runs to the Senators in a 6–4 loss. This defeat evened his record at 7–7. Patsy Donovan brought Eddie back in relief in the second contest, but in his fourth inning of work, Eddie collapsed on the mound. His "stomach had gone back on him," said the *Globe*, and Eddie's teammates had to carry him off the field as Joe Wood finished up. Eddie pitched a complete-game win over St. Louis on July 9, but lost eight of his next ten decisions as the Red Sox faded in the standings. A win in his final game of the season against Detroit left Eddie with a record of 11–15, the reverse of his 1910 log.

Eddie Cicotte remained on the team, though his status for 1912 appeared uncertain. Other, younger Red Sox pitchers had passed him, including Joe Wood, who won 23 games in 1911 and emerged as Boston's ace. Rookie right-hander Buck O'Brien, who won 26 games at Denver, joined the club in September and won five games with two shutouts. O'Brien threatened to displace Eddie on the Red Sox staff.

By this time, the increasingly erratic team president grew tired of the spotlight and the constant controversies and criticisms surrounding the Red Sox. John I. Taylor and his father, Charles, were ready to sell the club, and devised a plan that would not only assure them a healthy profit, but also give the Boston fans a new ballpark. The Taylors owned land in the Fenway section of Boston, and in late 1911 they began construction of a new home for the Red Sox. John I. Taylor named the new stadium Fenway Park. To finance the park, the Taylors sold half of the club to a group headed by Washington manager Jimmy McAleer and American League secretary Robert McRoy. The Taylors gave up the day-to-day operation of the team but retained ownership in the park, which they rented to the new owners for $30,000 a year.

Despite the change in ownership, the Red Sox were still actively shopping Eddie, and other American League teams expressed interest. One such team was Detroit. In those pre-tampering days, Frank Navin, the owner of the Tigers, told the *Detroit Times* in February, "I'd like to have Cicotte on the

Tigers' pitching staff, but they want too much for him." Eddie replied, "I'd like to be with the Tigers. I'd like to play with the bunch to be in my home town."[18] The Cincinnati Reds of the National League pursued Eddie, but every other American League team would have to waive their rights to him. The Chicago White Sox, Washington Nationals, and St. Louis Browns refused to do so, claiming Eddie every time his name appeared on the waiver wire.

In early 1912, new team president Jimmy McAleer told *Sporting Life* that Eddie had come to terms with the club. McAleer, as manager at Washington, had coveted Eddie, claiming him on waivers more than once, but he, too, was concerned about the knuckleball pitcher's physical condition:

> Eddie Cicotte has also signed and McAleer is confident that the Detroit man will prove to be on the winning list next season. There is no doubt but that he pitched in hard luck a number of times last year. The trouble with Cicotte, according to the club officials, is that he doesn't keep his underpinning in condition. His arm may be strong enough, but his wind is apt to be bad and his legs weak.[19]

Eddie's star had fallen so sharply since his successful 1909 season that new manager Jake Stahl, the former Boston first baseman, assigned him to play with the reserves (called the Yannigans), not the regulars, during spring training. With the Boston club boasting a rapidly maturing staff of young pitchers, Eddie had to earn his place on the team once again. He made his first start of 1912 at Philadelphia on April 15, losing to the A's, 4–1, and then remained idle for more than a week.

After nine days on the bench, Eddie pitched poorly on April 24, when he gave up runs in the first inning once again. He had trouble controlling the ball on a wet day in Washington, and in the first inning, Danny Moeller singled, Eddie Foster walked, and both moved up on a passed ball. Clyde Milan bounced to Eddie, who trapped Moeller in a rundown as Foster and Milan took second and third. A wild pitch brought both runners home, and the Senators led, 2–0. In the third, Foster walloped a double over Speaker's head in center; it probably would have rolled for an inside-the-park home run had the wet grass not slowed it down. Germany Schaefer drove Foster home with a single. All the while, Walter Johnson, a 33-game winner for the Senators in 1912, was hardly bothered by the bad conditions. Eddie was pulled in the fourth inning, and Johnson completed an easy 5–2 win.

The next day, the Washington papers buzzed with rumors that that Nationals were willing to trade veteran right-hander "Long Tom" Hughes for Cicotte. "Eddie Cicotte has never had any luck with the Boston club," said the *Washington Times*, "though rated as one of the best pitchers in the American League. He has been pursued almost continually by a jinx, and he would welcome a change of base."[20]

With three losses in his first four decisions, Eddie was the forgotten man

2. Boston

of the Boston rotation. He pitched only four times in May, and another disaster for Eddie occurred at Fenway on May 29. Joe Wood pitched the first game of a doubleheader against Washington that day and won, 21–8. Eddie started the second game but failed to get out of the first inning. He faced five batters and gave up three runs on two walks and three hits. Larry Pape came in and allowed three more runs, putting Boston behind, 6–0. The Red Sox fought back for a 12–11 win, shortened to eight innings due to rain.

A crossroads for Eddie Cicotte came when the Red Sox faced the Naps in Cleveland on June 4. It was "Lajoie Day," a celebration of Cleveland star Nap Lajoie's tenth anniversary with the club. Hugh Bedient started and gave up a run in the first inning when Jack Graney walked and scored on Lajoie's double. After that, Bedient pitched well for three innings as the Naps flailed away against his wide, sweeping curves. In the fourth, the Naps decided to move up and attack the ball in front of the plate before it broke too much. This tactic worked. After Joe Jackson smacked an inside-the park homer over Speaker's head in center, three singles in a row by Lajoie, Joe Birmingham, and Roger Peckinpaugh filled the bases with none out. That's when Jake Stahl brought Eddie into the game. Neal Ball's sacrifice fly scored Lajoie, and after Eddie retired Steve O'Neill, Vean Gregg's single scored Birmingham and Peckinpaugh. The score was now 5 to 0.

Eddie shut down the Naps the rest of the way, and as the *Boston Herald* stated, "Cicotte was in fine form for the next four innings, his showing being the only encouraging feature of the frolic from the Boston standpoint."[21] However, Eddie did not pitch again for more than a month. Perhaps the Red Sox were upset at him for allowing all three inherited runners to score, or perhaps the relationship between Eddie and Boston management had broken down completely, even with John I. Taylor gone. Whatever the reason, Eddie sat on the bench during the rest of June and the first few days of July.

The Red Sox did not miss Eddie during his four and a half weeks of idleness. Joe Wood appeared headed to a 30-win season, while Ray Collins and Buck O'Brien gave the team two more solid starters, with Hugh Bedient and Charley Hall in both starting and relief roles. After a loss in Detroit on June 7, the Red Sox reeled off 19 wins in their next 22 games to grab first place, which they held for the rest of the 1912 season. The Red Sox did all this without Eddie Cicotte. The Boston club no longer needed Eddie, so he landed on the waiver wire again. Surely some American League team could use a pitcher who won 15 games only two years before.

The Washington club needed pitching. Nationals manager Clark Griffith owned the best pitcher in the game in Walter Johnson and a solid number two man in Bob Groom, but the Nats needed depth if they expected to challenge the Red Sox. Griffith scanned the waiver list for pitchers and claimed Gene Krapp of Cleveland, Barney Pelty of St. Louis, and Eddie Cicotte of

Boston. Each time Griffith claimed Eddie, the Red Sox withdrew him from the list, so Griffith wound up buying Pelty from the Browns instead. With Washington no longer interested in Eddie, Jimmy McAleer still hoped to get something for his disappointing knuckleballer, but by mid-season it was clear that no deal was imminent. Eddie's poor pitching, bad luck, and 31-day layoff reduced his value so drastically that a sale, not a trade, was the Boston club's best option.

Eddie pitched one more game for Boston against the A's in Philadelphia on July 6. Perhaps McAleer was showcasing him, hoping that a good performance would raise his price. With his career in Boston on the line, Eddie only lasted four innings. In the first, Bris Lord singled, and Rube Oldring laid down a sacrifice bunt. Eddie fell down trying to field it, and Oldring was safe. Eddie Collins drove Oldring home, and the A's led 1–0 before Cicotte registered an out. He retired the A's in the first and second innings, but in the third, Eddie tried to pick Oldring off second base. The ball caromed off Oldring's leg and bounced into right field as Oldring took third. He came home on a single by Frank Baker. Later, a triple by Chief Bender and a single by Lord brought another run home. After four innings, the A's led, 5–2, and Olaf Hendricksen pinch-hit for Eddie in the fifth. Charley Hall and Hugh Bedient shut out the A's the rest of the way, and the Red Sox pulled it out, 11–5.

This game was Eddie's last in a Red Sox uniform. On July 9, 1912, the Red Sox sold Eddie Cicotte to the Chicago White Sox for a reported sum of $1,500. They could have sent him to Chicago several weeks earlier, but the White Sox held first place in early June, and the Boston club did not want to give a potentially good pitcher to their rivals. One month later, with the White Sox eight games out and sinking fast, Boston pulled the trigger on the transaction.

The Red Sox won the American League pennant and the World Series without Eddie, and the pitcher could not resist indulging in some sour grapes. In December of 1912, a Detroit reporter got an earful of Eddie's feelings about his former team.

> There is all difference possible between the Boston and Chicago clubs. The Boston club is made up of two men, Carrigan and Wagner. They are the only players who work in unison; the others work for personal glory. One thinks solely of his batting average; another of his fielding percentage, and still another of how many games he can win by his pitching.
>
> You never heard anything like coaching on the Boston bench. If a pitcher is hit a trifle hard or if a fielder makes a blunder the other players criticize instead of slapping the fellow on the back or yelling words of encouragement.[22]

Still, the article introduced Cicotte as the "dumpling pitcher," so perhaps Eddie still needed work on his conditioning.

3

Chicago

> *Edward Cicotte, the sturdy spitball flinger bought from Boston last night, was in the hotel here this morning for breakfast. He wasted no time in getting away from the Boston club and was greatly pleased to join the White Sox, declaring that he would work his head off to make a good record on the Chicago team.*—Chicago Tribune, July 11, 1912

The Boston Red Sox no longer wanted Eddie Cicotte, but the Chicago White Sox were happy to have him. The White Sox in 1912 were in the same place the Red Sox were in when Eddie joined them four years earlier—a once-dominant team fallen on hard times and seeking to rebuild with young talent.

The Chicago White Sox were founded by Charles Comiskey, one of the towering figures of baseball. Comiskey, a pennant-winning first baseman and manager for the St. Louis Browns during the 1880s, managed at Cincinnati for awhile, then bought the St. Paul, Minnesota, club of the Western League in 1896. He moved the club to the South Side of Chicago in 1900 as part of the new American League, and won the circuit's first pennant as manager and owner that year. In 1901, the new loop became a major league, and Comiskey's ballclub, which he named the White Sox, won the flag again with pitching star Clark Griffith as manager.

The pinnacle of Comiskey's career came in 1906, when the White Sox, called the "Hitless Wonders" for their anemic offense, rode their pitching to another pennant and shocked the powerful crosstown Cubs in the World Series. This unexpected triumph made Comiskey and his White Sox the kings of baseball in Chicago. In 1910, he built a grand baseball palace called Comiskey Park, which housed the club for more than 80 years.

Comiskey was an impatient man, hiring and firing several managers who failed to repeat the magic of 1906. His field boss for the 1912 season was James "Nixey" Callahan, a popular former pitcher and outfielder who had managed the White Sox in 1903 and was fired in the middle of the 1904 season. Now in his second term as manager, Callahan's job was to rebuild the White Sox, who finished in fourth place under Hugh Duffy's leadership in 1911. It was time to leave the Hitless Wonders behind and enter a new era of Chicago baseball.

Four members of the 1906 championship squad were still with the team in 1912, and the most important was pitcher Ed Walsh. A spitballer, Walsh was the workhorse of the pitching staff. He won 40 games in 1908 and nearly led the White Sox to the pennant by himself, pitching in a league-record 464 innings with 42 complete games. Walsh was so dominant and durable that his managers could not resist using, and overusing, him. Walsh pitched between 368 and 464 innings each year but one from 1907 to 1912, and most observers believed that it was only a matter of time before the veteran pitcher broke down. When the White Sox started the 1912 season with 28 wins in their first 40 games, Detroit manager Hugh Jennings dismissed them as contenders. "They're using Walsh in every game," he said. The overworked spitballer made 41 starts that year and, due to the lack of an adequate bullpen, 21 relief appearances. The White Sox imported Eddie Cicotte, among others, in an attempt to reduce Walsh's workload.

Cicotte, at age 28, was not the only new face. George "Buck" Weaver was an enthusiastic 21-year-old shortstop from Pottstown, Pennsylvania, who showed promise, but was so error-prone that the fans called him "Error-a-Day" Weaver. He batted only .224 in 1912 and led the league's shortstops with 71 errors, but he was young and showed exceptional range. His smiling good nature on the field made him one of the most popular White Sox. Another new recruit was catcher Ray Schalk, who made his debut on the day before his 20th birthday. Schalk, who was short for a catcher at five feet, nine inches, was not a strong hitter, but his defense was top-notch, and he took over the starting job within a year.

Cicotte often credited Schalk with much of his success. His catchers in Boston had trouble holding his trick pitches, but Schalk was quick and active enough to save knucklers and spitters from rolling to the backstop. Eddie expressed his admiration for his catcher to *Baseball Magazine* in 1916.

> Schalk showed what he was made of on the first day he joined our club. Walsh was pitching at the time with all his old speed and strength. The spit ball is notoriously hard to catch, and Schalk being new to the game had difficulty in getting Walsh to read his signals. Finally he said to Walsh, "Never mind any more signals, just cut loose with whatever you want and I will hold you," and he did. That was some stunt for any catcher, let alone a youngster just breaking into the league.[1]

Manager Callahan's chief assistant was the 45-year-old coach, William "Kid" Gleason, an enthusiastic baseball lifer who pitched and played second base for several teams during the 1890s and early 1900s. Gleason was a prankster—he loved to sneak into Eddie Collins' room at night and tie the star in-

Ray Schalk, who caught most of Eddie Cicotte's 156 wins in a Chicago uniform (Library of Congress).

fielder to the bed with a razor strop[2]—who kept the clubhouse lively. He was also a smart baseball man, highly skilled in teaching the finer points of the game. He worked with Eddie Cicotte, not only on his pitching but also on his attitude and confidence after his failure at Boston.

Eddie was always friendly to the press, but got along especially well with one Chicago sportswriter. That writer was Ring Lardner, whom Eddie had met when the pitcher was with the Red Sox and Lardner wrote for the *Boston American*. Lardner moved to Chicago not long after Eddie joined the White Sox, and the two men became friends, often dining and drinking together. Lardner found Eddie to be a good companion and conversationalist. When Lardner began publishing his "Jack Keefe" stories, tales of a fictional White Sox rookie interacting with the real-life ballplayers, Lardner gave Cicotte many of the best lines and jokes. In the stories, much of the wisest advice Keefe, a not-too-bright pitcher, receives comes from the mouth of Eddie Cicotte.

Ring Lardner admired Eddie not only for his pitching success, but also because of the grit and intelligence he displayed in fooling hitters with trick pitches and a mediocre fastball. Eddie possessed no world-beating talent, but appealed to Lardner as a normal Everyman succeeding against the odds. In 1915, Lardner named four pitchers to his all-time All-Star team. The four were Christy Mathewson, Walter Johnson, Grover Cleveland Alexander, and Eddie Cicotte. Lardner explained his selection in his vernacular prose. "They ain't a smarter pitcher in baseball," he wrote, "and they's nobody that's a better all-around ball player, no pitcher, I mean."[3]

Cicotte lost his first game for the White Sox, a 4–2 defeat to Walter Johnson at Washington on July 13. Five days later, Eddie's worst game of the year, and perhaps the worst pitching performance of his career, was fortunately washed out by rain. On July 18, Eddie faced the Red Sox for the first time since his departure from Boston. Despite threatening skies and a steady drizzle, the umpires started the game. While sheets of rain fell, the White Sox went out in order in the first. In the bottom of the inning, the Red Sox batted around and then some, scoring ten runs off Eddie and his replacement, rookie Ralph Bell. The umpires called the game with two out in the first when the rains reached monsoon proportions, saving Cicotte from a huge bump in his earned run average.

The next day, in the second game of a doubleheader, Eddie pitched one of his best games, holding Boston to one run in 11 innings before Hugh Bedient singled and Harry Hooper doubled him home in the 12th to end the contest, 2–1. The White Sox made five errors behind him—two by shortstop Buck Weaver—but Eddie pitched out of one jam after another. He also received a warm welcome from the fans at Fenway Park. "Cicotte was the hero of the day, though he was beaten," said one paper. "He gave a wonderful exhibition of pitching and was applauded time after time for his gallant work. It was no fault of Cicotte that he was licked, for he was given about the most bunglesome support that it would be possible to give a pitcher and still keep his team in the fight for the game."[4]

Eddie rebounded in Chicago, after a period of adjustment, and his move to the Midwest agreed with him. He lost his first four decisions with the White Sox, dropping his record to 1–7, but then won five in a row for the fourth-place Chicago club. He ended the season with nine wins in his 16 decisions for the White Sox and finished 10–10 overall. He had proven his worth in Chicago after his failures in Boston and established himself as a capable second starter, sharing the pitching load with the overworked Ed Walsh.

The White Sox and the crosstown Cubs of the National League regularly played a post-season series for the championship of Chicago in years in which neither team played in the World Series. Other cities staged similar October matchups, officially sanctioned by baseball's National Commission, but none were as fiercely contested as the White Sox—Cubs tilts. After the conclusion of the 1912 regular season, the two Chicago teams met in a seven-game set, Eddie's first taste of post-season action.

Eddie's knuckleball grip (author's collection).

Nothing illustrated the Chicago club's dependence on Ed Walsh more than the City Series of 1912. Walsh pitched a one-hit shutout in the first game, which ended in a scoreless tie after nine innings due to darkness. In Game Two, Eddie Cicotte allowed three runs in nine innings, then was relieved by Walsh, who pitched three more frames before the game was called in a 3–3 tie after 12 innings. The Cubs then took a 2–0 series lead, defeating Doc White and Walsh on consecutive days. This left it up to Eddie, who started the fifth contest and gave up three runs in the first inning and three more in the third. Eddie left the game at that point as the Cubs won, 8–1, for a lead of three games to none.

Eddie did not pitch again in the series because manager Callahan turned most of the pitching chores over to Walsh. "Big Ed" kept the Sox alive with a 5–4, 11-inning win in Game Six, while Doc White and Joe Benz took Game Seven for the White Sox. The Sox were now behind 3 games to 2, and when

Walsh saved a 5–4 victory in relief of Frank Lange in Game Eight, the White Sox tied the series. Callahan could have put the well-rested Eddie Cicotte on the mound for the deciding game, but instead started Walsh for the fourth time. The result was a laugher for the White Sox, who embarrassed the Cubs with a 16–0 win to sweep the city series after being down, 3–0.

This humiliating loss stunned the Cubs fans, many of whom loudly complained that the City Series must have been fixed. Perhaps the Cubs players were bought out by gamblers, they said, or else the Cubs threw the series to get their strict manager, Frank Chance, fired. *Chicago Tribune* writer Hugh Fullerton found it necessary to refute these wild claims. "The muckerishness of the 'fan' is exceeding itself in muck this fall," wrote Fullerton. "Boston howled that [the World Series] was 'all fixed,' then raved over the team when it won … and now Chicago accuses the Cubs." Fullerton went on to say, "If they will invent some system by which baseball games CAN be made crooked without being detected in two innings they can make fortunes."[5]

After a brief holdout, Eddie signed his contract for the 1913 season in mid-January and reported on time to spring training in Paso Robles, California, where the Red Sox had trained two years before. Now a veteran beginning his seventh season of major league play, Eddie took three young Chicago pitching prospects—Phil Douglas, Mellie Wolfgang, and Kid Smith—aside and taught them the secrets of the knuckleball. He conducted "a post-graduate course in the manly art of knuckleball slinging,"[6] said the papers, and Professor Cicotte declared himself pleased with the progress of his students.

The White Sox pitching staff now included several solid performers to support Ed Walsh and Eddie Cicotte. Ewell "Reb" Russell, who spent 1912 in the Texas League, impressed the White Sox in spring training after working with coach Kid Gleason to refine his curveball. Callahan wanted to send Russell to the Pacific Coast League, but Gleason convinced the manager to keep the rookie. Joe Benz, 13–17 in 1912, was slotted for both starting and relief roles, and Jim Scott, in his fifth season with the Sox, was ready to come back after an attack of rheumatism limited him to six games the previous season.

The White Sox leaned heavily on these pitchers, because years of overwork finally caught up to Ed Walsh. "Big Ed" pitched 434 innings in 1912 (393 during the regular season and 41 in the City Series), and in early 1913 he complained of a sore arm. Walsh was never the same after that, and in 1913 he appeared in only 16 games, with long stretches of rest in between. Russell, Cicotte, and Benz now formed the core of a new White Sox staff, one that Charles Comiskey hoped would soon bring a World Series title to Chicago.

Comiskey was determined to build a winning team, and in mid-1913 he found one of the game's best players on the trading block. The New York Yankees were willing to part with veteran Hal Chase, the best-fielding first sacker in the game, and were not asking for much in return. The White Sox,

3. Chicago

The White Sox pitching staff in 1913. From left: Ed Walsh, Jim Scott, Eddie Cicotte, Joe Benz, Reb Russell, Bill Lathrop, Red Faber, and a member of the support staff. Notice how much shorter Eddie is than his fellow hurlers (courtesy Ernie Harwell Sports Collection, Detroit Public Library).

disappointed with Babe Borton's play at first, made a deal. Comiskey sent Borton and reserve Rollie Zeider to New York for Chase on June 1.

In the words of his biographer, Martin Kohout, Hal Chase "was the most notoriously corrupt player in baseball history. He was also, according to many of those who saw him play, the greatest defensive first baseman ever."[7] Chase was a brilliant glove man at first base, and many of his contemporaries rated him as the greatest first baseman of all time. Babe Ruth, in his autobiography *The Babe Ruth Story*, selected Chase, not fellow Yankee Lou Gehrig, to his all-time team at first. Chase was also a good hitter for average, if not for power, and won the National League batting title in 1916 with Cincinnati.

"Prince Hal" should have been one of the biggest stars in the game, on the same level as Ty Cobb, Tris Speaker, and Walter Johnson, but controversy and accusations followed him throughout his career. In New York, where he began his career with the Highlanders (later called the Yankees), manager George Stallings accused Chase of "laying down." Stallings suspected Chase of purposely making errors and missing signs at the most damaging times, presumably to win bets. The team owners, one of whom ran New York City's biggest illegal casino, did not want to dismiss their most popular player and biggest gate attraction. They fired Stallings and made Chase the manager. His tenure was unsuccessful, and he directed the team for only one season.

His next manager, Frank Chance (hired by the Yankees after his dismissal by the Cubs), also accused Chase of "throwing down me and the team" and forced his trade to Chicago for two nonentities. When Chase joined the White Sox in June of 1913, Charles Comiskey was thrilled. "That deal means the pennant for the Sox," said the Chicago owner. "Chase is just the man we needed and he will give the team one hundred percent additional strength."[8] However, Chase's arrival made little difference, as the Sox held fourth place when he joined them and fifth at season's end. No one knows if his game-throwing followed him to Chicago, but suspicion certainly did. As *The Sporting News* put it, "Players like Chase come about once in a century. That he can play first base as it never was and perhaps never again will be played is a well-known truth. That he will is a different matter."[9] Still, despite Chase's notoriety, Comiskey wanted him, and Comiskey got him.

Chase solidified the first base position, though questions followed him everywhere. Sometimes he showed flashes of brilliance, as when he helped win a game for Eddie with an inspired piece of baserunning. He advanced from first base on a single, trotting nonchalantly into second. When Yankees right fielder Roy Hartzell lobbed the ball lazily back to the infield, Chase turned on the jets. He sailed around third and slid home safely. However, on July 23 he committed five errors in a 7–1 loss to Washington. His 33 errors in 1913 led the league for the third year in a row. One could never tell what kind of effort Prince Hal would choose to give on any particular day.

The 1913 season was Eddie's best in the major leagues so far. He finished the campaign with 18 wins and sported a sterling 1.58 earned run average, second-best in the American League behind Walter Johnson's 1.14 mark. He teamed with Reb Russell (22–16) and Jim Scott (20–21) to form a solid starting rotation. However, the White Sox owned the weakest offense in the league, finishing last in runs and batting average. The Sox were fortunate to finish in fifth place at 78–74, 17.5 games behind the pennant-winning Athletics. At least the 1913 campaign ended on a high note with another win over the Cubs in the post-season City Series. Eddie Cicotte pitched poorly in the second contest, a Cubs win that lasted 13 innings, but won the fourth game, 5–2, as the White Sox defeated their crosstown rivals in six games. This victory gave Eddie and his teammates $807 apiece, the winning share of the gate receipts.

At season's end, Charles Comiskey and New York Giants manager John McGraw took two teams of players on an ambitious world tour to spread baseball around the globe. Eddie was not part of it; perhaps he preferred to spend the winter in Detroit with his family, or maybe the cost was too high (each man was required to put up $250 of their own money to participate, while the organizers split the profits among themselves). Only five White Sox made the trip, including shortstop Buck Weaver and pitchers Joe Benz and Jim Scott. The two teams augmented their rosters with stars of other clubs, such as Boston's Tris Speaker and Detroit's Sam Crawford. In late November, they sailed to Japan for a series of contests—the first by major leaguers in that country—and then traveled through China, India, Egypt, and Europe, where they played for the King of England in London before returning to America in March of 1914.

On the tour, Comiskey discovered a pitcher who would be a fixture for the White Sox for the next two decades. Urban "Red" Faber, a 25-year-old spitball hurler who spent the 1913 season with Des Moines of the Western League, was a late addition to the world tour when Giants star Christy Mathewson dropped out at the last minute. Comiskey, who bought Faber's contract from Des Moines, lent the youngster to McGraw's Giants for the duration of the trip. Though Faber suffered mightily from seasickness, he pitched so well that McGraw offered to buy him at the end of the tour. Comiskey kept Faber instead and plugged him into the Chicago rotation.

Eddie Cicotte performed so successfully in 1913 that, while Comiskey was occupied with his round-the-world trip, the Federal League came calling. The Federal League was the brainchild of John Powers, a baseball promoter and businessman who saw a need for a third major league. This upstart league operated as a six-team independent circuit in 1913, and in 1914 a Chicago manufacturer named James M. Gilmore ousted Powers, took over as president, and proclaimed a new major league. Backed by wealthy investors such as oil baron Harry Sinclair and St. Louis ice magnate Phil Ball, the Federal League set out to steal the stars of the American and National Leagues. When the world tour returned to New York in March of 1914, Federal League agents, contracts in hand, made offers to the players as they disembarked from the ship.

The new league signed a few established players. Joe Tinker, longtime shortstop of the Chicago Cubs, became the playing manager of the Chicago Whales, while the St. Louis Terriers lured Tinker's teammate, pitching star Mordecai "Three-Finger" Brown into the fold. One White Sox player who made the jump was Edd Roush, a promising outfielder from Oakland City, Indiana, who saw action for the Sox in nine games in 1913. The Feds drew some other well-known names, but most of the stars took a wait-and-see attitude. Ty Cobb, Walter Johnson, and Tris Speaker all turned down the Feds and decided to remain in the established circuit for the time being.

The Feds courted Eddie Cicotte, who held out for a higher salary once again in early 1914, but Eddie was unwilling to make such a radical career change at this time. Both the Pittsburgh and Indianapolis Federal League teams wanted to sign Eddie, but lost all interest when they heard the pitcher's requirements. Eddie, with the success of 1913 behind him, drove a hard bargain, demanding a $10,000 signing bonus and a three-year contract at $8,000 per year. "They told me to go jump in the river when I told them my terms," said Eddie to the *Chicago Tribune*. "I didn't jump. I figured it was worth $10,000 to take a chance with them, for I am a long way from being through as a pitcher. The $8,000 three year contract would be a gamble, anyway, because they could let me go at any time. Then where would I have been?"[10]

Cicotte traveled to spring training in Paso Robles in February without a contract, but on March 10, after a conference with coach Kid Gleason, Eddie agreed to terms for the 1914 campaign. He was the next-to-last White Sox player to sign; Hal Chase, who was busily playing Comiskey and the Federal League against each other, finally decided to remain in Chicago, signing his contract on March 22.

The White Sox started the 1914 season with seven wins in their first eight games, but followed with eight losses in a row and never mounted a challenge for the pennant. Once again, poor offense did them in. Rookie Red Faber won ten games, but Reb Russell won only seven after winning 22 in 1913. Eddie Cicotte, Joe Benz (15–19), and Jim Scott (14–18) suffered from a lack of offensive support as the Sox fell to sixth place, tied with the New York Yankees at 70–84.

In June, the Sox received a jolt when Hal Chase abruptly quit the team and signed with Buffalo of the Federal League. The first baseman told the press that he broke his contract with the White Sox because it had the standard "ten-day" clause in it, under which the team could release a player on ten days' notice. Chase declared that the clause should be reciprocal; he should be allowed, in turn, to quit the White Sox on ten days' notice for a better offer. Comiskey fought the matter in court, slapping an injunction on Chase after "Prince Hal" played in two games for Buffalo. One month later, a Buffalo judge sided with Chase, citing an "absolute lack of mutuality" in the standard major league contract.

Despite Chase's departure, the Sox soon enjoyed their best stretch of the 1914 season. In late June and early July, a 17–2 streak lifted Chicago briefly into second place. But reality set in, and a disastrous eastern road trip dropped the White Sox back into sixth position. The Philadelphia Athletics grabbed first place on June 8 and never relinquished it, and by early August the pennant race was virtually over.

The entire 1914 season was a bad one for Eddie. He suffered from hay fever during the summer months, and one day in Detroit he let out a loud kerchoo as he released a pitch. The umpire called a balk on him. "Balk nothing," Eddie complained. "That was a sneeze!"[11] He improved his record to 11–10 with a five-hitter at St. Louis on August 16, but that was his last win of the season. Eddie lost his final six decisions to end at 11–16, though his 2.04 earned run average was the best among the team's main starters.

3. Chicago

The White Sox now owned a solid core of pitchers, and the arrival of Red Faber added depth to a strong pitching staff. However, the offense was still a weak spot, and team defense was lacking. Jack Fournier, who took over at first base after Hal Chase jumped the team, hit .311 but was subpar in the field, while a parade of third base prospects failed to solidify that position. Shortstop Buck Weaver improved his average to .246, but second baseman Lena Blackburn, at .222, added little at the plate. Once again, the Sox finished last in the league in runs scored, and Charles Comiskey recognized that the White Sox would not escape the second division, much less challenge for a pennant, without a marked improvement in the team's offense.

Fortunately for Comiskey, Connie Mack was ready to break up his championship team. The A's had won four pennants and three World Series titles during the previous five seasons, but their poor performance in the 1914 World Series—a stunning sweep by the underdog Boston Braves—convinced Mack that it was time to start over. Also, clubhouse grumbling over salaries and offers from the Federal League had destroyed team morale. Mack, who was losing money despite his club's on-field success, was now willing to sell or trade some of his high-salaried men.

Mack's biggest star was the top second baseman in the game. Eddie Collins, 27 years old in 1914, was the linchpin of Philadelphia's famous "$100,000 infield" that also featured third baseman Frank Baker, shortstop Jack Barry, and first baseman "Stuffy" McInnis. Collins, a perennial .300 hitter and prolific base stealer, ranked with Ty Cobb and Tris Speaker among the top three players in the American League. In 1914, Collins batted .344, stole 58 bases, and scored 122 runs, leading the club in all three categories. Now he was available, and Comiskey was determined to get him. On December 8, 1914, Connie Mack announced that he had sold Eddie Collins to the White Sox for $50,000, the largest amount ever paid for a player up to that time.

The addition of Collins, the top infielder in the game and the 1914 Most Valuable Player Award winner, showed the rest of the American League that Comiskey was serious about building a pennant winner. The White Sox owner, however, was dissatisfied with Jimmy Callahan as his manager. He dismissed Callahan for the second time, and many speculated that Collins, the star of Connie Mack's three-time world champions, would take the job. However, Collins was not interested, writing in a letter to a friend, "I don't want to have any such job as long as I am good enough to be in the batting order regularly."[12] Comiskey then surprised the baseball world by choosing a career minor leaguer, Clarence "Pants" Rowland, to lead the White Sox in 1915.

Rowland, a 36-year-old former catcher, earned his nickname when he slid into a base one day and his too-large pants fell down. The youngster liked the name Pants better than his given name of Clarence, so the moniker stuck. Rowland had known Comiskey for years and impressed the White Sox owner with his skill at talent evaluation. While managing in the Three-I League, Rowland had urged Comiskey to sign Red Faber, who became a star for the Sox, and others such as Bobby Veach and Larry Doyle who became standouts for other teams. The new manager spent several years at Dubuque, where Comiskey had played three decades before, before transferring to Peoria and winning the 1914 pennant.

"Rowland is by no means a new man to me," Comiskey told the press. "I have been watching his work very carefully in the minor leagues for the past seven or eight years, and have been greatly impressed with his aggressiveness and his judgment. He is particularly good at picking ball players and he has sent quite a few up to the White Sox during that time."[13] Still, it was highly unusual for a manager to have no experience in the big leagues, and Rowland set out to earn the respect of his charges.

At the same time, Comiskey released coach Kid Gleason, who had served as Jimmy Callahan's assistant manager, coach, prankster, and buffer for three seasons. Perhaps Comiskey wanted to sweep away the old regime, but the Kid was a sparkplug, and the White Sox would miss his energy and enthusiasm. Rowland expressed confidence that he would motivate the Sox despite the loss of the popular coach. "A ballplayer is a human being," Rowland said, "and with an even break he will treat you as well as you treat him. I'll play the boys on a 50–50 basis and we'll be a happy little family together."[14]

Collins wrote letters to some of his new teammates, but the one he sent to Eddie Cicotte caused him no end of trouble. In it, Collins stated, "Here is one thing I have been waiting to say, I am glad to be away from Mack's team. I say this sincerely, and of all the cities in the American League, I prefer Chicago. The fans are loyal there,"[15] implying that those in Philadelphia were not. Athletics rooters were understandably upset at the apparent insult, and Collins spent the next few weeks issuing denials and backtracking. Why Eddie Cicotte chose to share a private letter with some of his sportswriter friends in Detroit is a mystery, but it needlessly complicated Collins' relationships with Connie Mack and the Philadelphia fans.

A few weeks later, the papers reported how Eddie Cicotte, who battled his weight in every off-season, controlled it during the winter months. One of Eddie's brothers owned a tavern, the Goodrich House in Goodrich, Michigan, northwest of Detroit, and Eddie helped out for two or three weeks by cutting ice. This, the pitcher explained, was great exercise.

> You're out there all day working for all that is in you, and thus reducing your weight without being forced to go through a weakening process. Handling ice puts muscle where fat once rested.
>
> I am in shape now. Of course, my arm isn't strong, but I am down in weight and I intend to keep myself there until reporting at Paso Robles for the spring training season. I figure it will take me about two weeks to get the whip in working order.[16]

4

Career Rejuvenation

> *There is always the inclination on the part of the young pitcher to experiment on freak deliveries. I suppose this tendency is the wish implanted in all of us to try short cuts to a definite goal.... Perhaps I should be among the last to discourage freak deliveries since I have been accused of depending upon them a great deal myself. My particular pride and joy is the knuckle ball, which I developed by a good deal of practice. But there are no patents on this delivery. In fact I have endeavored to teach it to several other pitchers.* —Eddie Cicotte, 1918[1]

The 1914 season ended in disappointment for the White Sox (though they defeated the Cubs in the City Series for the fourth year in a row), but the team appeared ready to escape the second division. The addition of Eddie Collins improved both the infield and the lineup, while the good-hitting (but poor-fielding) Jack Fournier at first base and the steadily improving Buck Weaver at shortstop promised to aid the Chicago offensive attack. Third base was still a problem area, with the light-hitting Lena Blackburn moving to the hot corner to make room for Collins at second, but Ray Schalk emerged as the best catcher in the American League. Two outfield spots were manned by the reliable John "Shano" Collins, no relation to Eddie, who joined the Sox in 1910, and Bob "Braggo" Roth, who struck out too much but hit for power.

A muscular, speedy rookie took over in center field. Oscar "Happy" Felsch, a cheerful 24-year-old from Milwaukee, starred for his hometown Brewers of the American Association during the previous two seasons, hitting for power and average and making incredible catches in the outfield. Comiskey bought Felsch's contract in August of 1914 for $12,000 and two players. Felsch completed the 1914 season with the Brewers, then reported to training camp with the White Sox the following spring.

The White Sox were on the rise, and the 1915 American League pennant race looked to be a wide-open battle. Connie Mack's reign at the top of the American League was over, as the financially troubled Philadelphia A's reacted to their stunning loss in the 1914 World Series by selling, trading, or releasing many of their star players. While Mack's decimated team plummeted to last place, the Boston Red Sox, led by Tris Speaker, and Ty Cobb's Detroit Tigers were expected to compete for the flag. Many newspaper columnists expected the White Sox to join the fight, and some even predicted a pennant for Comiskey's men.

The White Sox now boasted five solid starters (not counting the injured Ed Walsh, who pitched only three games in 1915), and Eddie Cicotte was the oldest of the group. Red Faber, Joe Benz, Reb Russell, Jim Scott, and Eddie competed for starting slots, and some observers wondered if the club had too many good pitchers to fit into the rotation. Rather than send one of the five to the bullpen, new manager Pants Rowland solved the problem by giving each man between 25 and 32 starting assignments, with a dozen or more relief appearances in between.

After a shaky start, this arrangement worked very well for the White Sox. They began the 1915 season by losing six of their first eight contests on the road against the Browns and Tigers but won their first seven in a row at home. In May, the White Sox won nine consecutive games and vaulted into first place, passing the Yankees, Tigers, and Red Sox. Red Faber, in his second season, came into his own and jumped to the top of the rotation, winning 24 games and becoming one of Comiskey's favorites. The veteran right-hander, Jim Scott, also won 24 games for the Sox.

The odd man out was Eddie Cicotte. Eddie saved the first game of the 1915 season, a three-and-a-half-hour marathon in St. Louis, when Faber allowed two runs in the bottom of the 13th inning. Eddie came in and got the last three outs to preserve a 7–6 win. Afterward, Eddie lost his first three decisions and entered June with a 1–4 record. His only shutout of 1915 came at New York on June 9 with a 13–0 win over the Yankees. Eddie gave up only two hits, both singles, and belted three hits of his own in five trips to the plate.

Faber and Scott paced the Chicago pitching staff in wins, but Eddie struggled with his consistency. He followed his shutout with four more wins in a row to boost his record to 6–4, but then lost four of his next five. The low point of Eddie's season came on August 4, when he pitched seven innings at Washington and stopped a hard grounder from Merito Acosta with his pitching hand. The blow dislocated a knuckle, the one that Eddie rested the ball against when he threw his knuckler. Mellie Wolfgang came in to finish the game, and the blow knocked Eddie out of action for two and a half weeks.

While Eddie recovered from his injury, Charles Comiskey dickered with the Cleveland Indians to bring another of the game's biggest stars to Chicago. The cash-strapped Indians teetered on the edge of insolvency after a last-place finish in 1914 and a poor start to the 1915 campaign, so they decided

Eddie in his Chicago road uniform. The White Sox wore these blue uniforms, with white piping on the hat, in 1914 and 1915 (author's collection).

to part with Joe Jackson, the popular outfielder some called the best hitter in baseball after Ty Cobb.

They called him "Shoeless Joe" because he once played a minor league game in his stocking feet. Connie Mack signed him in 1908, but Jackson, a small-town mill hand from South Carolina who could neither read nor write, failed to stick with the Athletics. Traded to Cleveland in 1910, he blossomed, batting .408 in 1911 and .395 in 1912 and giving Cobb a run for batting supremacy in the American League. Now Jackson, who sported a career batting average of .371 at the time, was on the market.

Several teams were interested, including the Yankees and Red Sox, so Comiskey gave his trusted assistant Harry Grabiner a blank check and sent him to negotiate with Indians owner Charles Somers. "Go to Cleveland," instructed Comiskey, "watch the bidding for Jackson, [and] raise the highest one made by any club until they all drop out."[2]

Comiskey offered to buy both Jackson and shortstop Ray Chapman, but Somers did not want to part with both of his biggest assets. Instead, soon after Jackson signed a new three-year contract with the Indians for $6,000 a year (keeping him safe from Federal League raiders), Comiskey purchased the outfielder for $31,500 in cash and three players from the White Sox reserve list—outfielders Larry Chappell and Braggo Roth and pitcher Ed Klepfer. These three players collectively cost Comiskey $34,000 to acquire, making the $65,500 transaction the most expensive deal in baseball up to that time. Jackson joined the White Sox on August 21 and played left field in a doubleheader against the Yankees. He went hitless in the second game, in which Eddie Cicotte returned to the mound after his knuckle injury and took the loss, dropping his record to 9–10. Four wins in his final six decisions put Eddie over the break-even mark at 13–12 at season's end.

The additions of Hall of Fame–level talents Eddie Collins and Joe Jackson improved the Chicago offense, and their pitching staff was already one of the best in the game. But the Sox were not yet ready to take over the American League. They won 93 games in 1915, the club's highest total since the world championship year of 1906, but finished the season in third place, 9½ games behind Boston and seven behind Detroit. Once again they dominated the Cubs in the City Series in October, but by now everyone in Chicago expected that. The fans wanted a pennant, and the steadily improving White Sox were getting closer.

Charles Comiskey, founder and owner of the Chicago White Sox (author's collection).

4. Career Rejuvenation

During the early 1910s, Eddie Cicotte was often called the unluckiest player in baseball. The Tigers sold him to Newark in 1906, just before the Detroit club won three consecutive pennants from 1907 to 1909. The Tigers lost all three World Series, but Eddie missed out on three Series checks. In 1912, he was shuffled off to the White Sox a few months before the Red Sox won the American League pennant. The Boston club appeared in four World Series during the decade, none of which included Eddie Cicotte. Though the money he made from the Chicago City Series each October was nice, Eddie was more determined than ever to appear on the game's biggest stage and cash one of those fat winning shares of the Series money.

But as the 1916 campaign began, Eddie's career was at a standstill. He had won 18 games for the White Sox in 1913, but his 1914 (11–16) and 1915 (13–12) campaigns were average at best. Cicotte was now 31, a few months away from his 32nd birthday, and his career record was 91–81. He was getting old for a pitcher.

Fortunately for Eddie, Charles Comiskey was not finished acquiring new talent. On September 28, 1915, the White Sox drafted pitcher Dave Danforth from Louisville of the American Association. Danforth, six years younger than Eddie, had pitched for the Philadelphia A's earlier in the decade. After a stint in the high minors with the Baltimore Orioles (where one of his teammates was a teenaged pitcher named Babe Ruth) and another with Louisville, Comiskey brought him back to the American League. Danforth reported to spring training in early 1916 at Mineral Wells, Texas, where he met Eddie Cicotte.

The two men had little in common, as Eddie had dropped out of school early and Danforth was a college graduate who attended dental school in the off-season, but they both loved to experiment with new pitches. Danforth, during his minor league years, had discovered that an imperfectly round baseball did tricks when thrown. He used this knowledge to strike out 11 men in a relief appearance for Louisville, and the local paper reported, "he kept scratching the ball and roughing the surface until the visitors kicked about it."[3] He could also loosen the cover of the ball with his huge, powerful hands (which must have been a drawback for a future dentist), or pry up one of the seams.

Eddie Cicotte knew all these tricks. Eddie needed a new pitch, so Dave Danforth showed him one. Danforth introduced Eddie to the shine ball.

The pitch that made both Dave Danforth and Eddie Cicotte famous was one that Danforth found quite by accident. Pitching in Louisville on an infield sprayed with oil (to keep down the dust), Danforth found the ball hard to grip. He rubbed the oil off the ball on his pants leg. He soon found that rubbing the baseball on only one side made half of it smoother and shinier than the other. Hence, the shine ball, which once again took advantage of an uneven surface.

Major league infields were not covered in oil, so Eddie and his new teammate experimented with other substances. They found that talcum powder, applied to the right leg of the uniform pants, shined up the ball just as well and was not visible on the white uniform. Paraffin, too, did a good job of it. Once again, Eddie had found a "dry spitter," one that broke like a spitball without the spit. Throwing the pitch with the smooth side up made the ball act like a rising fastball, and delivering it with the smooth side down made it break downward. As the *Washington Post* explained, "One side of the ball is rubbed smooth and shiny and there is less air resistance on this side than on the other. In that the smooth side does not catch on the air as the rougher opposite side does, there is more air pressure on the rough side. Consequently the ball on its flight is forced in the direction of the lesser amount of resistance."[4]

The ball gained even more movement when pitchers learned to make the rough side even rougher. The emery ball, in which a pitcher scuffed the ball with sandpaper or an emery board, had been outlawed after the 1914 season, but the infielders were willing to scratch and mar half of the ball with gravel and dirt. Eddie also found that grinding the ball into the grass made it darker; soon, he could make one side dark and the other white, giving the ball a flickering effect as it approached the batter. Eddie already owned an impressive bag of tricks, but Dave Danforth added a new weapon to his arsenal.

Both Danforth and Cicotte increased the shine ball's effectiveness with a simple psychological ploy. They denied that the shine ball existed at all and insisted that it was merely a figment of the batters' imaginations. Eddie always insisted, long after his retirement from baseball, that the shine ball was a myth. As the pitcher told *Baseball Magazine* in December 1917,

> The thing which amused me most and was a bother at times was the sensational reception which greeted my so-called shine ball. I have read various comic accounts of trick deliveries in the papers but I have never before played the role of villain in such a drama with actual flesh and blood people claiming that my delivery had magical properties. I can assure them all that I would gladly have imparted such magic properties to that ball had I possessed the ability to do so. But I am human like the rest. I pitched as good ball as I was capable of doing. But the so-called shine ball which created such a furore in the American League is one of those pleasing fairy stories we used to read about in the rhymes of Mother Goose.[5]

Frank Shellenback, a White Sox teammate in 1918 and 1919, insisted that Cicotte did, in fact, throw the pitch. "Eddie darkened the ball on one side by rubbing it in the dirt," he said. "Then he slickened the ball by rubbing it vigorously on his pants. The process camouflaged the ball perfectly. The ball, thrown with blazing speed, rotating quickly, and showing the white side only at split-second intervals, baffled batters completely."[6] It must have looked like the phases of the moon, coming at the batter in rapid succession. The process created an optical illusion dubbed "the mysterious flicker" by the *New York Times*.

Shellenback's description of the shine ball shows that it was similar to the emery ball, the pitch that vaulted Russ Ford of the Yankees to stardom in 1910. Ford always claimed that his signature pitch was a spitter, but other hurlers discovered his secret before long and began throwing it as well. Ban Johnson, president of the American League, outlawed the pitch, but apparently Cicotte, Danforth, and others had achieved the same effect without the telltale emery paper. In fact, the emery ball never really went away; some pitchers used a handful of gravel to rough up the ball and then tossed the gravel away, while infielders hid sandpaper in their gloves for the purpose.

Johnson hated all trick pitches and called Cicotte into his Chicago office on several occasions to grill him about his repertoire. Eddie said, years later, that the conversation always played out this way:

"You've got to quit using that pitch, Eddie."
"What pitch?"
"The one they're all complaining about."
"Well if you tell me what I'm doing wrong I'll be glad to stop doing it."
"You know what it is you're doing wrong."
"I'm doing nothing that is illegal."
"Well, quit doing it."
"What do you want me to do, pitch left-handed?"[7]

Though the shine ball was still a secret, and both pitchers denied that it existed, the pitch played a crucial role in the Chicago club's steady improvement. To further aid the pitching staff, Comiskey bought Claude "Lefty" Williams, 24 years old, from Salt Lake City of the Pacific Coast League. Williams, like Cicotte, had failed in a short trial with Detroit and owned a fastball that was mediocre at best. Williams' specialty was the curve ball, which broke so sharply that minor leaguers could not hit it. Williams used it to win 33 games for Salt Lake City in 1915.

Comiskey also bought two smooth-fielding infielders, Zeb Terry and Fred McMullin, from Los Angeles of the Pacific Coast League. Rowland planned to move shortstop Buck Weaver to third base and insert one of his new arrivals at short. Terry, a Stanford University product, won the job and opened the season in the lineup, while McMullin became Rowland's all-purpose substitute.

The White Sox got off to another slow start in 1916, as the offense failed to jell. On May 19, Eddie pitched ten innings of shutout ball in a masterful game at Philadelphia against the Athletics, but the Sox could not score either. In the bottom of the 11th, Eddie walked Amos Strunk, retired Stuffy McInnis on a sacrifice, walked Nap Lajoie intentionally, and got Jimmy Walsh to fly to right for the second out. He almost extended the game to the 12th, but Charlie Pick singled Strunk home to win the game. This defeat left Eddie's record at

3–3 and dropped the Sox, who managed only three hits, into last place. Even worse, Eddie strained a lower back muscle and missed a month of action. He went home to Detroit to recuperate and rejoined the White Sox in Chicago on June 18.

Eddie was reluctant to leave Detroit, as Rose Cicotte was nine months pregnant and due to deliver any day, but the Sox played 35 games in July with ten doubleheaders, and the White Sox needed him. Virginia June Cicotte was born on June 27, but Eddie and the Sox left Chicago for a three-week road trip shortly after. He did not meet his newest daughter until the trip concluded in Detroit on July 24.

Fortunately, the Chicago bats woke up while Eddie was on the sidelines, and in July, which was filled with doubleheaders due to a spate of early-season rainouts, the White Sox came together and started winning. Eddie's first start after his injury came in New York on July 8, and he pitched a four-hitter for a 2–1 win. On July 25, he could not get his knuckler over the plate against the Yankees, and after he allowed two runs and four walks in one and one-third innings, Reb Russell relieved him. The Sox had scored five in the first inning on the way to a 13–8 victory, so Eddie got credit for the win under the rules of the time. The next day, Eddie pitched his best game of the year, also against the Yankees, when he threw a one-hit shutout and defeated New Yorkers by a 2–0 score. Eddie gave up only one walk and a harmless single to Wally Pipp in the fifth inning. Eddie became a Yankee-killer in 1916, winning seven of eight decisions against New York.

Eddie's near no-hitter pushed the White Sox into third place, only 1½ games out of the lead, and as July turned to August, eight wins in five days against the A's in Chicago boosted the White Sox into first place. This set off a tense, two-month battle for the flag, Chicago's first pennant race in years, with the White Sox, Red Sox, and Tigers in the fight. Boston, which lost Tris Speaker when they traded him to Cleveland during a contract dispute, came up with a new sensation in Babe Ruth, a left-handed pitcher who also provided some sock at the plate. Ruth burst on the scene in 1916, winning 23 games, but some already believed that he would be even more valuable as a position player due to his powerful bat.

The White Sox made a strong effort, but weaknesses in the field and at the bat did them in. Zeb Terry hit so poorly during the season's second half that Pants Rowland moved Buck Weaver back and forth from third base to shortstop. Bothered by the constant position shifting, Weaver hit only .227 that season. First baseman Jack Fournier slumped at the plate too, and his poor fielding made first base a liability for the Sox. In late August, Charles Comiskey decided that the club needed a shot of adrenaline, so he brought Kid Gleason back to the White Sox as a coach. Gleason, with his jokes, advice, and enthusiasm, immediately added a jolt of energy to the club.

4. Career Rejuvenation

White Sox coach, morale booster, and general prankster Kid Gleason. In 1919, Gleason was named manager of the club (Library of Congress).

Eddie Collins, Joe Jackson, and Happy Felsch provided a powerful three-four-five combo in the lineup, and the strong Chicago pitching kept their pennant hopes alive. Eddie did his part, winning all five of his decisions in September and saving one game. His 3–2 win over Washington on September 15 brought the Sox to within half a game of the lead, shared by Boston and Detroit. But when Rowland's club lost two of three to the Red Sox immediately afterward, the White Sox fell 1½ games behind and never got any closer.

The White Sox stayed in the race until the final day, as the Red Sox clinched their second straight pennant on October 1 when Chicago lost the first game of a doubleheader at Cleveland. With nothing more at stake, Eddie defeated the Indians in the last game of the year, 8–4. The White Sox then staged their usual annihilation of the Cubs in the City Series, with Reb Russell, Red Faber, Lefty Williams, and Eddie Cicotte pitching consecutive complete-game victories.

Eddie followed his mediocre 1915 season with a much better one in 1916. Working in 44 games (19 starts and 25 relief appearances), Eddie won 15 and lost only seven. The team was slowly coming together, as Lefty Williams (13–7 in his first full season), Red Faber (17–9) and Reb Russell (18–11) joined with

Cicotte and Danforth to form a solid pitching corps. Joe Jackson batted .341 to reclaim his place among the league's top hitters, while Happy Felsch hit .300 and claimed the starting center field position.

Ed Walsh, however, came to the end of the line. The most famous spitball pitcher of all, Walsh had followed up his amazing 40-win season of 1908 with several more fine campaigns, winning 27 games in both 1911 and 1912. The heavy workload wore out his arm, and in 1916 Walsh pitched only twice before retiring to the sidelines with a sore arm. Except for a few games with Boston of the National League in 1917, Walsh's career was finished. But the White Sox owned a strong pitching staff, and Walsh, the final link to the 1906 world champions, would not be missed. Now it was up to Cicotte, Faber, Danforth, and the rest to deliver a pennant to Chicago.

The fans of Chicago were passionate about their steadily improving White Sox, now that they were winning, but the gamblers and bookmakers in American League cities were even more enthusiastic. Successful teams like the White Sox, who led the circuit in attendance, drew fans, and they also drew interest from the gambling community.

Eddie Cicotte and many other ballplayers crossed paths with scores of "sporting men," or gamblers. Baseball was, during the early years of the 20th century, the most popular sport in America by far, with some competition from horse racing and boxing. It was the only important professional team sport in the nation, as the National Football League did not yet exist (it was founded in 1920), and professional basketball was still several decades away. Baseball stood alone on the national sports scene, and because it was played every day and was covered in minute detail in the newspapers, it was a magnet for the gambling crowd. As baseball grew in popularity, an entire culture of gambling attached itself, like a barnacle, to the national pastime.

The gambling scene was populated by men who followed their favorite teams religiously, often traveling with the clubs on road trips and befriending the players and sportswriters. Some of them made their living, or attempted to, by betting on their favorite teams. Others were merely wealthy hangers-on who styled themselves as superfans, tossing off thousand-dollar wagers at the drop of a hat and boasting about it when they won. At Fenway Park in Boston, hundreds of gamblers occupied the right field seats at almost every game and spent the afternoon making bets with each other. On a national level, gambling was so widespread that some writers claim that baseball gambling, not the sport itself, was the real national pastime of that era.

Inevitably, many gamblers who followed baseball looked for ways to increase their chances of winning. Gamblers love a "sure thing," and the surest thing of all is to bet on a game for which one can predict the outcome. Inside information is essential to the sports gambler, and many of them befriended players, took them out to dinner, and bought them drinks while quizzing

4. Career Rejuvenation

them about injuries, slumps, and clubhouse turmoil. Other gamblers took a more proactive approach. They tried to "fix" games by bribing the players to lose.

Though incidents of bribery and dishonest play were common during the sport's infancy, the first major game-fixing scandal occurred during the National League's second season. The Louisville Grays held a four-game lead over Boston in the pennant race on August 13, 1877, then utterly collapsed, losing 11 of their next 13 contests (with one tie) and falling out of the race. Club management conducted an investigation and found telegrams that proved that four of the Grays took money from gamblers to lose the pennant. One of the suspected players was right-hander Jim Devlin, who pitched every inning for the Grays that year. League president William Hulbert, who recognized the danger that gambling posed to the sport, expelled all four players from the National League for life.

Hulbert's action in banning the four crooked Grays set a precedent that should have been a warning to every player, but the gamblers kept trying. The first World Series in 1903 between the Boston Americans and the Pittsburgh Pirates was rife with accusations of bribery and game-fixing, and before the pennant-deciding game between the Chicago Cubs and New York Giants in October of 1908, a Giants team employee tried to bribe an umpire. Many such attempts were made during the 1910s, and because dedicated gamblers loved to bet on any game, even meaningless late-season contests between teams that were long out of the pennant race, no doubt many bribery attempts were successful.

Boston was a major hub of baseball gambling, and one of the leading "sporting men" of the city, and one whom Eddie Cicotte knew from his tenure with the Red Sox, was James "Sport" Sullivan. Sullivan, the son of Irish immigrants, was born in 1870 and gave the appearance of a reputable businessman, dealing in real estate. In truth, his real estate business was a front for gambling and bookmaking. Personable and accommodating, Sullivan followed the Red Sox on road trips, chatting with players and sportswriters in hotel lobbies and bars. The Sullivan home in Sharon, Massachusetts, a Boston suburb, was always open to players and writers from out of town, who played cards, smoked cigars, and drank until the wee hours with Sullivan as their host. His easy access and the information he gleaned therefrom made him, by 1910, the uncrowned "King of Boston Gamblers."

The life of a gambler was not easy. Sullivan was arrested for bookmaking and gambling-related offenses several times, and on one occasion was accused of fixing a prizefight. In 1904, Sullivan made the mistake of offering a bribe to Cy Young, the legendary pitcher, before a game. "The fellow who tried to tempt me," said Young many years later, "was a man known as 'Sport' Sullivan. He offered to hand over more than my salary if I would 'throw' a ball game. My salary was only $1,500 a year, but I promptly handed Sullivan a punch in the jaw and kicked him out of my room."[8] As time went on, Sullivan learned to read his targets. He could tell which players might be receptive to a game-related proposition, especially those in financial distress.

Despite his checkered past, reputable newspapers like the *Washington Post* consulted Sullivan for his predictions. In 1911, he told the *Post* that he made the Philadelphia Athletics an even-money favorite to win the World Series over the New York Giants. The article noted that Sullivan openly "makes his living by betting on baseball, and these prices, printed in Boston newspapers, presumably are those that he is now prepared to lay against any team's chances, in his future book. Sullivan does a heavy handbook business on baseball through the season, and is a prominent figure at all of the world's series games."[9] In 1915 Ring Lardner reported that Sullivan had bet $10,000 on a single Braves-Pirates game, "the biggest amt ever bet on 1 game of ball."[10]

A Boston newspaper described Sullivan as follows:

> He had a remarkable memory. He'd go to a baseball game—back in the days when there was a special section for the gamblers—and he would make 20 bets or 30 bets during a game without making a written notation. All the time he knew just what he stood to win, what his eventual profit would be. For that was his way of operating, placing his bet so that if the game went one way, he would wind up with $300 profit, or if the game went the other way, he'd be making $180 profit. To him, the cardinal sin was being caught with a one-sided book that might cost him money.
>
> Gambling men consulted him about various sports events because of this keen analysis, his sound valuations and, not the least important, his sources of information.[11]

Gamblers always look for an edge, and to men like Sport Sullivan, fixing a game was merely a way for a smart bettor to improve his chances of a big payoff. He and other gamblers may have compromised dozens, if not hundreds, of contests in both leagues during the 1910s. The gambling problem was a stubborn one which threatened the very foundation of the sport itself, and the reckoning was not far off.

5

The Championship Season

> *Perhaps no pitcher in the world has such a varied assortment of wares in his repertory as Cicotte. He throws with effect practically every kind of ball known to pitching science.*
>
> *The real inside dope is that Cicotte is the best little mixer on the slab in the world. In pitching for a batter's weakness and cutting corners when he wants to he has no superior in the game. His success is founded on these little things. He was the same crafty Eddie on the hill before he even thought of rubbing the ball on his uni.—The Sporting News, 1918*[1]

By the end of the 1916 season, Charles Comiskey had lost all confidence in his first baseman. Jack Fournier suddenly stopped hitting, batting .240 in 1916 after a .322 mark the year before. Fournier's fielding was as abysmal as ever, prompting Rowland to try him in the outfield, where he was even worse, if such a thing were possible. Some of the Chicago papers suggested that the Sox should employ Fournier as a pinch-hitter only. Comiskey, the best-fielding first baseman in the game during the 1880s, recognized that Fournier had no range and that even an average first sacker would not only commit fewer errors, but reduce the number of throwing errors for his fellow infielders as well.

To that end, Comiskey bought Arnold "Chick" Gandil, a good hitter and a solid gloveman, from Cleveland for $3,500. Pants Rowland pushed for Gandil's acquisition, and after the trade, the *Tribune* described Gandil as "the ideal type of athlete—a fighter on the field, a player who never quits under the most discouraging circumstances, and so game that he is one of the most dangerous batters in the league when a hit means a ball game."[2]

Gandil was a roughneck, a onetime boxer who had earned $150 per bout. He had also spent some time working as a boilermaker in a Mexican copper mine. Unlike some of his teammates, he had attended high school, though he dropped out without a diploma. He was a hard man, quick to anger and prone to carrying a grudge. However, most of his teammates liked him, and he and Eddie Cicotte played billiards together, especially on the road. He was not a great hitter, but a solid one who represented an improvement over the departed Jack Fournier.

Gandil held a deep personal animosity toward Eddie Collins. In 1912, when Collins played for the Philadelphia A's and Gandil for Washington, Collins tagged Gandil in the face at second base and broke his nose. Gandil never forgave Collins for that; as Gandil's Washington teammate Clyde Milan said, "for the rest of his playing career, Gandil was out to get even. He went into the bag against Collins 200 times I guess, and always got the worst of it."[3] Gandil resented Collins' Ivy League background, his sometimes arrogant, cocky attitude, and his apparent closeness with Charles Comiskey. The fact that Comiskey paid Collins $15,000 a year and Gandil less than one-third as much added to the hostility. Though the two men played next to each other on Chicago's infield, they rarely spoke, at least not in polite terms.

Chick Gandil was also a friend and acquaintance of the ubiquitous Sport Sullivan. While Gandil played for Washington, Sullivan asked Gandil to tip him off whenever Walter Johnson, the top pitcher in the American League, was slated to pitch. "It was a tempting proposition," said Gandil years later, "but I was going pretty good at that time and I was afraid to get into a jam. Besides, there had been an incident the year before which made me gun shy. While I was playing for Montreal, some gambler had offered two other players and me $25 apiece to throw a game to Rochester. We reported the bribe to our club owner who, in turn, reported it to the league president. It created a big commotion."[4] Though Gandil claimed that he turned Sullivan down, the gambler and the first baseman remained on good terms.

Another new face on the 1917 White Sox belonged to a man even tougher than Gandil. The new shortstop was Charles "Swede" Risberg, a Californian who came to Chicago from Vernon of the Pacific Coast League. He replaced the smooth-fielding Zeb Terry, who did not hit enough (batting .190 in 1916) to hold the job. Risberg owned a strong throwing arm, and at six feet and 175 pounds, was one of the largest shortstops of the era. He also had a bad temper, littering his minor league career with a trail of fights and suspensions. He once punched an umpire who made a call he didn't agree with. Still, baseball people liked fiery players, especially on the infield, and Vernon manager Doc White, the onetime White Sox pitching star, recommended Risberg to Comiskey.

Risberg hit poorly at the start of the 1917 season and appeared to be homesick for his native California. He once asked Comiskey to send him back to the Pacific Coast League, but the owner refused. "[Risberg] is liable to be a sensation one minute and a crape hanger the next, for he can throw them away as far and as hard as anyone," Hugh Fullerton wrote. "The boy is high strung, nervous, and inclined to panic.... His fault is that he seems striving constantly to conceal his nervousness under a veneer of pretended carelessness and coolness."[5] He hit a little better than Zeb Terry, but not much. Risberg's defensive skill kept him in the lineup.

Risberg too grew to hate Eddie Collins, a man he could not possibly understand or abide, and the arrival of Gandil and Risberg portended a shift in the clubhouse dynamic for the White Sox. Collins and the Gandil/Risberg tandem became the two poles toward which the rest of the White Sox gravitated, a development that would cause much trouble in the future.

To be sure, Eddie Collins was not always an easy man to like. His Ivy League background (as a graduate of Columbia) and success at a young age had given him a foundation of self-confidence that many of his teammates took for arrogance. Tagging him with the nickname "Cocky" early on, some of his Philadelphia Athletics teammates resented him as well, even as the A's won four pennants with Collins in a starring role. For one thing, Collins, like other stars such as Ty Cobb and Christy Mathewson, wrote newspaper columns (or had them ghostwritten) in which he discussed the inner workings and strategies of the game. Collins' Philadelphia teammates complained that their opponents read these columns and used the information therein to improve themselves. Perhaps such complaints sound petty—the carping of less-popular players who were jealous of their teammate's fame—but by 1914 the A's, like the White Sox a few years later, had divided themselves into pro–Collins and anti–Collins factions.

But the divisions in the Chicago clubhouse were not yet apparent in early 1917, and many experts predicted the White Sox to wrest the American League crown from the Red Sox. I. E. Sanborn of the *Tribune* spoke for many when he said that, barring injuries, "Chicago's White Sox will have only themselves to blame if they do not win the American League pennant of 1917." Sanborn praised the acquisitions of Gandil and Risberg, plugging two worrisome holes in the White Sox defense. He also said the pitching unit was "conceded to be a great slab staff, [but] it is not so in the sense that it has a star like Ed Walsh or Walter Johnson, nor a lion-hearted standby like [Three-Finger] Brown or [Christy] Mathewson." Sanborn mentioned Eddie Cicotte almost in passing, listing him with Mellie Wolfgang and Joe Benz as those who "can be depended on to be just as good as in 1916."[6]

As the White Sox gathered in Mineral Wells, Texas, for spring training, a cloud of uncertainty hovered over the baseball world. That cloud was the war in Europe, which had raged since August of 1914 and now threatened to draw the United States into the conflict. In January of 1917, the German government declared unrestricted submarine warfare on all Atlantic ships, including American ones. Though President Woodrow Wilson had used the slogan "he kept us out of war" during his successful 1916 re-election campaign, Germany's attacks on American shipping led the United States to break off diplomatic relations on February 3. American participation in the war was now only a matter of time.

The White Sox and all other major league teams made a show of preparing for the upcoming conflict. On March 10, before an intrasquad game in Mineral Wells, an army sergeant divided the Sox into five squadrons of what the papers called the B. N. G. (Baseball National Guard). The sergeant promoted five "privates"—Pants Rowland, Eddie Collins, Ray Schalk, Reb Russell, and Jim Scott—to the rank of corporal and gave each a squad to drill into shape. The players had already received training in the manual of arms, which concerned the handling of weapons. In future months, the White Sox drilled in formation before games, carrying bats as rifles, sometimes dressed in full Army uniforms. These quasi-military activities may not have amounted to much, but they showed that the national pastime was patriotic enough to do its part in the war effort. The conflict became a reality on April 6, 1917, when Congress formally declared war on Germany.

The White Sox split their first two games of the season in St. Louis, but in the third contest, played on April 14, Eddie Cicotte threw the only no-hitter of his major league career, defeating the Browns, 11–0. This game was a laugher, with the White Sox pounding Browns starter Earl Hamilton out of the box and building an 8–0 lead after only two innings. Eddie held command the entire game, striking out five and walking three. The only trouble came in the seventh inning, when Jimmy Austin hit a sharp line drive that eluded Chick Gandil. The official scorer ruled the play an error, and though one St. Louis paper complained that "ordinarily this would have been scored a hit,"[7] the decision stood. In the ninth, Eddie retired all three Browns—Ward Miller, George Sisler, and Del Pratt—on easy pop-ups to complete the no-hitter.

Though Eddie employed a whole arsenal of pitches, including the spitter and the shine ball, John B. Sheridan of the *St. Louis Globe-Democrat* expressed admiration for Eddie's knuckler, which he called the "hobo of balldom." Wrote the admiring St. Louis writer, "It is a freak delivery; this knuckleball, Cicotte invented it, and is its greatest exponent. Many other pitchers have tried it, some with more or less success. Earl Hamilton did wonderful work with it in 1912. Then he lost control of it. Many others tried it. They use it now and then to this day, but Cicotte is the only pitcher who admits that the knuckleball is responsible for a greater part of his success."

Cicotte talked to Sheridan about the pitch after he threw his no-hitter against the Browns. Said Eddie,

> I use it very frequently during a game, I vary pace on it, and very frequently I do not ask it to break at all. I throw it with some rotation. When I know a batter is going to hit—when I know and he knows that I must lay a strike over the plate—I pitch the "knuckle ball" with as little rotation as possible, so that it may break as well as

Eddie Cicotte and manager Pants Rowland in conference, 1917 (author's collection).

possible. The different paces deceive the batter, and the break simply makes it impossible to hit safely save by the greatest fluke.

The spitball has but one pace—fast. The "fadeaway" had but one pace—medium slow. I can pitch the knuckleball at any pace from medium fast to dead slow.

I began using this ball when I was a kid. It was always impossible to hit, but I found it very hard to obtain control of it. It was not until I joined Boston in 1908 that I began to get control of the "knuckle ball." Even then it evaded me for months at a time. When I got it going right I was hard to beat. Even now I often lose control of it.[8]

Eddie also told Sheridan that his weight was a factor in controlling the pitch. He had often been called "stocky," or even "stubby," and losing some poundage helped him.

> I joined Chicago in 1912 and began to do better with the difficult delivery. I had trouble, however, with my general control. I had been a slim kid, but I was growing fat. I weighed 135 when I had my first engagement with the Sault Ste. Marie team, way back in 1903. I weighed 190 pounds in 1912. Since that time I have tried to keep it down to 170 pounds, but I find it hard to do so.
>
> This year I made a special effort to reduce my weight. I am down to 170 pounds, lighter than I have been in 10 seasons; I find that my control is better than it has ever been. To this I attribute my early success this season. You see, when I am fat I can't get my arm to follow through with my pitch. My upper arm hits my right breast and won't go any farther. Thus, I have been pitching with a short, jerky motion, which is not good for control.[9]

The White Sox struggled to score runs early on. The Browns got revenge for Eddie's no-hitter by doing the same to the White Sox twice in two days in early May. On May 5, Ernie Koob no-hit the White Sox, and on May 6 Bob Groom turned the trick in the second game of a doubleheader. But the bats soon came around, and the Sox swept their next three games against St. Louis. In the first contest, Eddie relieved Jim Scott in the seventh inning to stop a Browns rally, then pitched a scoreless eighth when the White Sox went ahead. Dave Danforth, who emerged in 1917 as Chicago's relief ace saved the game in the ninth. This game kicked off a 19–3 run, in which Eddie won seven games and saved two others, that swept the White Sox into first place.

The Sox stayed afloat in the early part of the season mainly due to Eddie, who took the role of staff ace because of the injuries that plagued the other starters. Reb Russell hurt his arm with the first curveball he threw in spring training at Mineral Wells, and Rowland had to pace him carefully in starting and relief roles all season. Lefty Williams won his first nine games, but streaks of wildness bothered him, and he followed up his great start with seven losses in his next nine decisions. Red Faber, after lasting less than six innings in a start at Detroit on April 29, sat out for the next month and a half with arm and back soreness. On the positive side, manager Rowland employed Dave Danforth as his closer, and Danforth used his shine ball to compile his best season, leading the league in appearances and saving seven games.

The pennant race put Eddie in the spotlight, and the 33-year-old pitcher delivered the best season of his career. Despite Eddie's age, Pants Rowland often started him with only two days' rest, and he gave him plenty of relief assignments as well. Though Eddie's complete-game win over Detroit on June 29 left his record at 11–5 and his earned run average at 0.95, many wondered if he could keep it up. As the *Day Book*, a Chicago sports publication, warned, Eddie "is apt to fade after July 1 if his strength is not conserved. Eddie is no

5. The Championship Season

Eddie in 1917 (Library of Congress).

youngster and never was an iron man. He can stand only a certain amount of work. Recently he has been appearing frequently, and though his work so far scintillates, too much rescue work will kill him off."[10] But Eddie never faded, and the White Sox took control of the race. Cicotte matched his career high of 18 wins on August 4 with a 7–3 win at Philadelphia, and he became a 20-game winner for the first time on August 27 by beating the Yankees, 3–0.

How did Eddie do it? He was famous for his mastery of the knuckleball, which was still a rarity among American League pitchers, and the spitter, but he had more tricks in his bag. One was the shine ball that Dave Danforth taught him in 1916. The other was the "sailer," or "sailor," a pitch that Ty Cobb said would "start out like an ordinary pitch and then would sail much in the same manner of a flat stone thrown by a small boy." About Cicotte, Cobb said, "Nobody knows to this day ... what it was that Eddie Cicotte did to a ball to make it sail in that peculiar manner so completely puzzling to batters."[11]

The sailer was a mystery, but it was almost certainly achieved by distorting the surface of the ball. Eddie may have thrown it by prying up a seam on the baseball or by filling some of the seams with mud or paraffin. Some suspected Eddie of hiding paraffin on his uniform pants, or in his glove, and rubbing the seams against it. Others suggested that he had a tool hidden in his glove to break and raise the seams. As Washington manager Clark Griffith said, "Cicotte, who uses the delivery better than any of the other twirlers, never leaves his glove in the pitchers' box. If he did that would give away the secret of the substance used in doctoring the ball."[12]

Washington pitcher Walter Johnson found that Eddie used powder, concealed on his pants leg, to shine up the ball. "One day," said Johnson in 1925, "I got hold of a foul ball, which I inspected. I found it to be doctored with a powder. Cicotte and I were both pitching, so I determined to use some of his own methods. I soon had the ball hopping all over the place, and after I had, by accident, nearly hit Eddie Collins and Oscar Felsch, Cicotte quit using that shining substance."[13] Indeed, Eddie's teammates would often beg him and Danforth not to doctor the ball when pitching against Johnson. They did not want to give the fastest pitcher in baseball any more weapons.

Cicotte's sudden ascent to the first rank of American League pitchers, and Dave Danforth's new status as Chicago's relief ace, did not sit well with the rest of the league, who openly accused the White Sox of cheating their way into first place. As New York writer Damon Runyon complained, "There is a firm belief among many managers and players in the American League that the success of the White Sox pitchers has been due to trickery—to 'monkeying' with the baseball.... It has been quite openly charged for some time that Commy's carvers have been using vaseline and other substances." Runyon also said that players had told him that the White Sox tampered with the baseballs before their home games. "They claim that a nail file is employed to lift just enough of the seam of the ball to give it a 'sailor' effect when it is thrown."[14]

The public criticism of White Sox pitching gained momentum on August 13, when Dave Danforth pitched five innings of relief and earned the win in a 13-inning win at Cleveland. The Indians lodged a steady stream of complaints to the umpires about Danforth's deliveries, and the next day, the Indians delayed the first game of a doubleheader several times with protests against Lefty Williams. It got worse in the second game when a Danforth pitch hit Tris Speaker in the face, knocking the Cleveland star unconscious and putting his season in jeopardy. Said Speaker after the incident, "The game will go to the dogs unless a stop is put to the doctoring of the ball by Cicotte and Danforth.... If the Sox win, that is what will give them the pennant."[15]

I. E. Sanborn defended Eddie in the *Tribune*:

> Those jealous persons who have been attempting to cast suspicion on the pitching ability of Eddie Cicotte this year need to study baseball history.
>
> The veteran of the White Sox slab staff has been accused of using various kinds of dope to make the ball do funny stunts, and his accusers include players and managers of most of the opposing teams, with the exception of the Athletics, whose manager tells his players to go out and take a wallop at Cicotte's stuff, just as at anybody's else. And the Athletics have given Cicotte more trouble than any other team, in consequence of that mental attitude.

5. The Championship Season

Several American League teams have hypnotized themselves into the belief they could not touch Cicotte with a barn door... one frequently hears from rival players the charge that it is impossible for him to become a winning pitcher, after so many years of mediocre success, without the aid of some magic.

Those who talk that way simply do not know the facts. The official records of the game show that Cicotte, with the exception of one year, has been among the leading pitchers in the American League ever since the present system of ranking hurlers by their effectiveness, instead of by games won and lost, was adopted. In that time Cicotte has been the second best pitcher in the league two different seasons and eighth once.

The averages for this year show that Cicotte is only a little more effective than in previous seasons, consequently he is only a shade better pitcher than he has been.[16]

The wildest game of 1917, and an omen of things to come, occurred on June 16 in Boston when the White Sox sent Eddie Cicotte to the hill to face Babe Ruth. The White Sox, who held third place in early May, were on the rise with a 19–3 run that vaulted them past the Red Sox and into the league lead by June 11. Two losses to the Yankees followed, but on June 15 Lefty Williams shut out the Red Sox by an 8–0 score to boost Chicago's lead over Boston to two and a half games. At the same time, the fading Red Sox had lost six in their previous seven games, and though they hoped to break their skid behind the sensational young lefty Ruth, they had to do so against Cicotte, the hottest pitcher in the American League. A thunderstorm had drenched the field the night before, and wet grounds, threatening skies, and the prospect of another loss put the 9,400 fans in a bad mood from the start.

The surliest fans of all were the gamblers. At every game at Fenway Park, hundreds of "sporting men" straight out of a Damon Runyon short story occupied the right field stands, soliciting bets and passing money back and forth. This collection of Nathan Detroits and Sky Mastersons plied their trade openly and loudly, and though league president Ban Johnson vowed to get rid of gamblers in his league's ballparks, Red Sox owner Harry Frazee turned a blind eye. Frazee did not want to alienate the sporting men who bought several hundred tickets for every Boston game, so he ignored Johnson and allowed the gamblers to operate virtually unmolested. Now, with the gamblers bleeding money during the Boston losing streak, the atmosphere at Fenway Park was a sour one. The general mood grew worse when Pants Rowland refused to name a starting pitcher until the last possible minute before game time. He had the right-handed Cicotte and the lefty Reb Russell warming up side by side before he finally chose Eddie.

A light drizzle fell on the field as the Sox, Red and White, battled during the first few innings. Chicago scored a run in the first when Joe Jackson belted a double off Ruth to drive in Shano Collins. They struck again in the fourth when Ruth walked Happy Felsch, who went to second on a passed ball and scored on a single by Chick Gandil.

Eddie Cicotte looked unbeatable, and his dominance and the increasingly bad weather brought chants of "Call the game!" from the right field stands. Those cries grew louder in the top of the fifth inning, as Ray Schalk flew out to center and Eddie bounced out weakly to the shortstop. According to the American League rules at the time, a game was complete at the end of four and a half innings, no matter which team was ahead. Now, with one out to go, Shano Collins stepped into the box to face Ruth.

That's when the gamblers took matters into their own hands. Several hundred men, led by "some tall fan in a long rain coat," poured out of the right field seats and made a dash toward the infield. "They didn't rush at the players or umpires," said James Crusinberry in the *Chicago Tribune*. "The latter stood gazing in amazement. The grand stand crowd became absolutely still. But instead of fighting, the mob simply surged out upon the field, clear up into the diamond and stood around."[17] They stopped the game in its tracks, hoping that the worsening rain would cause the contest to be called.

Red Sox manager Jack Barry confronted the mob and threatened to forfeit the game to the White Sox if they did not clear the playing surface immediately, so some of the gamblers shuffled off the field, climbing into the grandstand box seats. But a new wave of humanity poured out of the right field seats before play could resume, and now fans surged onto the field from the left field stands as well. They overwhelmed the six police officers on hand. Umpire Barry McCormick called time and ordered the players to their benches, and that's when the riot broke out.

Several dozen fans attacked the White Sox, who grabbed bats from the bench area to defend themselves. Buck Weaver swung in all directions, striking a few of his assailants, but Fred McMullin preferred a more direct approach. The utility infielder slugged one fan on the jaw. The players all made it to safety, but the fans milled about for more than half an hour as the rain continued to fall. After a while, the rioters drifted away and the police and umpires restored order and cleared the field. The groundskeepers spread sawdust on the wet infield, and play resumed after a 45-minute delay.

Eddie Cicotte allowed two runs in the eighth inning, but the outcome was never in doubt as the White Sox won, 7–2. Buck Weaver added an exclamation point in the ninth when he walloped a majestic homer over the 31-foot barrier in left field (now 37 feet tall and known as the Green Monster). At game's end, as the players left the field, some fan hit Weaver with a pop bottle and set off another melee that the police broke up.

The nation's sporting press condemned the rioters. As George S. Robbins wrote in *The Sporting News*:

> The result is one of the most disgraceful scenes ever witnessed in a major league ball park. A riot of fans incensed at what are believed to be unfair decisions by umpires is one thing … but when a horde of gamblers, permitted to run riot in a major league ball park, seek to stop a ball game, and urge hoodlums to attack visiting players to save

their dirty coin—that is still another thing. All the rowdyism that could be crowded into a season, all the beating up of umpires, can not do the game half as much damage as the one incident that occurred in Boston last Saturday.[18]

Ban Johnson pledged again to stamp out gambling and bookmaking at Fenway Park. "If the Boston owners can not handle the situation, the league as a whole will go after the gambling clique,"[19] he declared. But nothing much happened in the wake of the riot, and the gamblers and bookies went about their business as before. (The only men who faced punishment for the affair were Buck Weaver and Fred McMullin, who were charged with assault. The charges were later dropped.) This unsettling incident showed that baseball lacked the will to confront its biggest problem. The leaders of the sport did not understand that wherever big-money sports gambling flourishes, game-fixing is never far away. By the time they recognized it, it was too late.

The White Sox battled the Red Sox through August and September, but though Boston crept to within half a game of the lead on August 17 (when they defeated the Indians while Eddie lost to the Philadelphia A's), the Red Sox could never get past the Chicago juggernaut. Even an injury to Buck Weaver, a broken finger suffered on August 10 that sidelined the infielder for more than a month, failed to slow the White Sox down; Pants Rowland simply moved Fred McMullin off the bench and into the lineup at third base. The White Sox entered September with a lead of three and a half games, and a sweep of two doubleheaders over the Tigers on Labor Day weekend extended their margin to six and a half. Eddie won the first and last contests of that four-game series, his 22nd and 23rd victories of the season, and from then on, the White Sox coasted to the flag.

The White Sox clinched the pennant when Red Faber pitched a 10-inning win over the Red Sox on September 21. The Sox rested many of their regulars during the season's final eight games, but Eddie made both of his remaining two starts. He pitched the first six innings of a 7–5 win at Washington on September 25, and four days later completed an eight-hit, 3–1 victory in New York. This win over the Yankees was his 28th of the season and brought his earned run average down to 1.53. Both of these marks were career bests for Eddie and led all pitchers in the American League.

The 1917 World Series began in Chicago on Saturday, October 6. It was the first World Series game ever played at Comiskey Park, and 32,000 fans filled the eight-year-old stadium to see Eddie Cicotte square off against the Giants' left-hander Slim Sallee. A downpour the previous afternoon left the field soggy, but, as the *Philadelphia Evening Bulletin* reported, "Groundskeepers worked all morning upon the playing field. Gasoline was poured over the ground and set afire to take up the moisture, and when the teams took the diamond for practice they found it fairly fast."[20] The weather was perfect, with sunny skies and a light breeze fluttering the patriotic decorations around the ballpark.

Before the game, Pants Rowland made a lineup change, moving Swede Risberg (who batted .203 in 1917) to the bench and shifting Buck Weaver to shortstop, with Fred McMullin taking over at third base. Rowland sacrificed some defense to put McMullin's bat into the lineup. On the New York side, manager John McGraw started the lefty Sallee (18–7 during the regular season) instead of his right-handed aces, Jeff Tesreau (13–8) and Pol Perritt (17–7), because he feared the slugging power of Joe Jackson and Eddie Collins. Jackson batted only .301 in 1917, the lowest average of his career, but was the hottest hitter in baseball in September with a .438 average. To neutralize Jackson and Collins (who also caught fire in September), McGraw started a left-hander in every game of the Series.

Though the teams played in different leagues, they had a history of bad blood stemming from the 1913–1914 world tour. The tour featured a lot of vicious backbiting and needling between Chicago's Buck Weaver and the Giants. Now, on the game's biggest stage, the Giants promised to give the Sox all the insults, profanities, and rough play they could handle and then some. The New York papers reported that the Giants filed their spikes down to sharp, dangerous points to intimidate their rivals. The Sox, however, decided to ignore them. McGraw's men razzed the White Sox all day, but the Chicago club pretended not to notice. They got down to business and refused to respond in kind.

The Giants did not, however, complain about Eddie Cicotte's bag of tricks. Though Chicago's American League rivals protested mightily all season against the shine ball, the sailer, and other unusual deliveries from Eddie and Dave Danforth, John McGraw did not make an issue of it. The Series proceeded without any challenges to the legality of Eddie's pitches. Perhaps McGraw did not know what he was up against. "If the Detroiter is right," said the *Detroit Free Press*, "the Giants are going to see the baseball perform some stunts that it is hard for a sober man to believe possible. Should Eddie have one of his real good days, he is mighty likely to convince the Giants that they are opposed to an exhibition of black magic."[21]

Eddie Cicotte, an 11-year veteran, was not fazed by his first taste of World Series pressure. His first pitch to New York leadoff man George Burns was a called strike. Burns rapped Eddie's third pitch to center for a single, then stole second but advanced no further, as Eddie retired Benny Kauff and Heinie Zimmermann on fly balls. The White Sox failed to score in their half of the first, and both Cicotte and Sallee made it through the first two innings without allowing a run.

With one out in the third, Cicotte started a rally with a single. Shano Collins followed with a single, but Eddie was thrown out when he tried to advance to third. McMullin doubled to score Collins, and the Sox took a 1–0 lead. They made it 2–0 when Happy Felsch belted one of Sallee's deliveries over the left field fence for a home run. The Giants scored in the fifth inning when Lew McCarty tripled, then came home on a single by Sallee.

In the seventh, with the Sox holding a 2–1 lead, Joe Jackson saved the game for Cicotte. With Walter Holke on first and one out. Lew McCarty whacked a sinking liner to left that Jackson caught with a diving, tumbling circus catch. Eddie kept the Giants off the board the rest of the way, leading the White Sox to a 2–1 victory and a one-game lead in the Series. I. E. Sanborn sang Eddie's praises in the *Tribune* the next day. "Everybody knew what to expect from Cicotte," wrote Sanborn. "Win or lose, he was sure to be there with a brand of hurling that would be almost invincible. He was. And the mere fact that that it was expected of him should not detract one whit from the greatness of his performance on the slab.... But for Sallee's handle hit in the fifth, the Giants would not have scored off the American League's premier pitcher."[22]

Game Two, the first World Series game ever played on a Sunday, saw Red Faber face New York's Ferdie Schupp. Faber gave up two runs in the second when Dave Robertson and Walter Holke singled. Lew McCarty then singled to left, and Joe Jackson's throw to the plate got past Ray Schalk as both Robertson and Holke scored. The White Sox got those two runs back in the bottom of the inning on singles by Jackson, Felsch, Gandil, and Weaver. There matters stood until the fourth, when six singles by the White Sox brought in five runs and gave Faber a 7–2 lead. Faber made the lead stand up—though he killed a rally in the fifth when he tried to steal third base with Weaver already occupying the bag—and defeated the Giants to put the Sox ahead, two games to none.

The Series moved to the Polo Grounds in New York for Game Three. After a travel day on Monday and a rainout on Tuesday, Eddie took the mound on Wednesday, October 10 against Rube Benton. Because left field in the Polo Grounds had one of the most difficult "sun fields" in baseball, manager Rowland put Shano Collins in left and moved Joe Jackson to right. This move backfired when Collins lost two fly balls in the sun, though neither error led to any Giants runs. The New Yorkers broke through in the fourth when Robertson tripled to right and Holke doubled him home for a 1–0 lead. Bill Rariden sacrificed Holke to third, and Cicotte struck out Benton for the second out. George Burns then hit a tap to Eddie, who threw wildly to first as Holke scored the second run.

Eddie pitched well, allowing only two runs on eight hits, striking out eight Giants and walking none. But Benton was better, scattering five hits and shutting out the White Sox, 2–0. On Thursday, the Giants evened the Series when Ferdie Schupp shut out the White Sox on seven hits for a 5–0 win.

White Sox outfielders Eddie Murphy, Shano Collins, Joe Jackson, Happy Felsch, and Nemo Leibold at the 1917 World Series (Library of Congress).

After losses in Games Three and Four, the White Sox decided to change tactics. Now they would retaliate in kind for all the insults and profanities the Giants tossed their way. "We were wild," said Buck Weaver. "They had us on the ropes. We'd kept it in so long that we just had to let it out of us."[23] Weaver and two other Sox infielders made a production of sharpening their spikes before Game Five (Eddie Collins declined to participate), and Weaver sliced line drives into packs of Giants on the field during batting practice. If the Giants wanted to see a fighting team, figured the Sox, now they'll see one. As a result, the fifth game of the 1917 World Series was one of the nastiest ever played in the fall classic.

Game Five in Chicago on Saturday, October 13 was played in bitter cold, with icy winds whipping across the field and freezing the 27,000 fans at Comiskey Park. As waves of profanities and heckling wafted forth from the New York bench, Reb Russell started for the White Sox but failed to make it out of the first inning. Russell faced only three batters. He walked Burns to start the game and gave up a single to Buck Herzog which moved Burns to third. Benny Kauff doubled Burns home, giving the Giants a 1–0 lead with no outs and two men on. Rowland called Eddie Cicotte into the game.

Eddie almost managed to retire the Giants with no further damage. Zimmermann bounced to Weaver, who threw Herzog out at the plate for the first out. Art Fletcher grounded to McMullin, who threw Kauff out at home. Dave Robertson spoiled the effort by singling home Zimmermann for a 2–0 lead. The White Sox scored in the third when Felsch doubled home Eddie Collins, who had walked, but the Giants reached Cicotte for two more runs in the fourth inning on two singles and three Chicago errors. In all, the White Sox committed six errors, three by shortstop Buck Weaver, and the Giants three on the cold, windy day.

Cicotte pitched through the sixth inning, when Rowland sent Swede Risberg to the plate to pinch-hit for him. Risberg delivered a single that scored Weaver and narrowed the Giants lead to 4–2. The Giants scored their fifth run off Lefty Williams in the seventh, but the Sox tied it in the eighth when Chick Gandil belted a two-run single and scored when Ray Schalk attempted to steal second and catcher Bill Rariden's throw sailed past Buck Herzog and into the outfield. Three more Chicago runs in the eighth put the game out of reach, and Red Faber shut down the Giants in the eighth and ninth to seal the 8–5 victory and a 3–2 Series lead.

The papers complained about the error-filled contest, and the *New York Tribune* called it "one of the most horrible examples of the national pastime ever spilled before an audience anywhere."[24] But the victory left the White Sox one win away from their first World Series title in 11 years, and Eddie Cicotte played a major part in it. Faber received credit for the win, but Eddie turned in six solid relief innings on short notice, when Rowland pulled out Russell because the game appeared to be getting out of hand after only three batters.

Eddie would have started Game Seven, but Red Faber made it unnecessary. With 33,000 in the stands at the Polo Grounds for Game Six, Faber dominated the National League champions, allowing two runs in the fifth inning and shutting out the Giants the rest of the way. The White Sox took the lead for good with three runs in the fourth inning, when the Giants imploded with two egregious errors and the most famous botched rundown play in baseball history. Eddie Collins reached first when shortstop Art Fletcher threw wildly to first, and Joe Jackson was safe when Dave Robertson dropped an easy fly ball in right field. With Collins on third and Jackson on first, Happy Felsch tapped the ball to pitcher Rube Benton, who caught Collins in a rundown between third and home.

Collins ran back and forth, avoiding a tag from third baseman Heinie Zimmermann and catcher Bill Rariden, but when Rariden tossed to Zimmermann, Collins saw that home plate was uncovered. Both Benton and first baseman Walter Holke were nowhere to be found, so the speedy Collins dashed past Rariden toward home. Zimmermann, with no one to throw the ball to, had no choice but to chase Collins down the line with the ball in his outstretched hand. Zimmermann, a big, lumbering infielder, lost the race as Collins scored the first run of the game. "The White Sox fairly screamed with glee," said Walter Turnbull in the *Chicago Tribune*. "As the crowd realized the absurdity of the play there was a roar of laughter from the stands, although many a man who had bet on the Giants swore as he laughed."[25] Chick Gandil then drove in Jackson and Felsch with a single and the Sox led, 3–0.

This play made Zimmermann the goat of the Series, though Holke and Benton should have shouldered the blame. It also took the fight out of the Giants, who scored twice in the fifth inning and never threatened thereafter. McGraw's men were uncommonly quiet for the rest of the afternoon, as Faber completed a 4–2 win, his third victory of the Series. The White Sox won the World Series four games to two, giving Charles Comiskey his long-awaited second Series title.

Faber, with three wins, was the hero of the Series, but several other White Sox deserved credit as well. Eddie Collins batted .409, Joe Jackson hit .304 and saved Game One with a diving catch, Chick Gandil drove in five runs, and Happy Felsch swatted the only home run by the White Sox. On the pitching side, Faber and Eddie Cicotte threw all but two of the 52 innings in the six games. Eddie won the first contest, pitched well in a losing effort in Game Three, and righted the ship in Game Five with six strong innings of emergency relief. His Game Five heroics may well have saved the Series for the White Sox.

One day after the team returned to Chicago, Eddie and former White Sox pitching star Nick Altrock traveled to Litchfield, Illinois, for a "Ray Schalk Day" baseball game, an annual event in the popular catcher's hometown. Eddie pitched and Schalk caught for the local nine against a club from nearby Mount Olive. The major leaguers also collected money for the Clark C. Griffith Ball and Bat Fund, which bought baseball equipment for the troops overseas. More than 3,500 fans paid to see the game and to cheer their local hero after Chicago's World Series victory.

The game organizers urged Eddie to "cut loose" and show how a real major leaguer pitched, and Eddie took them at their word. He pitched the first eight innings and struck out 16 batters. In one inning he struck out the side on nine pitches. The mood was so jovial that day that Eddie did not even mind when he was called out on the bases after hitting an apparent home run. The pitcher walloped a ball into the parking lot beyond the outfield fence, but someone retrieved it among the cars and threw it back to the infield, where the third baseman tagged him.[26] It was the best play Mount Olive made all day. Altrock, a onetime pitcher turned baseball "clown," pitched the ninth inning and entertained the crowd, even acting as his own umpire and pantomiming an argument with himself. The fans ate it up, and as the local paper reported the next day, "It is impossible to say which was the greater attraction, Cicotte, Altrock, or Schalk."[27] A banquet at the Litchfield Elks Club closed the day's festivities.

6

War and Turmoil

> *This fall I am going away from Detroit. I am going to buy me a farm a hundred miles out in Michigan where I can have the kind of home I want. Baseball is a lonesome job. It takes a man away from his family more than he could wish.*—Eddie Cicotte, 1917[1]

After the successful conclusion of the Series, the *Chicago Herald* decided to put the issue of Eddie's last name to rest once and for all. Fans, teammates, and opposing players had mangled Eddie's surname for years; he was "see-COTT-ee" to some, "see-COAT-ee" to others, and "CY-cott" to even more. Some of his teammates, jokers that they were, liked to address Eddie with every pronunciation except the correct one. To set the record straight, the *Herald* went to the source.

> Since the World Series started there has been almost as much argument over the pronunciation of Eddie Cicotte's name as there was about the famous problem, "How old is Ann?" Out in Chicago the announcer at Comiskey Park calls him "Sigh-Cotty." The manager, Clarence Rowland, calls him "Sigh-Cott," and so do all the players. Coming back on the White Sox special from Chicago he was looking over a game of draw, when the Herald reporter asked him what he really called himself. He wrote it down on a piece of cardboard, and, as he ought to know, it should settle all arguments. The star pitcher of the White Sox calls himself "See-Cot," and he affixed his signature to the affirmation of that. He said that his ancestors over in France used to spell their name with an initial "S" and that they were never known by any other pronunciation than "See-Cot."[2]

That confusion has existed to the present day. In the popular 1989 film *Field of Dreams*, the players are razzing each other while warming up on the field:

> BUCK WEAVER (TO CHICK GANDIL): Show-off.
> EDDIE CICOTTE: Yeah, Gandil. If you'd have run like that against Detroit, I'd have won 20 games that year!
> GANDIL: For Pete's sake, see-COAT-ee, that was 68 years ago! Give it up, will ya?

After winning 28 regular season games in 1917 and one more in the Series, Eddie, at age 33, was suddenly a star. He had never previously led the

6. War and Turmoil 69

American League in any pitching category (except for hit batters in 1908), but in 1917 he stood at the top of the list in wins, earned run average, and innings pitched. Thanks to modern baseball researchers and statisticians, we know that Eddie faced more batters (1,287) than anyone else in the league, and his ballpark-adjusted earned run average (ERA+) and walks and hits per innings pitched (WHIP) were the best as well. He was a good, if not spectacular, pitcher before 1917, but now the newspapers and magazines wanted to feature him in their pages. Eddie enjoyed the attention, and when *Baseball Magazine* came calling, Eddie sat down for an interview.

> I am an old man, as pitchers go, though I never felt better in my life, and am confident the next five years will be better than the last five. In any case the season which has just closed has been by long odds my best. And there's a reason. I have never been one of those ball players who could fairly be reproached for dissipation. But I have not denied myself a glass of beer when I felt like taking it, and I was usually satisfied to win what I considered a fair percentage of my games. The season which showed me a winner by twelve or fifteen contests was satisfactory so far as I was concerned.
>
> But this year I took account of stock I found myself on the shady side of thirty, on the down grade. If I were ever going to establish a record which would look nice in print, I had best begin with the least possible delay. Conditions were unusually favorable. Our pitching staff was shot to pieces. Faber was sick, Russell had a bad arm. Wolfgang was sick. Danforth was young and while a great help to the club, used mainly as relief twirler. Benz was not enjoying one of his good years. Scott was more interested in war prospects than in the matter in hand. Williams was good but often unfortunate. I was the leading twirler of the club for once in my life and could work as often as I wished so long as I could demonstrate my capacity to fill the job.
>
> We had been dreaming of the pennant for three years. But you can't win a pennant without pitchers and somebody had to carry an unusually heavy pitching load if we were to come through for Comiskey. Obviously I was "it" and I accepted the role without hesitation and determined to pitch ball as I had never pitched before.[3]

He credited his sudden ascent to his improved physical condition. His weight was a problem earlier in his career, especially in Boston, but by now, said Eddie, he had learned to take care of himself.

> This has been my best season not because of any ridiculous shine ball or any other mysterious kind of a ball. I use fast balls, curves, spitters and knuckle balls and am known to do so by every batter in the American League. That's enough of a variety, coupled with good control and long experience to give any pitcher all he can handle to advantage. If he plays those cards well, he doesn't have to have any joker stuck up his sleeve to win his fair percentage of the jackpots.
>
> It has been my best season mainly because of my improved physical condition and determination to work at top speed from start to finish. Last year I found myself beginning to puff and blow along about the seventh inning. I was carrying too much fat around the waist line. A corporation may be all right in its place but it's no help to a pitcher. This year I had no such handicap. I could breeze through nine innings just as I used to breeze through six or seven.[4]

Because of the World War, no one knew what would happen during the 1918 baseball season. The United States entered the war in Europe in April of 1917, but the full brunt of war preparation was not to be felt for nearly a year. Germany had already knocked out Russia, winning the conflict on the Eastern front, and the Kaiser's generals were now able to concentrate their forces in the West. The Americans were desperately needed to help the exhausted British and French hold off the Germans, and the American war effort swung into action. These international developments promised major consequences for baseball, both at the box office and on the field.

Eddie Cicotte was not required to enter the military, at least not yet. He was a 33-year-old married man with two children, and the draft board in Detroit was not yet inclined to call on men in similar circumstances. He was not affected by the Selective Service Act, passed by Congress on May 18, 1917, that required all men between ages 21 and 31 to register for the draft. He did, however, watch as his younger teammates dealt with their war responsibilities. Veteran pitcher Jim Scott voluntarily entered the Army in mid-season of 1917, and now other White Sox debated whether to do the same or wait to be drafted.

One player who did not wait was Red Faber. The spitball pitcher was a 29-year-old bachelor and virtually certain to be called, so he announced during spring training that he had signed up with the Navy (an odd choice for a man who suffered greatly

Eddie warms up in 1917. Note the dirt on his right leg where the shine ball artist rubbed the baseball on his pants (Library of Congress).

6. War and Turmoil

Red Faber, hero of the 1917 World Series. Eddie Cicotte won the first game, while Faber won the second, fifth, and sixth (author's collection).

from seasickness during the 1913–1914 world tour). Faber would leave the White Sox sometime during the season, though no one knew exactly when. Several other White Sox had already been classified as 1-A by their local draft boards, and they no doubt would be going too. The Sox would have been the favorites to defend their world title in any other year, but like every other team in both leagues, the men who played on Opening Day would most likely not be the same ones who ended the season.

Baseball made a display of support for the war effort in 1917, with flag patches on uniforms, military-style drills before games, lots of red, white, and blue decorations, and the like, but the public was not happy that so few players had volunteered for service. Only about 40 major leaguers had done so during 1917.[5] Major league ball went on with little disruption, although several minor leagues closed up early, and the World Series proceeded as normal. Things would be very different in 1918. Ban Johnson knew it, and the American League president leaned on his friends in the press to paint baseball as a morale builder and a necessary patriotic diversion for a nation at war. Johnson, now 54 years old, overweight, and diabetic, even offered to enlist in the Army and fight overseas himself.

Due to wartime travel restrictions, the White Sox spent only three weeks in training camp at Mineral Wells, Texas, beginning on March 18. Despite the abbreviated spring schedule, some of the Sox still found trouble. On March 20, Eddie Cicotte and three other players—Joe Jackson, Ray Schalk, and Chick Gandil—rode in a friend's new car for an outing at the local golf course. On their return to camp, they were struck by another car that ran through a stop sign. Eddie complained of a sore neck, though none of the other White Sox were hurt. Charles Comiskey reacted with anger. "Their place was on the ball field this morning if they were able to be there," he said, "not out experimenting with golf sticks and looking at scenery."[6] The owner banned golf and automobile rides for the rest of camp.

Eddie Collins, who spent most of March coaching the team at the University of Pennsylvania, joined the White Sox on March 30. He fell easily into the groove, belting three hits in his first exhibition game in Houston, but his health took a turn for the worse with a severe cold, probably worsened by the rainy weather and the drafty Pullmans that the players rode in while playing their way north. Collins fainted during an examination by a doctor on April 11 and was diagnosed with tonsillitis. Comiskey sent his second baseman ahead of the team to Kansas City, the next stop on the trip, and assigned Eddie Cicotte to accompany him and wait for the rest of the team to arrive.

No one knew how long Collins would stay with the Sox in 1918. The Chicago captain had written Ban Johnson the previous December and stated that he was thinking of entering the service at that time. Collins admired the Marines, and though he was a 31-year-old married man and probably safe from the draft, he wanted to enlist in the Marine Corps. His loss would be a huge blow to the club. Another setback came when Kid Gleason, after a salary dispute with Comiskey, sat out the 1918 season. Both the White Sox owner and his longtime coach were stubborn and strong-willed, and because neither man would budge, the Sox lost an important cog in their championship machine. Gleason was the man who smoothed over tensions between the two cliques on the ballclub, and now Pants Rowland had to manage that task by himself.

Eddie Cicotte signed his contract for 1918 in January without his usual holdout, but his season began in disastrous fashion and never improved. On Opening Day, April 16, with 20,000 in the stands at Comiskey Park, Eddie lost to St. Louis 6–1. The Browns batted him out of the box in the fifth inning, and Danforth, Faber, and Russell finished up. Eddie never liked starting on Opening Day, believing the honor to be bad luck for him, and this game was his only Opening Day start with the White Sox. (He had pitched the season opener in 1910 for the Red Sox and left after seven innings without a decision.)

This loss was the first of seven in a row for Eddie Cicotte. On April 22, the Tigers roughed him up for seven runs in seven innings in a 7–3 win, and on May 1 the Indians touched him for six runs and 11 hits in Cleveland. After another loss to Detroit on May 4 dropped Eddie's record to 0–4, he left a game in the second inning on May 8 with a twisted ankle. He singled and hurt himself as his foot hit first base. The Sox won that game, but Eddie did not get the decision.

Eddie took eight days off to recover, and when he returned he was phenomenal, but as unlucky as ever. He took a shutout into the ninth at Washington on May 17, only to lose when Clyde Milan doubled and Joe Judge drove him home to win the game, 1–0. Five days later, Eddie pitched 13 scoreless innings in New York, matching zeroes with the Yankees' Hank Thormahlen. In the bottom of the 14th, Wally Pipp won it for the Yankees when he singled Frank Baker home. Eddie had scattered seven hits, all singles, but saw his record fall to 0–6. It went to 0–7 with his third 1–0 loss in a row, this time to Boston, before he finally won his first game on the last day of May.

On May 23, 1918, the Provost Marshal, General Enoch Crowder, issued a requirement that all men between the ages of 21 and 31 either volunteer for military service or find work in a defense-related plant. Eddie Cicotte, who turned 34 in June of 1918, was not affected by this "work or fight" ruling. The government also ordered all men between ages 18 and 35 to register for the draft, and Eddie did so in his native Detroit.

However, most major and minor league ballplayers were impacted by Crowder's edict, and the immediate future of baseball was suddenly in danger. Each team would have only a handful of available players if all the men between ages 21 and 31 went into the war effort. The Red Sox would lose every one of their players, and the White Sox would be left with Eddie Cicotte, two other pitchers, and one outfielder. The situation was so dire that Pants Rowland, a minor league catcher who never played major league ball, volunteered to suit up if necessary, as did Hughie Jennings, the 48-year-old manager of the Tigers.

Still, baseball went on, and as the season progressed, the White Sox had trouble scoring, partly due to injuries. Buck Weaver tore cartilage in his right foot on May 15, while Eddie Collins, still not completely recovered from his illness in the spring, was spiked in a loss at Cleveland on May 1. The pitchers suffered from lack of support, and on May 15, Lefty Williams pitched 17 innings of shutout ball at Washington, only to lose 1–0 to Walter Johnson in the 18th. The biggest blow to the Chicago offense, however, came on May 11, when Joe Jackson left the team to take a job in a shipyard. After Jackson was reclassified as 1-A by his hometown draft board in Greenville, South Carolina, his number came up and he was told to expect induction into the United States Army. Instead, Jackson found employment at the Harlan and Hollingsworth shipbuilding plant in Wilmington, Delaware.

Perhaps Jackson's decision to do war work instead of Army service would not have caused so much controversy had the shipyards and defense plants not fielded their own highly competitive baseball teams. The defense plants made offers to major league stars, and some, unwilling to be sent to France for an indeterminate time, opted to remain stateside. Jackson was the first prominent player to opt for war work instead of induction, and in early June, Lefty Williams and Byrd Lynn joined Jackson at the same Delaware shipyard. At the end of June, Happy Felsch went to work at a defense-related factory near his hometown of Milwaukee. Swede Risberg, who told both Comiskey and the press that he planned to enter the Army in August, changed his mind and went home to California to work at a nearby shipyard run by Bethlehem Steel in Alameda. According to media reports, all these men spent more time playing ball than building ships, drawing censure from the press and public.

Lefty Williams and Eddie Cicotte. These two Chicago pitchers won 52 games between them in 1919 (author's collection).

Though Jackson and the others made these decisions legally, in full accordance with General Crowder's order, the players came in for scathing criticism. Ban Johnson made a show of his patriotism when he declared that Jackson and the others should be "yanked into the Army by the coat collar. The American League ... does not approve of players trying to evade military service."[7] Johnson was engaged in a desperate battle to keep baseball going lest the government shut it down, and the bad publicity resulting from players avoiding the Army could only damage his efforts.

Comiskey, not to be outdone in patriotic fervor, reacted angrily when Lynn and Williams left the team on June 11. Williams was slated to pitch that day's game, but Comiskey ordered him and Lynn to leave the ballpark immediately. The White Sox owner fumed to the press:

6. War and Turmoil 75

I don't consider them fit to play on my ball club. I would gladly lose my whole team if the players wished to do their duty to their country ... but I hate to see any ball players, particularly my own, go to ship yards to escape army service.

There can be no other reason for their act, as they can not honestly earn as much building ships as they can playing ball.[8]

Ban Johnson's politicking came for naught on July 20, when Secretary of War Newton D. Baker declared that baseball players held a "non-essential" occupation and would not be deferred from service. Theater performers, however, were granted "essential" status, perhaps because they mostly worked at night, and perhaps because they did not generate the bad publicity that baseball players had. Johnson rashly ordered the circuit to shut down for the year, but the owners ignored him and kept playing. President Woodrow Wilson threw the game a lifeline on July 27 when he wrote a letter to the National Commission in which he allowed the sport to continue. But as more players left for the service, the quality of play deteriorated, and the club owners decided to cut the season short. They received an extension of the work or fight order from the War Department and announced that the 1918 campaign would end on Labor Day, with the World Series to be played immediately afterward.

Eddie Cicotte won four games in a row after his 0–7 start, but his streak ended on June 13 when the Red Sox shut out the White Sox for the third time in four days, 6–0, behind Dutch Leonard. The Chicago offense disappeared with Joe Jackson, as the Red Sox gave up only one run in the four-game series. The White Sox sank steadily in the standings after that disastrous series, and by the end of June they were effectively out of the race.

Lefty Williams' departure for the shipyard and Red Faber's call-up by the Navy, both in mid–June, left the pitching in the hands of Eddie Cicotte, who was over the draft age, and 19-year-old rookie spitballer Frank Shellenback, who was under it. Reb Russell and Joe Benz made some starts but were ineffective, as was reliever Dave Danforth, who followed up his great 1917 season with a poor one in 1918. With little offense to back their pitching, the White Sox stumbled into the middle of the pack of the American League, settling into fifth place in late June and falling to sixth soon after.

The White Sox did, however, receive a boost from a 33-year-old minor leaguer. Jack Quinn was a right-handed spitballer who had pitched in the American, National, and Federal leagues, with varying degrees of success, earlier in the decade. In 1916 he landed with Vernon of the Pacific Coast League, and in 1918 his 1.48 earned run average led the circuit.[9] When the Pacific Coast League closed up shop for the season on July 14, the National Commission allowed all its players to sign with major league teams. Charles Comiskey signed Quinn, who joined the Sox on August 1 and posted a 5–1 record in six games. However, the Vernon club, though temporarily disbanded, sold Quinn's contract to the New York Yankees on July 19, setting off a bitter two-team battle for the spitballer's services. Quinn finished the year with the White Sox, but the National Commission now had to decide who owned him.

Quinn's pitching was the sole bright spot for the White Sox in August, the season's last month. Eddie Collins belted two hits in his final game on August 15, then joined the Marines. The captain played with injuries all year, and his .276 batting average (with only 12 extra-base hits) was the worst of his career so far. Collins' departure spelled the end for the White Sox, who won only four of their final 16 games and ended the 1918 season with eight consecutive losses. Eddie Cicotte briefly rallied with three complete-game wins in early August, but he closed the campaign with four losses in a row. The final two games, a Labor Day doubleheader in Detroit, were a disaster in which Dave Danforth gave up 16 hits in the opener and lost, 11–5. In the nightcap, Eddie Cicotte allowed 21 hits in eight innings and fell to the Tigers, 7–5. At least Buck Weaver was happy at day's end. He belted eight hits in the twin bill, lifting his average to the .300 mark for the first time in his career.

Eddie Cicotte finished the 1918 season with a 12–19 record, leading the American League in losses. It was the worst year of his career, but the constant turmoil and lineup shuffling played havoc with the team and made consistency impossible. Of the regulars, only Schalk, Gandil, Weaver, and Cicotte remained for the whole season, with the rest of the slots filled by minor leaguers, some of whom never played big league ball again. Still, some thought that his win-loss record indicated that Eddie was finished. He was 34 years old, and his career was at another crossroads. Would the Eddie Cicotte of 1919 resemble the Eddie of 1917 or the Eddie of 1918?

Eddie went home to Detroit and, to assist in the war effort, took a job at the Ford Motor Company's plant in River Rouge, Michigan. Ford had turned over much of its production capacity to the government, and Eddie went to work as a stock manager in the plant boatyard. Thus began Eddie's association with the Ford Motor Company that lasted for nearly three decades. When the War Department required all men not in the service between the ages of 18 and 45—those born between 1873 and 1897—to register once again for the draft in early September, Eddie filled out his card and listed his employer as the Ford Motor Company, not the Chicago White Sox. If the war forced a delay or cancellation of the 1919 campaign, the Ford job assured Eddie of a steady source of income.

During the late stages of the 1918 season, an incident occurred in the National League that would have great consequences for baseball, and for Eddie Cicotte, in the future. It concerned gambling and game-fixing, and, not surprisingly, it involved Eddie's old Chicago teammate, Hal Chase.

Chase, who joined the Cincinnati Reds in 1916 after he wore out his welcome in the American League, was still fixing games. In August of 1918, his manager, Christy Mathewson, suspended Chase for what the papers called "indifferent play," but was actually Mathewson's discovery that Chase was offering bribes to teammates and opponents alike. Reds pitcher Jimmy Ring later charged that Chase had given him a $50 bill after a loss, presumably after Chase won a bet against his own team. Mathewson also suspected that Chase and teammate Lee Magee bet on the Reds to lose against the Boston Braves on July 25, 1918. The Reds won anyway, and both Chase and Magee lost their $500 wagers. Magee admitted to this indiscretion two years later. Other National League players, including New York Giants pitcher Pol Perritt, claimed that Chase had offered them money to "lay down" in 1918 as well.

In January of 1919, league president John Heydler held a hearing on the matter. Ring and two other Cincinnati players testified against Chase, while Perritt sent a deposition. Mathewson, then serving with the Army in France, was not available, and without Mathewson's testimony, Heydler cleared Chase of wrongdoing. "The testimony showed that Chase acted in a foolish and careless manner," reported Heydler, "both on the field and among the players, and that the club was justified in bringing the charges in view of the many rumors which arose from the loose talk of its first baseman.... There was, however, no proof that he intentionally violated or attempted to violate the rules in relation to tampering with players or in any way endeavored to secure desired results in the outcome of games.... He has been proved not guilty of the charges."[10]

Heydler believed that he had no choice but to exonerate Chase. As an editorial in *Baseball Magazine* explained, Heydler "found a mass of rumors, half rumors and bare suspicions mixed in with a few suggestive facts and nothing more. Of evidence in any technical sense, there was none, and without evidence it would have been a criminal act to blast the reputation of any ball player."[11] But Heydler also issued a stern warning. "Any player who during my term as President of the National League," he said, "is shown to have any interest in a wager on any game played in the league, whether he bets on his club or against it, or whether he takes part in the game or not, will be promptly expelled from the National League."[12]

Despite Heydler's tough words, baseball was still unwilling to address its gambling problem, partly because the personable Chase still carried a degree of popularity within the game. Even *The Sporting News* tried to excuse Prince Hal's behavior. As the "Bible of Baseball" reported in August of 1918, "There is unquestioned evidence showing that during the Cleveland-Red [post-season] series last fall, Hal put up a flock of coin on [pitcher Hod] Eller to beat Cleveland twice, and won each time—betting honestly on his own team. When a player bets honestly on his own club, he'll surely do his best to win, but it is a bad practice just the same."[13]

Though Chase was exonerated, the only major league manager who wanted him was Mathewson's old mentor, John McGraw of the Giants. McGraw convinced himself that he could control the smooth-fielding first baseman. "I have found him a most agreeable chap, and I am sure we will get along without a hitch,"[14] said an optimistic McGraw. He traded infielder Walter Holke and catcher Bill Rariden to the Reds for Chase, returning the tainted star to New York, where he began his twin careers in baseball and game-fixing a decade earlier. What's more, McGraw then signed Mathewson as a coach. Mathewson, who hoped to manage the Giants someday, had no choice but to accept the situation.

There matters stood at the dawn of the 1919 season. Hal Chase evaded punishment for his special brand of dishonesty once again, and now Lee Magee was suspected of collaborating with Chase in the game-fixing business. The Boston Red Sox won the World Series in 1918, but the gamblers at Fenway Park conducted their business in the right field stands during the Series with little or no interruption. Some of the plays made by the Chicago Cubs in that Series looked suspicious, and rumors circulated that the fall classic may not have been played on the square. One could also find people who believed that the 1912 and 1914 Series, both of which were won by Boston teams, looked a little fishy too.

In December of 1918 the authorities in Boston arrested and convicted 33 men, some of whom were regulars at Fenway, for gambling-related offenses. Ban Johnson took credit for the convictions, but he was more interested in embarrassing Red Sox owner Harry Frazee than in making real headway against the gambling problem. Johnson, who dominated the three-man National Commission, was too busy battling his enemies, including Frazee and Chicago's Charles Comiskey, to provide effective leadership on the gambling front. Nothing short of a major scandal would force baseball to finally face the problem.

7

The 1919 Season

To me baseball is as honorable as any other business. It is the most honest pastime in the world. It has to be or it could not last a season out. Crookedness and baseball do not mix. It has become immeasurably more popular as the years have gone by. It will be greater yet. This year, 1919, is the greatest season of them all.—Charles A. Comiskey, 1919[1]

Babe Ruth hated facing Eddie Cicotte. The Babe walloped a league-leading 11 homers in 1918, a record-breaking 29 in 1919, and then, after a trade to the Yankees, 54 more in 1920. Not one of them came off Eddie Cicotte.

Ruth was a free swinger who loved to whale away at the hard fastball. Cicotte, whose speed was adequate at best, knew better than to give Ruth what he wanted. Instead, Eddie frustrated the Babe with his trick pitches, thrown up, down, inside and outside at varying speeds and in no predictable pattern. Eddie's approach worked, for Ruth batted only .178 against the White Sox ace, with eight hits and 12 strikeouts in 45 at-bats.

Cicotte also employed psychology against the fearsome slugger. "I'd say to Schalk, 'Who's that big bum up there?' and oh my, you should have heard the Babe. 'Why, you old pea-souper,' he used to say…. He'd get so mad he couldn't swing."[2] Ruth, who never could remember anybody's name, would be so busy bellowing invective against the pitcher he called "Froggy" that he would, much more often than not, drag his bat back to the bench in defeat.

Ty Cobb had trouble with Eddie too, at least early on. "Cicotte had everyone mystified," said Cobb later in life. "He began to win 18 to 29 games a season with a ball that looked softy-boiled when it came to the plate. But oh, brother! No matter how closely you focused on it, you could never see the thing break…. Even when he threw it letter-high, where I liked a pitch, I'd cut under the ball." However, Cobb discovered that his old Augusta teammate could be rattled. "So your middle name is Vivian, eh?" jeered the Detroit star from the batter's box. "My, what a pretty name."[3] Cobb found that his razzing unnerved the usually even-keeled Cicotte.

In one game, or so Cobb claimed, he found an even better way to get under Eddie's skin. He strode to the batter's box, turned his back on the Chicago pitcher, and carried on an animated conversation about duck hunting with teammate Sam Crawford, who was waiting in the on-deck circle. Cobb did not even look at the pitcher, but because his feet were legally placed in the box, Cicotte was required to pitch. The thoroughly flustered Cicotte threw four straight balls and lost his control so completely that he was pulled from the game shortly after. In all, Cobb batted .333 against Cicotte, with nine of his 34 hits going for extra bases.

Eddie's 12–19 record in 1918 was the worst of his career, but it was not an ordinary year, and Chicago fans hoped that Cicotte, at age 34, was not washed up. The uncertain status of the roster, with star players leaving for war and journeymen taking their places, had damaged every team, but none more than the White Sox. The Chicago club, with Collins, Jackson, Faber, and many others returning to the fold, would be expected to contend once again for the pennant and a spot in the World Series.

For a while, it looked as if the country would have no baseball at all in 1919. No one knew if the war would drag out for years on end, and because the game was stopped a month early in 1918, it would probably not resume for the duration. Fortunately for baseball, the World War came to an abrupt end in November of 1918 when the German war effort collapsed after four years of intense fighting. The 1919 campaign was saved, though the club owners, worried about how quickly the American appetite for sports and amusement would recover after the conflict, decided to slice 14 games off the schedule and stage a 140-game season.

The White Sox opened their 1919 spring camp at Mineral Wells, Texas, with virtually the same roster of players that had won the world title in 1917. Though Jim Scott decided to leave Chicago and play ball in the Pacific Coast League, Red Faber (Navy) and Eddie Collins (Marine Corps) returned from the service, and Happy Felsch, Lefty Williams, Swede Risberg, and Joe Jackson came back from the shipyards. These last four players had spent most of their time playing ball instead of doing war work, so they could be expected to round into shape quickly. Jackson, who won the batting title of the "paint and putty league," showed that his hitting eye was as sharp as ever.

The biggest change for the White Sox came on New Year's Eve, when Charles Comiskey dropped Pants Rowland as his manager and promoted coach Kid Gleason to the post. Rowland, despite his success, could never quite erase his reputation as a minor leaguer who lucked into the Chicago job, and his nickname, "The Busher from Dubuque," stuck to him like glue. When he tried to shake hands with Giants manager John McGraw after the 1917 Series, McGraw reportedly yelled, "Get away from me, you busher!" McGraw may have uttered an expletive or two in that statement as well. Rowland left Chicago for a job as manager and part-owner of the minor-league Milwaukee Brewers.

Kid Gleason, unlike Rowland, boasted a world of experience in major league ball. He began his career as a pitcher and won 38 games for the 1890 Philadelphia Phillies. When his arm gave out from overwork a few years later, Gleason moved to second base and played for another decade and more. He was a tough, scrappy fighter, in sharp contrast to the amiable Rowland. He had left the Sox in early 1918 after a pay dispute with Comiskey, but now all was forgiven. If anyone could keep all the cliques and factions of the White Sox from destroying each other, Kid Gleason was the man. The writers liked him too. As Jim Crusinberry of the *Tribune* wrote, "No one was ever shrewder in a game of ball.... There isn't a ballplayer in the game today or any of those who played with the Kid in the old days who will not declare him as fair and square a man on and off the ball field as ever lived."[4]

After leading the American League in losses in 1918, Eddie Cicotte could not expect a raise from Comiskey. He signed a contract in February that called for the same salary as the year before—$5,000 in base pay and a $3,000 bonus. His $8,000 total salary was, contrary to popular belief, not unreasonably low, nor was it evidence of Comiskey's skinflint ways. Indeed, according to research by Jacob Pomrenke, Bob Hoie, and others from the Society for American Baseball Research, Eddie's salary was the eighth-highest in the American League. He was the second-highest-paid pitcher in the league after Walter Johnson, and though he made barely half as much as Eddie Collins (whose $15,000 salary dwarfed that of every other member of the club), he had every reason to be satisfied with his pay.

He did, however, have money woes. Eddie and his wife, Rose, were expecting their third child, and the Cicotte house on Central Avenue in Detroit would soon have 12 people living in it. Rose's parents, along with her brother and sister-in-law and child, and Eddie's brother and sister-in-law, had all moved in with Eddie and Rose, and money was tight. Eddie bought a small farm in Farmington, on Seven Mile and Merriman Roads northwest of Detroit, to make room for the large extended family, and the farm carried a $4,000 mortgage. Another fat World Series check, like the one he cashed in 1917, would come in handy for the Cicottes.

The resentment between the cliques on the White Sox had never abated, and now that all the players were back from the war and the shipyards, the conflicts flared anew. Comiskey held a firm line on salaries after the seventh-place finish and poor attendance of 1918, so the money gap between Eddie Collins and most of his teammates remained. Also, the men who went into the defense plants, especially Williams, Felsch, and Jackson, were peeved that Comiskey had so viciously criticized them for their perfectly legal choice.

Eddie Collins, a Marine, and Red Faber, a Navy man, received special praise from the White Sox owner, further dividing the Chicago clubhouse.

As Eddie Collins described it later,

> [The club] was torn by discord and hatred during much of the '19 season. From the moment I arrived at training camp from service, I could see that something was amiss. We may have had our troubles in other years, but in 1919 we were a club that pulled apart rather than together. There were frequent arguments and open hostility. All the things you think—and are taught to believe—are vital to the success of any athletic organization were missing from it, and yet it was the greatest collection of players ever assembled, I would say.[5]

Years later, Buck Weaver told an interviewer of his dislike for Collins. During the 1917 World Series, Weaver and most of the other Sox made a show of sharpening their spikes "until they were like razors" to intimidate the Giants. Collins declined to join them. "Well, he was a different kind of ballplayer," said Weaver. "He never went in for that sorta stuff because he figured they might come back at him and he'd get hurt playin' there in the infield. He was a great guy to look out for himself. If there was a tough gent comin' down to second, he'd yell at the shortstop to make the play."[6]

Veteran Chicago reporter Warren Brown, in his book *The Chicago White Sox*, related a story in which Collins, the team captain, complained to manager Gleason that his charges often did the opposite of what he asked them. Gleason rolled his eyes. "If you want 'em to bunt, tell 'em to hit straightaway," the manager said. "If you want 'em to hit and run, tell 'em to bunt. Do I have to do all your thinking for you?"[7] Gleason respected Collins' baseball acumen and gave him much leeway in running the club on the field, which stirred the anti–Collins resentment even more.

Despite the turmoil, the White Sox looked good as they broke camp and headed north to start the season. The only holdout was Chick Gandil, who sat out most of camp but signed, reluctantly, just before the season started. On the weekend before Opening Day, the White Sox traveled to Cincinnati and played two exhibition games against the Reds of the National League. Lefty Williams beat them in the first contest, and Eddie Cicotte won the second. Eddie looked like he had put the troubles of 1918 behind him, as *The Sporting News* stated, "Cicotte looked every whit as good as he was in 1917, when he was a world-beater." Gleason offered Eddie the honor of the Opening Day start, but Eddie, superstitious as usual, declined it. *The Sporting News* said, "He says it augurs ill for him when he pitches the first game of the year."[8]

The 1919 White Sox were certainly talented enough to win their second world title in three years. Except for the bullpen, the Sox were solid everywhere. Red Faber, Eddie Cicotte, and Lefty Williams made perhaps the best top three of any pitching staff in baseball, with rookie Dickey Kerr and 20-year-old Frank Shellenback fighting for the fourth position. The infield,

Captain Eddie Collins (left) and manager Kid Gleason in 1919 (Library of Congress).

headed by future Hall of Famer Eddie Collins, was the best in the American League, and the outfield had Joe Jackson in left and Happy Felsch, a rising young star, in center. Nemo Leibold and Shano Collins shared right field, Ray Schalk was the best defensive catcher in the game, and the bench had solid performers in Eddie Murphy, Fred McMullin, and backup catcher Byrd Lynn. No team in the American League save perhaps for the defending champion Red Sox could match Chicago's personnel.

The Chicago club did not, however, have Jack Quinn, who won five games for the Sox in August of 1918. After the season, the Yankees demanded that the National Commission, led by league president Ban Johnson, award Quinn to them, as they had bought his contract from his Pacific Coast League team. Comiskey had made the mistake of merely signing Quinn without consulting his minor league club when the Coast League closed up shop for the season (though the Commission permitted teams to treat such minor leaguers as virtual free agents). The White Sox received a month of Quinn's pitching services for free (except for the pitcher's salary) and now the Yankees, who actually paid for him, wanted him. The whole mess was the National Commission's fault, but the Commission, quite reasonably, awarded Quinn to the Yankees.

This act not only harmed the White Sox, but it also turned the already shaky friendship of Johnson and Comiskey into bitter enmity. From then on, Comiskey opposed Johnson in almost everything related to the governance of the American League, and actively campaigned for his dismissal from office. Their acrimonious feud would have serious repercussions for both men, and for baseball itself, during and after the 1919 World Series.

The White Sox charged out of the gate with six wins in their first seven games against St. Louis and Detroit, all on the road. The home opener on Thursday, May 1, at Comiskey Park was rained out, and the Sox lost the next day behind Williams on a muddy field. After another rainout on Saturday, Eddie pitched on Sunday and defeated the Browns in a rain-shortened, five-inning game. After Frank Shellenback won a makeup game against the Browns on May 12, the Sox stood in first place by three games over Boston, with the Yankees and Indians trailing.

It was only May, but Eddie Cicotte was already in late-season form. Three shutouts in a row at home, against the Red Sox, A's, and Yankees, gave him a team record 29⅔ consecutive shutout innings. His first shutout on May 14 was a duel against Boston's Carl Mays. The Sox scored in the sixth inning when Jackson's double brought home Eddie Collins for the game's only run. In the ninth inning, with a man on and two out, Eddie got Babe Ruth to fly out to center for the last out of the game. Cicotte had allowed four hits, all singles, and pitched the only shutout of his career against his former team, the Red Sox. "You will live a long time before you see another battle of slabmen to equal that,"[9] I. E. Sanborn wrote in the *Chicago Tribune*. Eddie won all seven of his starts in May, though he took a loss in a relief role, and at the end of the month his earned run average stood at 1.02.

Eddie's pitching bag of tricks, some of which skirted the line of illegality, frustrated many teams, but none more than the Indians. On May 31, in a game at Comiskey Park, Cleveland outfielder Jack Graney kept up a steady stream of complaints to the umpires, claiming that Cicotte was doctoring the baseball. He even grabbed two baseballs and gave them to home plate umpire Dick Nallin, asking him to send them to the league office for analysis. Eddie

Sports cartoonist Robert Ripley drew Cicotte's likeness for the nation's newspapers in June of 1919 (author's collection).

allowed two runs in the second inning but toyed with the Indians the rest of way amidst increasingly vicious heckling.

Cleveland outfielder Tris Speaker, upset with Eddie and frustrated by his 0-for-4 performance, lashed out in the eighth inning. He slid hard into first base on a routine groundout, much to the dismay of Chick Gandil. The two men traded insults, and at the end of the inning, as Speaker and Gandil passed each other on the infield, a fight erupted. It was not the usual baseball fight, but a vicious, bloody brawl between the two men. As Jim Crusinberry described it in the *Tribune*,

> An old time fist fight such as probably hasn't occurred on a league ball field in the last 15 years or more broke loose at the White Sox park yesterday when Chick Gandil and Tris Speaker mixed at first base, just as the first half of the eighth inning came to a close. It started as a fist fight, but it was a rough and tumble tiger battle with claws, spikes, fists, feet, and possibly even teeth before the two finally were dragged apart. Both fighters were cut by spikes and apparently badly bruised, and Gandil's baseball shirt was almost torn off his back.

"Baseball fights," wrote Crusinberry, "generally are stopped after about one exchange of blows. This pair were tumbling over the earth from first base halfway to the pitcher's slab, then back toward second, and still nobody stopped them."[10] In *Eight Men Out*, Eliot Asinof stated that the other White Sox stood by and did nothing in order to see Gandil "get his lumps," but the Sox were probably so awestruck by the violent nature of the fight that they froze in place. The police on the scene had to pry the two fighters apart, and both men were ejected and suspended for five days by the league president.

Cleveland manager Lee Fohl blamed the fracas on Eddie Cicotte. "It was that 'shine' ball that started the row," said Fohl. "As long as things like that are permitted, there'll be fights. My players simply got mad. The rules declare there shall be no discoloration of the ball. Cicotte repeatedly discolors it. We appeal to the umpires and they do nothing."[11] Eddie later claimed that the Indians stole his uniform pants from the Chicago clubhouse and sent them off to a lab for testing, but found no talcum powder, paraffin, or other substances besides sweat.

Eddie's record stood at 12–1, best in the American League, in mid–June, and perhaps it was inevitable that the 35-year-old pitcher would fall into a slump. Though he defeated the Red Sox on June 10 and the A's in a 14-inning contest on June 14, he uncharacteristically walked five men in each game. He lost his next three starts against the Senators, Indians, and Browns, but righted himself with seven wins in a row through the end of July. With Red Faber struggling, Eddie emerged as the undisputed ace of the Sox rotation, as he had in 1917.

The Sox might have run away from the pack had Faber been healthy, but the spitballer never found his footing in 1919. He had contracted the Spanish flu while in the Navy, and though he survived the pandemic that killed millions around the world, Faber emerged from the service weakened and at least 15 pounds underweight. Faber won his first four decisions of 1919, but tired so easily that on May 24, Yankees right fielder Sammy Vick threw him out at first base on what should have been a clean single. Arm soreness, failing stamina, and an ankle injury led to five losses in a row. Faber's inconsistency put pressure on Lefty Williams and Eddie Cicotte to carry the team until Kid Gleason could find one more pitcher to fill out the rotation. In the meantime, Chicago's lead melted away and on July 1, the upstart Yankees held first place with the White Sox three and a half games behind. The Sox certainly could have used Jack Quinn, who was winning games for the Yankees thanks to Ban Johnson.

The Sox finally found a reliable third starter on July 4 when rookie left-hander Dickey Kerr filled in for Grover Lowdermilk, who had a cold. After Cicotte won the first game of the doubleheader that day, Kerr held Detroit to seven hits and one run in a 7–1 win. Kerr defeated Walter Johnson and the Senators on July 19 with eight strong relief innings, and he came into the game against the Browns on little notice on July 25 when Lefty Williams was hit in the head by a line drive off the bat of Hank Severeid. Kerr finished the game and got the win in that one. He solidified the rotation, and when the Chicago bats came alive in July, the Sox went on a 13–2 tear to reclaim the league lead. They hardly missed Chick Gandil, who sat out three weeks with appendicitis. Gleason moved Swede Risberg to first, shifted Buck Weaver to short, and put utility man Fred McMullin on third, and the White Sox did not miss a beat.

All the while, the two cliques on the team barely spoke to each other. Kerr joined the group of White Sox with "more schooling and less bravado," as Red Faber's biographer Brian E. Cooper put it, which included Eddie Collins, Ray Schalk, and Faber. The less-educated drinking men like Swede Risberg, Happy Felsch, and Chick Gandil went their own way, often joined by Eddie Cicotte, who enjoyed playing pool and hanging out in taverns. The rowdier White Sox caused headaches for manager Gleason, and their wild antics got the team booted out of their hotel in Boston early in the 1919 season.

During the first week of August, with the Sox holding a five-game lead, *The Sporting News* referred to the White Sox as "the coming champions," but the race was not over yet. The defending champion Boston Red Sox, even with pitcher-turned-outfielder Babe Ruth belting home runs at a record pace, faded into the second division, but the Indians remained within striking distance, and the Yankees, with Jack Quinn and the newly-acquired Carl Mays stabilizing their rotation, stayed in the hunt. Charles Comiskey had tried to swing a deal for Mays, who had quit the Boston team in a salary dispute, but the Red Sox were understandably reluctant to help the league leaders and sent Mays to New York instead.

Tris Speaker now managed the Cleveland club, which had fired Lee Fohl in mid–June after a game with Boston. The Indians held a 7–4 lead in the top of the ninth when Babe Ruth came to bat with the bases full. Fohl brought in left-hander Fritz Coumbe to face Ruth, ignoring Speaker's frantic signals from center field for a different pitcher, and Ruth promptly walloped a grand slam to put the Red Sox in the lead. Cleveland lost the game, 8–7, and that night, Speaker was named manager of the Indians. The new manager's energy and enthusiasm kept the Indians in the race.

During August, Eddie Cicotte and the White Sox clicked on all cylinders. As the Yankees faded in the summer heat, a ten-game Chicago winning streak at home against the Red Sox, A's, Senators, and Yankees put the Sox in the lead by eight games over Cleveland and the streaking Detroit club. Eddie won his 20th game of the season on August 7, 2–1 against the A's at Philadelphia. He was the first pitcher to reach 20 in 1919, and three days later, he pitched 12 innings of shutout ball against the Senators, allowing only four hits in a 1–0 win. He zoomed through the rest of August with five more wins, then won the first game of a Labor Day doubleheader in Detroit on September 1 to put his record at 27–7. With one month to go in the season, Eddie appeared to be on the cusp of winning 30 games.

The 30-win plateau was not nearly as major a milestone at the time as it would be today. During the 1910s, four pitchers reached the 30 mark seven times in all (with Grover Alexander doing so three times and Walter Johnson twice). During the previous decade, Ed Walsh and Jack Chesbro reached the 40-win mark, while Christy Mathewson won 30 or more four times. By contrast, as of the start of the 2020 campaign, no pitcher has won 30 in a single season since Denny McLain of Detroit in 1968. In the present day, 30 wins by a pitcher in two seasons is a respectable total. Still, not many pitchers won 30 in a season even then, and Eddie, at age 35, had a chance to be the oldest to do so since Cy Young in 1902.

After the results of Labor Day, the races in both the American and National Leagues were effectively over. The White Sox held a seven-game lead over Cleveland, and the Cincinnati Reds stood seven games ahead of the fading New York Giants. The World Series matchup was all but official, barring a disastrous collapse by either the White Sox or the Reds, and sportswriters across the country began their prognostications on the outcome of the 1919 World Series one month hence.

The only bad news for the White Sox involved their pitching ace. Eddie Cicotte had carried a heavy load in the absence of Red Faber, and in early September it caught up to him. On the Friday after Labor Day, Eddie's usually pinpoint control failed him while pitching against the Indians at Comiskey

Park. Eddie won his 28th victory of 1919 by a score of 9 to 1 that day, but he gave up six walks, his highest total of the season.

With the pennant virtually assured, Kid Gleason decided to let Eddie rest his arm for two weeks. Reports vary as to what was wrong with Eddie. Some reporters said that his arm was sore, others that it was merely tired. With Eddie on the shelf, some of the second-stringers filled in; during a six-game winning streak on the road in mid–September, six different Sox pitchers, including Grover Lowdermilk, Roy Wilkinson, and Bill James, earned wins. Eddie warmed up on September 12 at Philadelphia with every intention of pitching that day, but decided to stay out. Wilkinson, recently acquired by the Sox to fortify the bullpen corps, pitched instead and delivered a five-hit shutout in his second major league game.

On September 17, with Eddie still out of action, an explanation appeared in the *Philadelphia North American*:

> The mystery has been solved. The Indians have discovered why it is that Eddie Cicotte, the star pitcher of the White Sox, has not worked since Sept. 5, when he beat the Indians. His arm, which bothered him in that game, causing him to pass six batsmen, an unusually large number for him, has troubled him ever since. He thought yesterday that it was nearly right and planned to pitch against the Athletics, but after warming up he declared it did not feel good enough to warrant his going in.
>
> He told friends it was not lame, but very tired. Gleason is confident his big winner will be rested enough when the World Series starts.[12]

Gleason certainly hoped so, because his other workhorse was unavailable. Red Faber tried to make a comeback, taking the mound against the last-place Athletics in Philadelphia on September 15 after a one-month layoff. The A's battered the spitballer for 13 hits and 10 runs, and though Faber won the game, 11–10, his arm hurt so badly that he did not pitch again in 1919. He would ride the bench in the Series, but was definitely out of action. Faber's absence left the Chicago pitching in the hands of the overworked Cicotte, the steady Williams, and the rookie Kerr, with Wilkinson and others in reserve.

Eddie's 13-day hiatus ended on September 19 in Boston. He pitched a complete game, winning 3–2 for his 29th victory. Eddie gave up seven hits but, most significantly, no walks. This performance quieted some of the more fretful White Sox fans. Now he had two starts remaining to clinch his 30th win.

That's when Eddie's old friend Sport Sullivan entered the picture.

The creation of the Black Sox fix is still a matter of much debate and disagreement, but the fact remains that during the last month of the 1919 season, Eddie Cicotte and seven of his teammates held several meetings with gamblers and fixers. We'll never know the exact sequence of events, as there are many accounts of which players met with which group of fixers on which dates. However, we can say with certainty that Sport Sullivan and his good friend, White Sox first baseman Chick Gandil, were intimately involved in the planning and execution of the fix. They were the key players in the game-throwing scheme that ruined the careers of Eddie Cicotte and seven other White Sox.

As Gandil told his version of the story many years later, he and Cicotte were leaving their hotel on their way to the Boston ballpark during the third week of September when Sullivan greeted them. The gambler came right out with his proposition—that a band of seven or eight Chicago players could make a lot of money by throwing the World Series. Gandil expressed his doubts at the possibility, but Sullivan dismissed Gandil's reservations with a wave of his hand. "Don't be silly," he said. "It's been pulled before and it can be again."[13]

Sullivan had set the hook, and now he reeled in his catch. He offered $10,000 in cash to each participant in the scheme. The gambler was well aware that no one on the White Sox except Eddie Collins made $10,000 per year, or anything close to it. Gandil, who resented his low salary, and the debt-ridden Cicotte listened intently. They told Sullivan that they would think about it, and, as Gandil recalled, won their game that afternoon. This would put the date of the proposal on Friday, September 19, the day Eddie Cicotte won his 29th game.

Perhaps Sullivan's scheme did not seem so outlandish because of suspicions surrounding the previous World Series. The general public knew little about it, but rumors of a 1918 Series fix between the Boston Red Sox and Chicago Cubs floated freely within baseball circles. This was the Series that took place right after Labor Day, when the owners cut the season short due to the World War. It was also the one in which the players threatened to strike before Game Five in a dispute over distribution of the gate receipts. The teams played anyway, partly because there were injured soldiers in the stands, but also because Ban Johnson showed up at the park that day too drunk to discuss the issues.

There were a lot of strange-looking plays in the 1918 Series, and Cubs outfielder Max Flack made several of them. In Game Four, won by the Red Sox, Babe Ruth picked Flack off base in the first inning, and catcher Sam Agnew picked him off again in the fourth. Later that same game, Ruth stepped to the plate with two men on base. Other Cubs frantically waved at Flack, the right fielder, to move back, but Flack pointedly ignored them. Ruth belted a screaming liner right over Flack's head. Ruth made it to third with a triple that drove in two runs, and the Red Sox never trailed after that. In Game Six, Flack dropped a fly ball that let in two Boston runs, which were all the Red Sox needed in a 2–1 win that clinched the title.

(One play in the 1917 Series looked shady as well. Everyone laughed as the lumbering Heinie Zimmermann chased the speedy Eddie Collins down the third base line, but what choice did Zimmermann have? The Giants catcher was involved in the rundown, but where were the pitcher and first baseman? Why was nobody covering home?)

Therefore, Sullivan's "It's been pulled before and it can be again" sounded like a reasonable statement.[14] Besides, if Eddie's later testimony can be believed, the players had already discussed the possibility of a fixed Series. In September of 1920, Eddie Cicotte gave a deposition before his grand jury appearance and stated, under oath,

> The way it started, we were going east on the train [Note: the last Eastern swing for the White Sox began on September 8 in Washington]. The ball players were talking about somebody trying to fix the National League ball players or something like that in the World's Series of 1918. Well anyway there was some talk about them offering $10,000 or something to throw the Cubs in the Boston Series. There was talk that somebody offered this player $10,000 or anyway the bunch of players were offered $10,000 to throw this series. This was on the train going over. Somebody made a crack about getting money, if we got into the series, to throw the series. The boys on the Club got talking over there in New York about the fellows getting too much money and such stuff as that and said that they would go ahead and go through with it if they got this money.[15]

One wonders if Sport Sullivan, the well-connected Boston gambler, helped to fix the 1918 championship. He certainly would have known about it, if the fix was real, and probably made money from it. Sullivan's air of confidence helped convince Gandil and Cicotte that the scheme would make them all rich.

Gandil needed little convincing. The first baseman, who joined the White Sox in 1917, came to despise Comiskey more with each passing year. The Chicago owner, said Gandil, "was a sarcastic, belittling man who was the tightest owner in baseball. If a player objected to his miserly terms, Comiskey told him: 'You can take it or leave it.' Under baseball's slave laws, what could a fellow do but take it?"[16] Gandil took it, but he didn't like it. Perhaps Sport Sullivan would help him get even.

Cicotte, for his part, needed the money. His $8,000 annual salary was not enough to support the dozen members of his immediate and extended family who relied on him, and at age 35 he knew that his career would last only a few more years at best. With the World Series scheduled to start on the first day of October, Eddie Cicotte made the decision that he would regret for the rest of his life. He threw in his lot with Sullivan and Gandil and agreed to lose the Series.

Gandil and Cicotte went to work. In Gandil's words,

> Cicotte and I tried to figure out first which players might be interested. And of those who might be, which ones would we care to cut in on this gravy. We finally decided on Jackson, Weaver, Risberg, Felsch, McMullin and Williams—not that we loved them,

because there never was much love among the White Sox. Let's just say that we disliked them the least.

That night Cicotte and I called the other six together for a meeting and told them of Sullivan's offer. They were all interested and thought we should reconnoiter to see if the dough would really be put on the line. Weaver suggested we get paid in advance; then if things got too hot, we could double-cross the gambler, keep the cash and also take the big end of the Series cut by beating the Reds. We agreed this was a hell of a brainy plan.[17]

Fred McMullin, a bench player and good friend of Gandil, would have little opportunity to affect the outcome of the Series, but the other conspirators were all key performers. The fixers now claimed three-fourths of the Chicago infield (Risberg, Gandil, and perhaps Weaver), two hard-hitting outfielders (Jackson and Felsch), and the top two starting pitchers (Cicotte and Williams). Only Collins, Schalk, third-string starter Dickey Kerr, and right fielder Nemo Leibold were certain to be playing to win, and they were outnumbered.

Buck Weaver was a special case. He knew of the fix and sat in on at least two meetings of the conspirators, but insisted for the rest of his life that he played his best all through the Series. His claim is bolstered by the fact that Weaver received none of the crooked money. Gandil and the rest could not count on Weaver to join them, but they knew he would keep his mouth shut. Weaver was not a tattletale, and he counted Gandil, Risberg, and the others as his friends.

At about the same time, another group of would-be fixers made an offer of their own. Bill Burns was a former pitcher who played for the White Sox a few years before Cicotte joined the club. Called "Sleepy Bill" for his lackadaisical demeanor on the mound, he pitched for five major league teams in a career that ended in 1912. Now he made a living selling Texas oil leases, but his real passion lay in the murky underworld of sports gambling. He wanted to meet with Cicotte, an old friend of his. Because news traveled fast in the gambling world, Burns asked Eddie if the rumors of a fixed World Series were true. Cicotte allowed that they were, and Burns then asked to meet Gandil and lay out a new proposition.

Gandil, Cicotte, and Burns met at the Hotel Ansonia on Broadway, where the White Sox always stayed in New York. According to Burns' later testimony, Gandil offered to throw the Series for $100,000, and Burns asked for time to round up the money.[18] Burns then brought in a friend of his, a former boxer from Philadelphia named Billy Maharg.[19] Maharg was well known in the Philly baseball scene, as a go-fer and unofficial trainer for the Phillies who was even allowed to play the outfield in one game three years earlier.[20] Maharg asked around his hometown, but this scheme was too big for anyone in Philadelphia to handle. So Maharg and Burns decided to approach the "Big Bankroll," Arnold Rothstein, the most powerful gambler in New York.

Rothstein curtly rejected the idea, but Eddie Cicotte's old Chicago teammate Hal Chase, whose tenure with the Giants lasted only one season, heard about the proposal and put Burns in touch with Rothstein's lieutenant, a shady ex-boxer named Abe Attell. A former featherweight world champion, Attell promised to provide the money if the players went through with the scheme. Now the White Sox had commitments from two different groups of gamblers, each with assorted hangers-on and middlemen working the phones and conducting furtive meetings to iron out the particulars. The fix was getting bigger, and too many people knew about it to keep it under wraps for long. By the time the White Sox clinched the pennant on September 24, the rumor mill was spinning wildly with word that the Sox had been compromised.

Many people heard the rumors, but Arnold Rothstein acted on them. Thanks to Burns and Maharg, the two small-timers from Texas and Philadelphia, Rothstein now knew that a fix was in the works. While Burns scoured the country, chasing cash from gamblers in places like Des Moines and St. Louis, Rothstein made contact with Sport Sullivan, a real player in the sports betting game, and started funneling money through him. Besides, Burns and Maharg had presented the Big Bankroll with an alibi. If the cops came calling, Rothstein could tell how he had rudely dismissed these two losers, as indeed he had.

When Eddie Cicotte told the story later, he said that he agreed to take part in the scheme only after much agonizing and soul-searching. He claimed in his 1920 testimony before a Chicago grand jury that Gandil and Fred McMullin presented the fix idea to him, as if the scheme were well along before he heard of it. This is, regrettably, not the truth. All other accounts of the affair place Cicotte in it from the beginning. He and Gandil made the initial contacts with both the Sullivan group and the Burns group. Eddie's decision to join the fix was not an impulsive mistake; rather, it was a conscious effort to make some quick, easy money to pay down his debts. He was as enthusiastic about the scheme as anyone.

Eddie was the oldest of the Black Sox, and perhaps the smartest as well. He demanded a payment of $10,000 in cash, to be delivered before Game One of the Series. Eddie was not interested in promises; he wanted cash on the barrelhead before he threw a pitch. Eddie knew that the whole plan depended on him. With Faber unable to pitch, the Sox would probably need three wins from Cicotte and two from either Williams or Kerr to win the Series. Without Eddie, the fix could not possibly succeed. With him, it could. Eddie was indispensable, and he knew it.

As the season wound down, Eddie's quest for 30 wins fell short. On September 24, Eddie pitched seven mediocre innings against the St. Louis

Browns, giving up 11 hits and five runs and leaving for a pinch-hitter with the Sox behind, 5–4. The White Sox won the game in the ninth when Joe Jackson singled in the winning run in a 6–5 win. This victory clinched the 1919 American League pennant for the White Sox and put them in the World Series seven days hence. Cicotte's final start of 1919 came against Detroit on September 28, but that was merely a tune-up for the Series. He pitched the first two innings in a game that the Tigers won, 10–9, in the last game of the regular season. Had the 1919 campaign not been cut to 140 games (instead of the regular 154) by the team owners, Eddie would likely have joined the 30-win circle.

The 1919 campaign may have been Eddie Cicotte's best. He led the American League in wins with 29, five more than anyone else, and led in winning percentage (.806), complete games (30), and innings pitched (306⅔). Eddie also made five relief appearances and saved one game. He and Washington's Walter Johnson towered over all other hurlers in the circuit that year, and if the Cy Young Award had existed in 1919, either Johnson or Cicotte would have won it.

With Red Faber unable to pitch for much of the season, the Sox asked Eddie to carry a heavy workload for a 35-year-old. No wonder Kid Gleason gave him nearly two weeks off in September, especially after Cicotte gave up six walks to the Indians on September 5. However, one oft-repeated story of the Black Sox Scandal says that Charles Comiskey had promised Eddie a bonus for winning 30 games—some say $5,000, others $10,000—and held him out of the lineup when he got too close to it. This story is one of the central themes of Eliot Asinof's *Eight Men Out*, which depicted Cicotte as embittered because Comiskey cheated him out of a sizable bonus. This, they say, is why Eddie threw in his lot with the fixers. The tale is one of the pivotal incidents in the movie version of *Eight Men Out*, which was released in 1988.

Some suggest that the story actually took place in 1917, when Cicotte won 28 games, falling two short of the magic 30-win mark. However, this is refuted by the fact that Eddie pitched regularly, and very well, in September. He had 21 wins at the start of the month and made six starts (and two relief appearances) thereafter, winning seven games and losing one. He started three of Chicago's last 10 games of the 1917 season, and took no appreciable time off that month.

Though the tale of the missing bonus is an enduring part of Black Sox lore, and though Eddie told the story to his family,[21] we can be reasonably certain that it never happened. Comiskey was not in the business of handing out large bonuses to his players, especially not for $5,000 or more in an age in which most ballplayers earned far less than that. And why would Comiskey offer a huge bonus for winning 30 games to an aging pitcher who won 12 the year before? Eddie had 28 wins at the time of his layoff, and he won his 29th

7. The 1919 Season

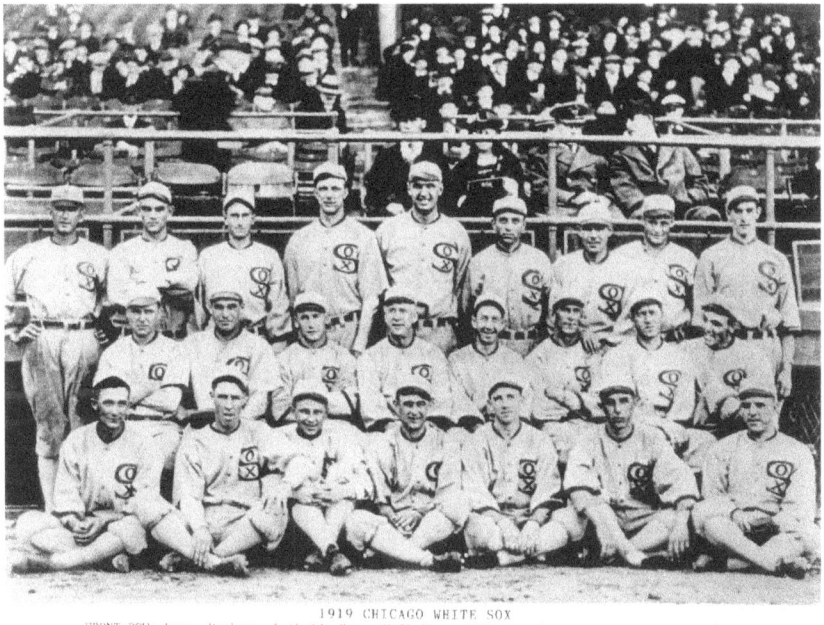

1919 CHICAGO WHITE SOX
FRONT ROW: Lynn, Risberg, Leibold, Kerr, McClellan, Williams, Cicotte.
MIDDLE ROW: Schalk, Jenkins, Felsch, Gleason, E.Collins, J.Collins, Faber, Weaver.
BACK ROW: Shoeless Joe Jackson, Gandil, McMullin, Lowdermilk, James, Mayer, Murphy, Sullivan, Wilkinson.

The 1919 Chicago White Sox, American League champions. Eddie is in the bottom row, far right (author's collection).

in his first start back. He made two more starts, and was no world beater in either of them, but both represented legitimate chances to notch his 30th. Charles Comiskey may well have been a cheapskate, and he definitely took advantage of his less educated players—like Joe Jackson, who had been earning the same $6,000 annual salary since 1914, and Lefty Williams, a 20-game winner making only $3,000 per year—but the tale of a bonus being unfairly withheld from Eddie Cicotte appears to have no basis in truth.

8

The 1919 World Series

> *[Cicotte] has had less than a week to rest up for his first start.... And that may not prove to be enough. If he blows up for a single inning it may cost the White Sox the championship, for I think the first battle is going to have a very strong bearing on the outcome, especially if the Reds win it.*—Christy Mathewson in his newspaper column, October 1, 1919[1]

From Labor Day onward, a World Series matchup between Chicago and Cincinnati appeared inevitable, and most observers declared the White Sox the heavy favorites, almost prohibitively so. The American League had won eight of the previous nine World Series, and the White Sox, with most of the same players, had defeated the Giants soundly to win the title only two years before. The Reds were a very good team, solid in most aspects of the game, but boasted only one player, center fielder Edd Roush, who eventually gained election to the Baseball Hall of Fame. Many of their other starters were very good, including third baseman Heinie Groh, two-time batting champ Jake Daubert at first base, and former White Sox second baseman Morrie Rath, but they had no stars to match Eddie Collins and Joe Jackson. Their strength lay in their pitching. The Reds had five legitimate starters (Ray Fisher, Jimmy Ring, 19-game winners Hod Eller and Dutch Ruether, and 21-game winner Slim Sallee), backed by Cuban-born fastballer Dolf Luque as their relief ace. Eller was a shine ball artist like Eddie; in fact, Eller, while the property of the White Sox in 1916, once asked Eddie to teach him the secrets of the shine ball. Cicotte refused and left Eller to figure it out himself.

The Sox could expect little help from their bullpen. Erskine Mayer, Grover Lowdermilk, Bill James, and Roy Wilkinson were mediocre at best; indeed, the 1919 White Sox owned one of the weakest relief units of any pennant winner in history. The whole pitching corps was short-staffed. Gleason had sent Charlie Robertson and Frank Shellenback to the minor leagues in mid-season and released both Reb Russell and the sore-armed Dave Danforth, while onetime stars Joe Benz and Jim Scott were long gone. Gleason would have to ride Eddie Cicotte and 23-game winner Lefty Williams as far as they could take him, and because the Series was a best-of-nine affair in 1919, it appeared that Cicotte would have to win three games and Williams two for the title. Charles Comiskey had campaigned against stretching the Series to nine games because he knew that the longer fall classic would tax his overworked pitching staff. Comiskey lost the vote, and the White Sox resigned themselves to the nine-game schedule.

No one knew what to expect from Chicago's third starter, Dickey Kerr. The papers called the 155-pound pitcher "Little Dickey Kerr," but in reality, Kerr was a tough, no-nonsense athlete who had fought as an amateur boxer as a teenager. Gleason was initially wary of him, though the Kid was once a small pitcher himself, but by season's end Kerr had won his manager over. Still, despite a fine 13–7 record during the regular season, he was a rookie in the World Series, and one win from Kerr would be a blessing.

Nonetheless, the pitching problems of the White Sox could not explain the sudden shift in gambling odds in the days leading up to the Series. Bookies usually increase the odds to encourage gamblers to bet on the underdog, but during the last few days of September, so much money suddenly came in on the Reds that no increase was necessary. Arnold Rothstein reportedly bet $270,000 (more than $4 million in modern dollars) on the Reds to win the Series, and the posted odds favoring the White Sox fell from 8–5 to 6–5 in a single day. The word was out that the "smart money" was going Cincinnati's way, and when Sport Sullivan laid down $29,000 on the Reds, he could get no better than even odds.

In the crowded lobby of the Hotel Sinton, where the Chicago players, team officials, and newspaper reporters set up camp in Cincinnati, gamblers waved fists full of thousand-dollar bills, almost begging out-of-town fans and passers-by to bet on the White Sox. Many did so, mainly out of Chicago civic pride but also because the fix rumors had not yet circulated to the general public. The newspapermen, however, knew that something was amiss. Hugh Fullerton of the *Chicago Herald-Examiner*, distressed at the wild scene, sent a message by telegram to all the papers that carried his column. The message read ADVISE ALL NOT TO BET ON THIS SERIES. UGLY RUMORS AFLOAT. None of his papers printed the message, and the average gamblers, blissfully unaware of the dark currents that ran under the surface, lay down their bets with total confidence.

Charles Comiskey was alarmed at the shift in odds. A gambler had called him on the morning of Game One, mere hours before game time, and warned him that the bookies were now taking odds at 10–7 in Cincinnati's favor. The White Sox owner sent several Chicago team officials to investigate, and when they returned from the lobby of the Sinton with news of the commotion there, Comiskey knew something was wrong.

However, Eddie exuded confidence to a reporter from the *Brooklyn Eagle*. He blamed his troubles in September on a cold:

> Sure, I am in shape. I had a bad cold toward the end of the season, and felt miserable all over, but that was the result of the general depression of the system and had nothing to do with my arm. I was beaten the last time out, but Gleason told me to go in and pitch and not to care a hoot whether I won or lost. He gave orders that I was not to try to pitch with might and main, and would not have sent me in at all if he had not thought it necessary to keep my muscles limbered. I worked the cold out of my system and now I am all right again.[2]

Eddie had already received his bribe money. Three days before the start of the 1919 Series, six of the conspirators (all but Jackson and Risberg) met at the Warner Hotel in Chicago, where the players stayed during the season. Eddie repeated his demand for $10,000 in cash, telling the others, "there is so much double crossing stuff, if I went in [on] the Series [fix] I wanted the money put in my hand."[3] He then left to go out with some teammates, and when he returned to his room late in the evening, he found ten $1,000 bills under his pillow. He had no idea who left it there, but the fix was real now, and there was no turning back. Eddie hid the $10,000 in the lining of his jacket.

October 1, 1919, was a beautiful, sunny fall Wednesday in Cincinnati. The stands in Redlands Field, which was later called Crosley Field and served as the home of the Reds until 1970, were full of excited fans, thrilled to see their team in its first World Series. Eddie Cicotte nervously warmed up on the sidelines. He had been instructed to either walk or hit the first Cincinnati batter as a signal that the fix was on.

Shano Collins opened the game for the White Sox with a single. Eddie Collins tried to bunt him to second, but Reds pitcher Dutch Ruether threw Shano out, with Eddie safe at first. Eddie then lit out for second with Buck Weaver at bat, only to be thrown out easily by catcher Ivey Wingo. Collins believed ever after that Weaver missed a bunt signal, either accidentally or on purpose. Weaver flied out to end the inning.

"What's the matter? Were you asleep?" asked Collins.

"Quit trying to alibi and play ball,"[4] snarled Weaver. The Sox failed to score in the first, and the Reds came up to bat.

Cincinnati's leadoff man was Morrie Rath, Eddie's old teammate from his early days in Chicago. His first pitch to Rath was a called strike. His second pitch hit Rath in the back. Legend has it that when Arnold Rothstein, following the Series on a large play-by-play board in the lobby of the Ansonia in New York, heard that Cicotte hit Rath, the Big Bankroll went out and bet another pile of money on the Reds.

Rath came around to score after Jake Daubert singled him to third and Heinie Groh drove a sacrifice fly to Jackson in deep left field. This gave the Reds a 1–0 lead, but the White Sox tied it in the second when Jackson reached second on an error, Happy Felsch bunted him to third, and Chick Gandil drove him home with a single.

There matters stood until disaster struck the White Sox in the fourth. Eddie retired Edd Roush on a fly to center, but Pat Duncan followed with a single. Larry Kopf hit a hard liner that Eddie knocked down, but he hesitated (possibly while waiting for either Risberg or Collins to cover second), then threw to Risberg. The throw forced Duncan, but Risberg's relay to Gandil at first was too late to complete the double play which would have ended the inning. The Reds had new life, and Greasy Neale hit a popup behind shortstop that at Risberg failed to reach, sending Kopf to third. Then the wheels fell off. Ivey Wingo singled Kopf home, and Dutch Ruether blasted a triple to left-center between Jackson and Felsch, driving in Neale and Wingo. Rath doubled Ruether home, and it looked as if Eddie had totally lost it. A single by Daubert scored Rath, and now the Reds led, 6–1.

Kid Gleason called Roy Wilkinson into the game, and Eddie's day was finished. In three and two-thirds innings, he had given up six runs (all earned), seven hits, and two walks. It was, perhaps, his worst performance of the year. Wilkinson and Grover Lowdermilk finished up, allowing three more runs, and the Reds won, 9–1.

After the game, Eddie faced the reporters and tried to make sense of his poor showing:

> It is hard to explain, but I was in no condition to pitch the game that I had expected. I felt perfectly confident before the game started and appeared to have everything when I was warming up, but when I hit Rath it seemed to have a strange effect on me. I felt so badly about it that I trotted with him down the first base line to see if the ball had hurt him. When Rath assured me that he was all right I went back to the pitching mound, but I did not seem to be right.[5]

Eddie's sudden blowup in the fourth inning of Game One has puzzled fans and writers ever since. In *The Great Baseball Mystery*, published in 1966, author Victor Luhrs blames Risberg for the botched double play, which would have gotten the White Sox out of the inning with no runs scored. On the next play, Eddie should have had the third out again, but Risberg misplayed Neale's popup behind the infield. Only then, said Luhrs, did Cicotte fall apart. Still, Eddie allowed four hits in a row, two for extra bases, after Neale reached first. A 35-year-old veteran should not have suffered an epic meltdown in such circumstances.

It was a devastating loss for the White Sox. Gleason was counting on Eddie Cicotte to win two or three games in the Series, and now his star pitcher had laid an egg on baseball's biggest stage. One man who was roundly disappointed at Cicotte's performance was Cleveland Indians outfielder and manager Tris Speaker, who wrote a column on the Series for the *Cleveland Plain Dealer* (actually, Speaker dictated it to local sportswriter Henry Edwards, who put Speaker's thoughts into print form). This column also appeared in the Boston Post and other papers. Speaker lamented,

> The Chicago team that led us to the wire had Eddie Cicotte working like one of the greatest pitchers I had ever seen in action. The Sox, who showed us the way, played smart ball. If the Cicotte who pitched against Cincinnati today looked like the Cicotte who beat us so often during the American League campaign, then I better quit center-fielding and go to pitching myself. If the White Sox played smart ball today I am going to recruit the Indians for next season from some place over in Europe, where they never saw our national game played.
>
> The Cicotte of today was not the Cicotte who faced us during the season.... It is almost beyond comprehension to believe that any National League team was able to make five runs off Eddie Cicotte, the best pitcher in the American League, after two were out.[6]

Ring Lardner, Eddie Cicotte's good friend, knew what was happening. He accosted Eddie after the game and asked, "What was wrong? I was betting on you today."[7] Eddie waved the question off, but Lardner sensed the truth in the pitcher's demeanor. While Eddie went to bed early, complaining of a headache, Lardner and some of his fellow writers entertained themselves in a bar on the Kentucky side of the Ohio River with some new lyrics they wrote to a popular tune of the day, "I'm Forever Blowing Bubbles."

> I'm forever blowing ballgames,
> Pretty ballgames in the air.
> I come from Chi,
> I hardly try,
> Just go to bat and fade and die.
> Fortune's coming my way,
> That's why I don't care.
> I'm forever blowing ballgames,
> And the gamblers treat us fair.[8]

Charles Comiskey reportedly cornered Gleason after the game and demanded to know if his players were throwing the Series. Gleason said he didn't know, but would keep a close eye on things. The next afternoon, with Lefty Williams starting for the Sox, Gleason drew Schalk to one side. "Watch him," commanded the manager.

Williams had not yet received any money, but the fixers had promised him $10,000, and because Cicotte received his payout, Williams trusted that he would soon pocket the cash as well. He knew he would have to lose, but not as egregiously as Cicotte.

Williams took the mound in Game Two for the White Sox against Cincinnati's Slim Sallee. Williams looked like a world-beater during the first three innings, with one Red (Edd Roush) reaching base on a walk, only to be erased on a double play. Meanwhile, Sallee, the former Giant whom the White Sox beat twice in the 1917 Series, put a string of zeroes on the board. In the Chicago half of the second, Jackson doubled and was sacrificed to third by Felsch, but was stranded there when Gandil and Risberg failed to bring him home. In the third inning, Weaver and Jackson singled, but once again Gandil and Risberg failed to drive them in. The game was scoreless when the Reds came to bat in the bottom of the fourth.

That's when Williams, renowned for his control, lost it in a hurry. Walks to Rath and Groh put runners

Joe Jackson in 1919 (author's collection).

on first and second, and then Roush, the National League batting champion, drove in Rath with a single. Schalk threw Roush out stealing, but another walk to Duncan and a triple by Kopf brought in two more runs. It was now 3–0, and the game was getting out of hand. The Reds scored again in the sixth inning when Roush walked, Williams' fifth free pass of the game, and scored on a single by Neale. The White Sox scored twice in the sixth, but all that did was make the score a little closer. Williams pitched a complete game and allowed only four hits, but his six walks doomed the Sox to another disastrous defeat.

Ray Schalk was furious after the game. Eliot Asinof, in *Eight Men Out*, has Schalk yelling at his manager, "The son of a bitch! Williams kept crossing me. In that lousy fourth inning, he crossed me three times! He wouldn't throw a curve."[9] Charles Comiskey was now more convinced than ever that some of his men were playing to lose. "I was startled at the apparent nonchalance with which my players played," he recalled shortly before his death in 1931. "They lacked the dash and fight that was so prominent when I watched them win the pennant in our league. Were they selling out on me?"[10]

The White Sox owner, troubled by the scene in the Sinton Hotel before

Game One, had already approached John Heydler, president of the National League, with his suspicions, but Heydler dismissed the idea that the Series was being fixed. Now, after the Game Two defeat, Comiskey accosted Heydler again. This time, Heydler was more willing to be persuaded, so the two men decided to inform Ban Johnson, once a good friend of Comiskey but now a bitter, implacable enemy. That evening, Heydler knocked on Johnson's hotel room door and confronted his counterpart, who was tired and most likely inebriated. Johnson listened for only a moment before he rudely dismissed his guest and slammed the door on him.

The scene shifted to Comiskey Park in Chicago for Game Three. Looking for privacy, Eddie left his room at the Warner Hotel, which was full of reporters looking for quotes, and moved into a boarding house on Grand Boulevard, a few blocks from Comiskey Park, where he and other White Sox sometimes stayed during the season. The landlord, Mrs. Henrietta Kelley, recalled later that Eddie's brother and his teenaged daughter, Rose, stayed with him during the next few days.

With the Sox down two games to none, Gleason was on the fence about his starting pitcher. "I expect to start Kerr tomorrow," he told the *New York Times*, "but might use Cicotte, as I have every confidence in Eddie to trim Cincinnati."[11] If Dickey Kerr's later recollections can be believed, the manager had Eddie warm up while Kerr did some light tossing in the infield before the third contest, then surprised everyone by sending Kerr to the mound. "You should have seen the look on Cicotte's face," recalled the rookie pitcher years later. "Boy, was he put out!" Kerr also said that he sat in on the meeting where Eddie went over all the Cincinnati batters and discussed how he would pitch to them. Both Eddie Collins and Kid Gleason advised Kerr to do the opposite of whatever Eddie said.[12]

Bill Burns asked Chick Gandil which way to bet on Game Three. Gandil, according to later testimony, replied something along the lines of *We didn't win for Cicotte and Williams. We sure ain't gonna win for no busher.* So Burns and Billy Maharg bet every dollar they had on the Reds.

Dickey Kerr was unbeatable on that day. He held the Reds to three hits and no runs, while Gandil drove in both Chicago runs with a single in the second inning. Perhaps the conspirators expected the Reds to score more than two runs, or else Gandil and the rest decided to win to cross up the fixers. Whatever the reason, Kerr and the White Sox won the game by a 2–0 score. Burns and Maharg, the small-timers who thought they had hatched the scheme of a lifetime, were now dead broke. Maharg had to pawn his diamond stickpin to raise enough money for a train ticket home to Philadelphia. They were out, but the real professionals, Rothstein and Sullivan, were still in it. They were canny enough to bet on the outcome of the Series, not on the individual games.

8. The 1919 World Series 103

Sport Sullivan was now in contact with Arnold Rothstein, and he knew that the players were angry about the fact that with the exception of Eddie Cicotte, they weren't paid what they were promised. Sullivan was on the defensive and had to use all his charm to convince Gandil and the rest to lose Games Four and Five. Sullivan promised to deliver $20,000 after Game Four and $20,000 more after Game Five if the Sox threw them. This seemed fair to the players, so they agreed to lose both contests. Sullivan spent the morning of Game Four on the phone looking for funds, and by noon, after much cajoling, he had $20,000 in hand. As game time approached, the veteran Boston fixer realized that he could get two losses, not one, with a single $20,000 payment. He had no intention of giving the second installment to the players.

Game Four, played in front of 34,363 fans in Chicago on Saturday, October 4, was Eddie Cicotte's chance to atone for his embarrassing performance in Game One. He had no real reason to throw the game, because he had received all the money the gamblers promised him, but Gandil and the others were determined to lose, and lose they did. Eddie and Cincinnati right-hander Jimmy Ring matched zeroes through the first four innings, but it all fell apart for the White Sox in the fifth. Eddie retired Edd Roush on a tap in front of the plate for the first out, but when Pat Duncan hit a liner off Eddie's glove, the pitcher grabbed it and threw wildly to Gandil at first. The ball skipped away behind first base and Duncan wound up on second. Larry Kopf drilled a sharp single to left. Joe Jackson fired it home, and the throw had Duncan beaten at the plate, but Eddie unaccountably tried to intercept it. The ball clanked off Eddie's glove and bounded past catcher Ray Schalk for a two-base error. Duncan scored for a 1–0 Cincinnati lead while Kopf took second.

Years later, Jimmy Ring reflected on Cicotte's second error of the inning. "That's when we knew for sure there was some horseshit going on. I'll never forget Schalk standing there in front of home plate staring at Cicotte. Eddie went back to the mound and was standing there with his back to the plate, staring out to center field and rubbing the ball up very slowly, like he didn't want to turn around and face Schalk."[13] Dickey Kerr recalled, "Now, everybody knew that Cicotte had no business there [in the cutoff position]. He should have had his pants against the grandstand backing up the plate."[14]

With Kopf on second, Greasy Neale lifted a pop fly to left that Jackson misplayed; he stumbled around a bit before he caught up to it, only to have it bounce off his glove. Kopf scored to give the Reds a 2–0 lead. Ring made it stand up the rest of the way, and the Reds left the field with a lead of three games to one in the Series.

Eddie always maintained that he tried his best to win the fourth game. In a deposition he made a few years later, Cicotte was asked why he did so. He answered:

Well, because I didn't care whether or not I got shot out there the next minute. I was going to win the ball game and the Series. I didn't care for the money after that.[15]

Still, the two errors he made in the fifth inning cannot easily be explained away. Some writers suggest that he made those miscues out of nervousness; the wild throw to first could happen to any pitcher, especially one with a spitter or a shine ball, and perhaps he deflected Jackson's throw in a clumsy attempt to make up for the first misplay. Victor Luhrs, for one, exonerates him, offering the conclusion that the two errors were "too glaring to have been crooked."[16] However, Gleason fumed to the reporters after the game, "They shouldn't have scored on Cicotte in 40 innings.... There wasn't any occasion for Cicotte to intercept that throw. He did it to prevent Kopf from going to second. But Kopf had no more intention of going to second than I have of jumping in the lake."[17] Tris Speaker expressed his surprise in his daily column. Said Speaker, "We always have regarded Eddie Cicotte as one of the best fielding hurlers in our league, and I was amazed to see him pull two bad plays in the fifth inning. I doubt if Eddie ever made two errors in the same inning before in his life."[18]

Except for one bad inning, Eddie pitched very well. He gave up only five hits and walked no one. However, the White Sox batting attack, such as it was, made Jimmy Ring look like the second coming of Walter Johnson. Ring scattered three hits (though he walked three and hit two batters) and shut out the American League's most powerful offense.

After the game, Kid Gleason called his players together and ripped into them for their sloppy play. The manager accused the Sox of "throwing down" Charles Comiskey and their own teammates. Everyone knew what he meant, but only Gandil and McMullin offered weak objections ("You'd think we wasn't trying," whined Gandil). After the meeting, Gandil returned to the business at hand. He divided the $20,000 from Sullivan into four equal envelopes. He gave one apiece to Risberg and McMullin and two to Williams, with instructions to give one to Jackson.

The writers knew what was happening, and Eddie's friend Ring Lardner was too intelligent to deny what he was seeing. Eddie was one of Lardner's favorites, if not his favorite player in the major leagues, and the writer's Jack Keefe stories were full of Eddie's humor and good nature. Now Lardner could tell that Eddie had sold out his team and violated what another great writer, F. Scott Fitzgerald, described in *The Great Gatsby* as "the faith of fifty million people." Lardner wrote much less often about baseball after 1919, though he continued to publish stories about the game every now and then, and his friendship with Eddie Cicotte did not survive the 1919 World Series.

A rainout on Sunday pushed the Series schedule back by one day, and Gleason lamented to Harvey Woodruff of the *Tribune*, "It's the best team that ever went into a World Series. But, it isn't playing the baseball that won the pennant for me. I don't know what's the matter, the players don't know what's the matter, but the team has not shown itself thus far. But we'll be there tomorrow."[19] Woodruff noted that the Chicago manager seemed nervous and restless.

The manager thought long and hard about starting Kerr in Game Five. When a reporter asked, "Will it be Williams tomorrow?" the manager replied, "No, I think I'll go in myself,"[20] only half-joking. In the end, he decided to go with Lefty Williams and hope for the best. Williams could not possibly look as bad as he did in the second game, figured Gleason.

Williams, with $5,000 in hand and the promise of more in short order, was only too happy to blow another game. He made it look better this time, breezing through the first four innings without allowing a hit. On the Cincinnati side, pitcher Hod Eller, a shine ball artist like Cicotte, struck out six White Sox in a row and had seven strikeouts by the end of the fourth inning. The Reds broke through in the fifth, when Eller's popup fell untouched between Felsch and Jackson in left-center field. Felsch picked up the ball and threw it wildly over the infielders' heads, and Eller wound up on third. Rath drove Eller home with a single, and after a sacrifice by Daubert and a walk to Groh, Edd Roush lifted a lazy fly to center that Felsch misplayed so badly that two runners scored. Happy's miscue looked every bit as bad as Eddie's two errors the day before.

Schalk, whose temper had reached the boiling point by this time, thought he had tagged out Groh at the plate, and he argued with umpire Cy Rigler so forcefully that Rigler tossed him out of the game. The little-used Byrd Lynn replaced him. The Reds scored four runs in the inning on their way to an easy 4–0 victory. Eller, like Ring the day before, had shut out the White Sox on three hits.

Gleason couldn't believe it, and he vented his feelings to James Crusinberry of the *Tribune*.

They aren't hitting. I don't know what's the matter, but I do know that something is wrong with my gang. The bunch I had fighting in

Happy Felsch, center fielder of the White Sox (Library of Congress).

August for the pennant would have trimmed this Cincinnati bunch without a struggle. The bunch I have now couldn't beat a high-school team. We hit something over .280 for the season in the American League pennant race. Now, that's the best hitting any ball club ever did in the history of baseball. The way those .280 hitters acted against Eller, they couldn't make a place on a high-school team.

I am convinced that I have the best ball club that ever was put together. I certainly have been disappointed by it in this series. It hasn't played baseball in a single game. There's only a bare chance they can win now. The gang I had in August might do it. The gang that has played for me in the five games of the World Series will have to have luck to win another ball game.[21]

Crusinberry noted that the Chicago manager "was mad enough to lick a lot of people and go to jail for it."[22]

The White Sox were in a hole now, and had the Series still followed a best-of-seven format, the Reds would already be the world champions. The heavy favorites were now down four games to one with the rookie Kerr on the mound. Kerr had pitched masterfully in the third game, but could he do it again? Gleason told Crusinberry, "It doesn't seem possible that the gang that worked so great for me all summer could fall down like this. I tell you, I am absolutely sick at heart."[23]

The manager did not know that the conspirators had held a conference on the morning of Game Six. Sport Sullivan failed to deliver the next promised installment of $20,000, and the players now realized that the money train had stopped for good. Gandil and Risberg debated their next move. If the Sox lost Game Six, the Series would be over, but Cicotte wanted a win to bolster his bargaining position for 1920. A win for Kerr in Game Six and one for Cicotte in Game Seven would allow the players to pad their stats a bit, to make them look a little more presentable. They could then lose the eighth or ninth contest to keep the gamblers happy. Gandil passed the word to go out and win.

Kerr came through a second time, but it wasn't easy. The Reds scored twice on a double by Pat Duncan in the second inning, and added two more in the fourth on a double by Dutch Ruether and a grounder that Risberg booted. The Sox chipped away, scoring in the fifth inning on a sacrifice fly by Eddie Collins to break their 26-inning scoreless streak. In the sixth, Joe Jackson finally drove in his first run of the Series, and the Sox scored three times to even it up. Cincinnati manager Pat Moran brought Ring in to relieve Ruether, while Kerr continued for the White Sox. The score remained tied until the tenth inning, when Weaver doubled, Jackson sent him to third while beating out a sacrifice bunt, and Gandil drove Weaver home for the go-ahead run. Kerr disposed of the Reds in the bottom of the tenth for a 5–4 win.

Now it was Eddie's turn again. The players knew that both Sullivan and the Burns-Attell group had stiffed them. Now Gandil and Risberg talked openly of double-crossing the gamblers and winning the Series after all, which would give every man an extra $1,900 in their Series shares. The Sox decided to go all-out for Cicotte and deal with the eighth game later.

With only 13,000 fans in the Cincinnati stands, Eddie finally looked like a 29-game winner. He held the Reds to seven hits and one run, while the Chicago bats came to life and battered Slim Sallee. Jackson drove in Eddie Collins in the first inning and again in the third with singles, while a single by Happy Felsch plated two more runs in the fifth. Eddie made it stand up, allowing one run in the sixth inning but coasting the rest of the way for a 4–1 win. The Sox had closed the gap, and a win in Game Eight would tie the Series. Then Gleason would start Kerr for the third time in Game Nine, and Eddie Cicotte, with a day of rest behind him, would be available in relief.

Arnold Rothstein was having none of that. He had invested $270,000 in bets on the Reds to win the Series, and by God, the Reds were going to win the Series.

Legend has it that someone visited Lefty Williams before the game and told him that it would be in his best interest, and that of his family too, to lose Game Eight.[24] Eddie Cicotte's descendants say that one or more dangerous-looking goons threatened both Cicotte and Williams. Whether it really happened or not, Lefty Williams failed to make it out of the first inning. He faced five batters, four of whom reached base, and threw 15 pitches before Kid Gleason came out to get him. He allowed four runs on four hits in one-third of an inning, and the fans barely had time to settle into their seats before the Reds grabbed a 4–0 lead. Bill James came in and retired the Reds, but he and Roy Wilkinson gave up six more runs. After the top of the eighth, the Reds held a 10–1 lead.

It really didn't matter that Joe Jackson walloped a solo homer in the third inning, a line drive into the right field stands. It also didn't matter that Cincinnati starter Hod Eller gave up five runs and ten hits. The Sox made it closer with four runs in the eighth inning, but they had little chance after that disastrous first inning. The Reds won the game, 10–5 and celebrated their first world championship, only the second for the National League in the last ten years.

The White Sox clubhouse was silent after the game, except for the bellowing of a furious Kid Gleason. While the players packed their equipment, Gleason shouted to his sportswriter friends, "The Reds beat the greatest ball team that ever went into a world's series." Then, shaking his head in frustration he said, "I tell you those Reds haven't any business beating a team like the White Sox. We played the worse baseball in all but a couple of games that we have played all year. I don't know yet what was the matter. Something was wrong. I didn't like the betting odds. I wish no one had ever bet a dollar on the team."[25]

Eddie Cicotte, $10,000 in hand, closed up his room at Mrs. Kelley's boarding house and returned to Detroit. He wanted to put this miserable experience behind him, but at least he could pay his debts. By his later account, he paid off the $4,000 he owed on his farm, bought animals and feed, and installed new flooring in his barn. Eddie could also expect a check for $3,154.27, the losers' share of the World Series money. That bonus would further relieve his financial pressures.

Some of Eddie's friends in Detroit were pretty steamed at him. The pitcher had told all his local buddies that the Sox were a cinch to win the Series, and many of them made wagers both small and large based on their friendships with Eddie and the air of confidence he exuded. At the same time, another Detroiter, Sox outfielder Nemo Leibold, refused to tell his pals which way to bet. Leibold sensed that something was amiss, and he didn't want his friends to lose their shirts. Eddie received a chilly post–Series reception in his home town, but as fall turned to winter, the memory of his Game One and Game Four failures faded. On January 6, 1920, the Boston Red Sox sold Babe Ruth to the Yankees in a blockbuster deal, perhaps the biggest in baseball history up to that time, and knocked the 1919 Series off the sports pages. The Roaring Twenties had begun, and the baseball world was ready to shift its collective focus to the upcoming 1920 season.

9

The 1920 Season

Let me tell you something: Eddie Cicotte had more speed last year [1919] than he did in 1912. Cicotte's pitching assets are there. He is a wonderful smart pitcher, has a good fast ball, a nice curve, one of the best slow balls in the world and perfect control. Cicotte bluffs the spitter and the shine ball ten times more than he uses it.—Ralph Works in *The Sporting News*, February 1920[1]

Eddie Cicotte spent the winter of 1919–1920 working on his farm, playing with his newest child (Eddie Junior, born in November of 1919), hunting, fishing, and tending to family obligations.

He had no idea what was happening back in Chicago.

Hugh Fullerton, the lead baseball reporter for the *Chicago Herald-Examiner*, was close to both Charles Comiskey and Kid Gleason. He was so close that he knew that the rumors of thrown games were true, and that Comiskey and Gleason knew it too. Fullerton, like Comiskey, had seen the gamblers waving fat wads of money around in the lobby of the Sinton Hotel in Cincinnati before Game One. The gamblers took all the action on the White Sox they could handle, and that, and the sudden shift in the betting odds, confirmed that there was something seriously amiss. In response, Fullerton sent a telegram to warn all the papers that carried his column. No one wanted to hear it, and not one of his papers published the warning.

Fullerton discussed the Series with Comiskey in the owner's office the day after the Series ended. The next day, October 10, Fullerton wrote in the *Herald-Examiner*: "Yesterday's game also means the disruption of the Chicago White Sox ballclub. There are seven men on the team who will not be there when the gong sounds next Spring." This line raised a howl of protest, and Comiskey, the unnamed source of the statement, quickly denied it. On October 11, the White Sox owner offered $20,000 "for a single clue to lead to evidence that any of his players had deliberately attempted to throw any of the world series games to the Cincinnati Reds." But Comiskey also doubted that was the case. "There is always some scandal of some kind following a big sporting event like the world's series," he said. "These yarns are manufactured out of whole cloth and grow out of bitterness due to losing wagers. I believe my boys fought the battles of the recent world's series on the level, as they have always done."[2]

Comiskey denied Fullerton's statement because he did not want to tip his hand. In public, Comiskey assured the Chicago fans that the unfortunate loss in the Series was nothing more than one of the bad breaks of baseball. Privately, his own investigation was in full swing.

Harry Grabiner was, at the time, the secretary of the White Sox and Charles Comiskey's confidante and right-hand man. Grabiner reportedly kept a detailed diary during his time with the White Sox. Two volumes of that diary, covered with dust, were discovered in the bowels of Comiskey Park in 1961, two years after Bill Veeck, the P. T. Barnum of baseball, bought control of the White Sox from the Comiskey family. No one knows where the diary is today, though a couple of pages can be seen on the Internet, but Veeck printed excerpts from it in his 1965 best-seller, *The Hustler's Handbook*. If those excerpts are truly Grabiner's words, then the diary provides a guide to the inner workings of the scandal and its aftermath. Grabiner's diary makes it clear that he, Kid Gleason, and Comiskey knew the whole story of the fix less than a week after the end of the Series.

Charles Comiskey had started investigating the 1919 World Series while it was still being played. According to Grabiner's notes, a gambler, alarmed at the sudden shift in betting odds in Cincinnati's favor, had warned the Chicago owner before Game One that the White Sox were compromised. Comiskey told National League president John Heydler what he had heard, only to be rebuffed because he had no solid proof. A day later, Heydler was rudely insulted by Ban Johnson when he took Comiskey's concerns to the American League president. Undeterred, Grabiner and Comiskey set to work gathering information from their network of contacts in the sporting and newspaper worlds. As soon as the Series was over, their investigation gained momentum.

Eddie Cicotte appeared in the diary early on when an informant told Grabiner that Mrs. Kelley, Eddie's landlady in Chicago, "overheard Cicotte state to his brother while in the bathroom, 'To hell with them, I got mine.'" Grabiner also recorded a meeting on October 12, three days after the end of the Series, with Kid Gleason, team official Tip O'Neill, and a St. Louis gambler named Redmon. This man refused to inform on his fellow gamblers but gave up the names of all eight players involved, including Buck Weaver. He claimed that Weaver and Cicotte were crooked in the first game and then turned honest. Redmon also detailed the amounts of money that the players received for throwing the Series. Comiskey and Grabiner continued their investigations, even hiring a detective to monitor the eight men and their spending habits, but they already knew the basic outline of the story. They

9. The 1920 Season

were now satisfied that Eddie Cicotte and his teammates were guilty of tanking the Series for money.

Hugh Fullerton did not want to let the story go. After stewing about the issue for several months, Fullerton let loose in December. No paper in Chicago would publish his article, but the *New York Evening World* did so on December 10, 1919. Wrote Fullerton,

> Professional baseball has reached a crisis. The major leagues, both owners and players, are on trial. Charges of crookedness among the owners, accusations of cheating, of tampering with each other's teams, with attempting to syndicate and control baseball, are bandied about openly. Charges that gamblers have succeeded in bribing ballplayers, that games have been bought and sold, that players are in the pay of professional gamblers and that even the World's Series was tampered with are made without attempt at refutation by the men who have their fortunes invested in baseball.... Some are for keeping silent and "allowing it to blow over." The time has come for straight talk. How can club owners expect writers, editors and fans to have any faith in them or their game if they make no effort to clean up the scandal?[3]

Once again, Comiskey, who was sitting on the whole story in hopes that it would simply go away, was forced to respond. "I can say that we have discovered nothing to indicate that the team double-crossed me or the public last fall," he said the next day. "Do not get the impression we have quit investigating. I am still working on the affair, and will go the limit to get any evidence to support the truth of these charges. And if I land the goods on any of my players I will see to it that there is no place in organized baseball for them. There will be no whitewashing or compromising with crooks, but as yet not one bit of reliable evidence has turned up."[4] The White Sox owner knew better, but was not going to expose what he knew and destroy his team for many years to come. Comiskey, like Richard Nixon 50 years later, chose instead to cover it up and ride it out.

Fullerton told the truth, but no one, in or out of the baseball world, wanted to hear it. As *Baseball Magazine* put it, Fullerton was an "erratic writer.... If a man really knows so little about baseball that he believes the game is or can be fixed, he should keep his mouth shut when in the presence of intelligent people."[5] Other writers accused Fullerton of claiming a Series fix due to embarrassment; the *Herald-Examiner* writer was a successful baseball prognosticator (he had correctly picked the Hitless Wonders White Sox over the powerful Cubs in 1906) who made the wrong choice in 1919 and refused to accept defeat.

One paper was not afraid to print the story. *Collyer's Eye* was a weekly tabloid, begun in Chicago in 1915 and focused on the local sports and gambling scene. On October 18, 1919, only nine days after the World Series ended, *Collyer's Eye* produced an article under the headline "Involve 7 Sox in World's Series Scandal." In it, writer Frank O. Evans stated that "no less than seven members of the Sox team are listed as 'under suspicion.'" Two weeks later, Evans reported that a woman, who may have been Lefty Williams' wife, made a large wager on the Reds, and on November 1 the paper said that "in fairness to the boys who gave their best to the game," Eddie Collins, Shano Collins, Dickey Kerr, Nemo Leibold, and Buck Weaver "came out of the series 'clean as a hound's tooth.'" If anyone doubted the identities of the seven suspected White Sox after this revelation, the article concluded with the sentence "You may write the other two lines yourself."[6]

Eddie Cicotte's name popped up for the first time in *Collyer's Eye* on November 8, when the paper claimed that Ray Schalk not only charged Eddie with crossing him up during the first game in Cincinnati, but that Schalk attacked the pitcher after the contest. On November 15, the paper finally named the seven suspects (excepting Weaver) and charged that the gamblers made the payoffs at a poolroom a few blocks from Comiskey Park. During the next few weeks, the paper made a raft of new accusations, claiming that Cicotte and Williams were drinking to excess before the start of the Series, and that Eddie "fell off the wagon" on the last Eastern trip in September. *Collyer's Eye* also stated that Kid Gleason considered benching Eddie and starting Bill James in Game Four.

The November 15 issue also aired, for the first time, Eddie Cicotte's claim that Comiskey had offered him a $10,000 bonus which the pitcher never received. On December 13, *Collyer's Eye* repeated a report from Detroit in which Eddie stated that the alleged bonus had been offered for winning 30 games. As Eddie closed the season with 29 wins, *Collyer's Eye* left it to the reader to deduce that Eddie's two-week benching in September of 1919 was intended to keep him from the magic 30 mark. The paper also said that Eddie was "through with the game."

No one paid much attention to *Collyer's Eye*, which most regarded as a scandal sheet, but the paper had pieced the story together with a fair degree of accuracy. The December 13 issue dropped another bombshell, when the paper quoted Ray Schalk as stating that none of the seven players—Cicotte, Williams, Jackson, Felsch, McMullin, Risberg, and Gandil—would play for the White Sox in 1920. It also said that Schalk, enraged that his pitchers deliberately ignored his signals, beat up both Cicotte and Williams after Games One and Two, respectively. Schalk quickly moved to deny the report, telling *The Sporting News* that he found nothing wrong with the Series.

Kid Gleason was a baseball man who had played, coached, and managed in major league baseball for 30 years. Gleason had seen it all, and as the Series unfolded he could clearly tell that his White Sox were throwing it. The manager's suspicions were confirmed when he sat in on the meeting with Redmon, so Gleason knew who the fixers were, too, and that one of them—perhaps the biggest culprit of all—was Eddie Cicotte. Eddie's awful performance in Game One and his two egregious errors in the fourth inning of Game Four were too much to ignore. However, the eight conspirators kept their mouths shut, and because of this, Comiskey elected to keep all the incriminating information to himself. So Gleason gritted his teeth and made plans for the 1920 campaign.

The White Sox would need a new first baseman. In early 1920, Chick Gandil demanded a raise to $6,500 a year. Comiskey, whose investigators had long since identified Gandil as the ringleader of the fix, turned him down, so the veteran went home to California and quit the game at the age of 32. He spent the summer of 1920 playing semipro ball for the Elks Club in Bakersfield for $75 a game. Gandil, the main instigator of the scheme and the point of contact between the players and the gamblers, escaped Chicago with the biggest share of the crooked money; some, including Eliot Asinof, author of *Eight Men Out*, claim that Gandil took as much as $35,000, more than half a million in today's dollars, back to California. Both Comiskey and Gleason were happy to see him go. They had no intention of keeping this troublemaker on the team for one more year. They could put Shano Collins or rookie Ted Jourdan on first base. At least Eddie Collins would have one fellow infielder who would talk to him.

They could not easily dismiss Eddie Cicotte. Comiskey knew that Eddie was as guilty as anyone in the scheme, but he could not simply release a man who won 30 games in 1919 (29 in the regular season and one in the Series). Cicotte had no trade value, because all the other American League teams harbored their own suspicions about his Series performance. The White Sox were stuck with Eddie. In fact, they were stuck with all seven of the suspects, because a wholesale housecleaning might set the wheels in motion to expose the fix.

The seven men remained on the team, and they knew that they had the upper hand in contract negotiations for 1920. Comiskey could not get rid of them or trade them, though the Yankees reportedly offered first baseman Wally Pipp in exchange for Happy Felsch. Comiskey probably knew by this time that he had made a major blunder by conducting his investigation. He could have traded off some of the seven if he had only suspected them of wrongdoing, but now he had knowledge of the fix, and the White Sox owner could not possibly trade a player that he knew was tainted. Also, Ban Johnson was looking into the rumors too, and it was only a matter of time before Johnson talked to the same people who gave information to Comiskey. Indeed, in late December of 1919, Grabiner found out that the St. Louis gambler, Redmon, had talked to Johnson's detectives as well as Comiskey's. Now Johnson, Comiskey's enemy, was hot on the trail of the scandal and knew of the White Sox owner's cover-up.

Most of the seven, Eddie Cicotte included, held out for more money.

Eddie demanded a raise to $10,000 per year and held out well into the new year. He traveled to spring training in Texas in March while still unsigned. So did Buck Weaver, who went to training camp but left after two days when Comiskey would not honor his request to be traded to the Yankees. Weaver was in the second year of a three-year contract, which severely limited his bargaining power. Risberg stayed away from camp entirely, demanding a raise despite entering the last year of a two-year deal. The shortstop, who batted .080 (2-for-25) and made four errors in the World Series, followed Gandil's lead and threatened to retire.

So Comiskey reluctantly handed out raises to his men. Eddie Cicotte signed a new contract for $10,000, while the chronically underpaid Lefty Williams' salary jumped from $3,000 to $6,000, with bonuses for winning 15 and 20 games. The White Sox owner nearly doubled Happy Felsch's pay to $7,000, and Joe Jackson accepted a three-year contract for $8,000 per year, a $2,000 raise for the man Bill Veeck called "the world's worst negotiator." McMullin also received a healthy increase, and Risberg and Weaver must have been satisfied somehow, for both eventually joined the team. Comiskey's sudden spree of generosity meant only one thing—that the owner was prepared to buy off the perpetrators. Comiskey was a businessman and apparently believed that the best way to deal with this festering problem was to throw money at it.

In most years, the White Sox would have entered the 1920 season as the favorite to repeat their pennant-winning performance of 1919. Gandil was gone, but Red Faber was healthy again and ready to resume his spot in the rotation. With the emergence of Dickey Kerr, the White Sox now boasted the best front-line pitching in the league, though the bullpen was still as weak as ever. The daily lineup was strong, with Joe Jackson and Eddie Collins playing at a Hall of Fame level in 1919 and Happy Felsch emerging as a star at age 26. Buck Weaver was ready for a breakout season, and Ray Schalk was still the top catcher in the American League. However, Chicago's pratfall in the World Series was so stunning that most writers expected Tris Speaker's Indians, not the White Sox, to win the 1920 pennant. The World Series loss was so devastating that many figured that the Sox could not recover from it. Cleveland's main challenge, they said, would come from the Yankees, who added Babe Ruth to an already formidable lineup.

At the start of the 1920 season, the 35-year-old Eddie Cicotte was the oldest player on the White Sox and the seventh-oldest in the American League. If the White Sox had any concerns about their pitching staff, they centered on their aging staff ace. How long could Eddie last, and could he continue to win 20 or more games a season? Many predicted that Eddie was finished as a top-rank pitcher because of his tired arm in September of 1919, resulting in his two-week layoff and his Series failures. As columnist Grantland Rice put it, "If Cicotte skids badly, as many think he will, the White Sox case will be next to hopeless."[7]

Gleason was not worried. Said Gleason, "Cicotte always takes the best care of himself and the way he performs on the mound he ought to go along for a few years more. He does not waste much effort in his pitching and he makes every ball count. This is why I believe he ought to be as valuable to us as he was in the last race."[8]

However, many figured that the veteran pitcher would be hard-pressed to repeat his 1919 performance without the shine ball, which was banned in February of 1920 by league president Ban Johnson. Gleason was not concerned about this either. "I do not think that Cicotte will worry about the elimination of the shine ball," said the manager. "It was never proved that he used it as a regular thing in his pitching. Of course he bluffed with it the same as all pitchers do, but that is another thing. I am sure Cicotte will not be bothered by any changes in the rules and I expect him to be as successful for the White Sox as he was last year."[9] Even now, with the shine ball banned, Eddie and his manager still denied that such a pitch ever existed.

The spitball was also on its way out, thanks to Johnson, who had campaigned against "freak deliveries" for years. During the winter of 1919–1920, American League managers agreed to a partial ban of the wet pitch, with each team instructed to designate two pitchers who would be permitted to throw it. The White Sox selected Eddie Cicotte and Red Faber as their spitballers. (They would be two of only eight legal spitballers in the league, as two teams did not choose anyone and two teams chose only one apiece.) They left out Frank Shellenback, who spent the rest of his career in the minors, where he was allowed to keep using the spitter. Shellenback won more than 300 minor league games, mostly in the Pacific Coast League, but his big league career was finished.

The White Sox trained in Waco, Texas, that spring. Training camp began a few weeks later than usual because Charles Comiskey decided that a veteran team like the Sox needed less time to round into shape. He probably saved a bundle in training expenses, too, but he had to pay for all those salary increases somehow. Because so many Sox held out that spring, even the ones who had taken the dirty money the previous October, Kid Gleason found it difficult to hold practice. Eventually they all signed, and the team set out to defend its pennant.

The writers noticed that this training camp was different from any other they had seen. In previous years, the Collins faction and the Risberg-Gandil faction on the White Sox spent the spring, and the season, sniping at and arguing with each other. At this camp, the two groups simply avoided all communication. Instead, an eerie silence prevailed. The seven conspirators did not speak at all with their teammates. The seven men stuck together on the field and off.

Many of their conversations, carefully hidden from the other Sox, concerned the fix. When Joe Jackson complained that he had received only $5,000 of the $20,000 he was promised, Eddie Cicotte told him that he was "a God-damned fool" for not getting it in advance. Risberg also claimed to have received only $5,000, an assertion which Jackson called, accurately, a "damned lie." It was obvious that the fix troubled the players greatly, because they could not stop talking about it.

Eddie and the White Sox started the 1920 season in fine form. After Lefty Williams defeated the Tigers in 11 innings in Chicago's home opener (Eddie, one again, did not want to pitch on Opening Day), Eddie shut out the Tigers, 4–0, the next day. The Sox grabbed the early league lead with wins in their first six games, and on May 3 they held first place with a 10–2 record. They followed this up with seven losses in their next eight contests, losing four of five to Cleveland, the pre-season favorites. Gleason's crew was now four games back, and after winning three straight over Washington, each with double-digit scores, the Sox went to Cleveland and lost three of four to the Indians, dropping all the way to fifth place.

The Sox were nothing if not inconsistent, and Eddie's performance mirrored that of his team. Cicotte struggled during April and May, and after giving up seven runs and 14 hits in six innings in an 8–1 loss to Boston on June 10, his record stood at 4–5. He rallied with seven consecutive wins, a streak which ended with his worst performance of the season, a 20–5 loss to the Yankees on July 17. Eddie surrendered eight runs in five innings, while relievers Spencer Heath and George Payne gave up 12 more in a lost cause. Eddie closed July with consecutive wins over the Red Sox and Athletics, and the White Sox ended the month in third place, five and a half games out.

On Sunday, August 1, 45,000 people jammed Comiskey Park to see Eddie face the Yankees. This was the largest home crowd in White Sox history up to that time, and team management set up rope barriers in the outfield and allowed fans to stand on the field behind them. The Chicago fans came to cheer for Joe Jackson, whose batting average hovered near the .400 mark, and Eddie Cicotte, who had boosted his record to 13–7 after his poor start. Cicotte was never better, allowing only five hits, all singles, and holding Babe Ruth hitless in a 3–0 win. Eddie walked four men, including Ruth, but completed his second consecutive shutout.

A bit of trickery by Joe Jackson helped Eddie preserve his shutout. In the fourth inning, Ruth belted a fly ball into the overflow crowd in left field. Jackson drifted back and leaped into the crowd with outstretched arms; moments later, he emerged without the ball, but loudly insisted that he caught it. Umpire Tommy Connolly believed him and called Ruth out. This ruling set off a long, loud argument among Connolly, Yankees manager Miller Huggins,

9. The 1920 Season

Eddie Cicotte (left) and Babe Ruth talk before a game at Comiskey Park, August 1, 1920. Eddie shut out Ruth and the Yankees that day with some help from left fielder Joe Jackson (author's collection).

and most of the Yankees, but the decision stood. Many years later, Jackson admitted to a reporter that he never caught the ball.

Lefty Williams lost to the Yankees on Monday as Ruth walloped his 38th homer, but on Tuesday and Wednesday Red Faber (who kept Ruth at bay by walking him three times) and Dickey Kerr held the powerful Yankees to one run each, winning by identical 3–1 scores. Three wins in four games against the Yankees left Chicago four and a half games out of the lead.

The Sox now made their move. They split four games at home against the Red Sox, then took five in a row from the Senators with Eddie winning the first and last games of the series to pull to within one game of the top. Three days later, Eddie took the mound on Sunday, August 15, in Detroit with a chance to put the White Sox into the league lead with a win. He delivered it, holding Ty Cobb hitless and belting a double to drive in a run in a 10–3 victory, his 17th of the season.

Eddie was good, but Dickey Kerr was sensational. Like Eddie, Kerr had started the season slowly, and after the Browns knocked him out of the box in the first inning on July 1, his record stood at 4–4. He won five of his seven decisions in July and saved two games, and won his first seven starts in August. Now, with Faber healthy, Williams pitching well, and Cicotte and Kerr finding their form, the Sox boasted four strong starters, backed by the powerful bats of Joe Jackson, Eddie Collins, Happy Felsch, and Buck Weaver, all hitting well above .300.

Despite the turmoil within the team, the White Sox now held control of the pennant race. A 16–4 win over the Yankees in New York behind Dickey Kerr on August 26, Kerr's 12th in his last 13 decisions, gave the Sox a 3 ½-game lead over Cleveland, with the Yankees four games back. The Indians were reeling from the death of their shortstop, Ray Chapman, after a beaning in New York ten days before, while Yankees slugger Babe Ruth sat out two games against Chicago to rest an injury. Both Cleveland and New York were fading, and some of the writers already conceded the pennant to Gleason's crew.

The Sox then lost seven in a row.

Eddie Cicotte started the second game of the New York series on August 27. He lasted eight innings, giving up four runs and walking three Yankees. Kid Gleason took him out for a pinch-hitter in the eighth, after which Roy Wilkinson came on in relief. The game went into extra frames, and the Yankees won with a run off Dickey Kerr in the 12th inning. Eddie belted two hits himself, but his pitching performance was disappointing, especially with Ruth out of the lineup for the Yankees.

The next day, the Chicago offense simply died. The White Sox managed only six hits in a 3–0 loss to the Yankees, and their sloppy and listless play could not be ignored. I. E. Sanborn of the *Tribune* complained in print that "Risberg and Weaver were the best players New York had today," and Joe Jackson ran the bases "like a high school boy."[10] Jackson singled with two out in the first inning but made the third out trying to stretch it to a double. He was out by a large margin, and this rash act stranded Eddie Collins on third. In the ninth inning, with a rally in the offing, Jackson singled with one out, but when Felsch lined out to third, Jackson wandered off first and was doubled up easily to end the game. Other misplays and fielding mistakes raised eyebrows, and by now, most, if not all, of the honest Sox were convinced that their teammates were purposely losing games in a repeat of the 1919 Series fiasco.

After an off-day, the Sox traveled to Boston and produced a mere five hits, three by Eddie Collins, in a 4–0 defeat to the fifth-place Red Sox. On August 31, Cicotte took the mound at Fenway Park and delivered another poor effort, losing, 7–3. This damaging loss left Cleveland only half a game back and the Yankees one game out. On September 1, Cleveland regained first place when the White Sox lost their fifth in a row, falling to Boston, 6–2, behind Kerr. I. E. Sanborn spoke for all the writers when he stated in his column, "There is no way of accounting for their slump in Boston and New York on any rational basis."[11]

During the third game of the Boston series, Dickey Kerr grew increasingly frustrated with the shoddy play behind him. As Eddie Collins later recalled, a lazy fly ball fell untouched between Felsch and Jackson in left-center field, and Weaver missed an easy grounder. Kerr was charged with an error on a throw to third, though Collins believed that Weaver's lack of effort caused the throw to get away. Neither Weaver nor the outfielders were charged with errors, but Kerr wasn't fooled. After the Red Sox scored six runs in the middle three innings, Kerr threw his glove in anger and confronted Risberg and Weaver. "If you told me you wanted to lose this game," shouted the pitcher, "I could have done it a lot easier." Risberg threw a punch, and the other White Sox and manager Gleason rushed in to break it up.[12]

The losing continued even after the White Sox returned to Chicago for a four-game set against St. Louis. The Browns beat Red Faber on September 3, and Eddie, in the first contest of a Labor Day doubleheader, pitched poorly once again, surrendering 14 hits in a 10-inning loss. The slide stopped at seven with a win in the second game, but the losing streak dropped the Sox to third place behind the Indians and Yankees. When Eddie Collins got back to Chicago with the team, he marched into Comiskey's office and told the owner that his teammates were throwing games again. Specifically, according to the captain's later recollections, he said that Eddie Cicotte "wasn't trying."

Kid Gleason also suspected Eddie, especially after his veteran pitching ace turned in another subpar performance against Boston on September 9. Eddie allowed five runs and nine hits, with four walks and a hit batter, and left the game for a pinch-hitter in the eighth, trailing 5–0. Eddie Murphy, batting for Cicotte, singled and started a five-run Chicago rally that tied the game. Roy Wilkinson retired the Red Sox in the ninth, and the White Sox scored in the bottom of the inning to win it. After this game, Eddie sat on

A close-up of Eddie late in his White Sox career (author's collection).

the bench for eight days. Gleason not only bypassed Eddie in the rotation (rookie Shovel Hodge took Eddie's place in a 7–0 loss to the Senators), but brought him and some of the other slumping White Sox in for early-morning workouts as well.

The Black Sox, Cicotte included, may have been tanking for several reasons. After the news of the scandal broke, Buck Weaver reported that Fred McMullin, the utility player, offered him $500 to help throw a game in mid-season. Weaver insisted that he turned down the offer, but there may have been many more such bribery attempts in 1920. Perhaps the suspected players made some extra money—a few hundred dollars here, another hundred or so there—by dropping the occasional fly ball or botching a rundown.

They also may have thrown games because they were afraid of the gamblers. During the early 1960s, a writer and college professor named Lawrence Ritter interviewed 20 old ballplayers for his iconic book, *The Glory of Their Times*. One of those long-retired players was Smoky Joe Wood, Eddie Cicotte's teammate in Boston from 1908 to 1912. While Eddie struggled with the Red Sox, Wood became a sensation, winning 34 games at the age of 22 for the 1912 World Series champions. Wood's arm went bad shortly afterward, probably from overwork, and the Red Sox sold him to Cleveland in 1917. There he reinvented himself as an outfielder for the Indians. Wood and Eddie remained friends, and visited with each other whenever their teams met.

Wood, who was well into his 70s when he spoke to Ritter, revealed one sensational piece of information about the 1920 season. This tidbit did not appear in the book, but one can hear it on Ritter's interview tapes, which were released to the public on audiocassette and later on compact disc. On the tape, Wood tells his interviewer, "But this thing in '20, it wasn't exactly on the up and up, I have to admit that. Because I knew from what Cicotte had told me in Cleveland that the White Sox didn't dare win."[13]

Perhaps Ritter left this item out of his book when it was published in 1966 because Eddie and two other Black Sox were still living at the time. It is possible that Ritter (or Wood) did not want to embarrass Cicotte, or that Ritter wanted to avoid a libel suit over the allegation. However, Wood's assertion would have been no surprise to any observer at the time. Eddie Collins and the rest of his faction on the club suspected their teammates of throwing games, with Eddie Cicotte as one of their main suspects.

The gamblers, not the players, now held the upper hand, and it would have been very easy for Sport Sullivan, the Boston-based fixer, to harass his old friend Eddie Cicotte. Sullivan had the goods on all the Black Sox, and could have exposed them at any time if they did not win or lose as he and other gamblers directed. The fact that Cicotte lost six of his seven decisions against the Red Sox and Indians in 1920, while posting a 20–4 mark against the rest of the league, looks suspicious in this light. (He went 15–1 against the three worst teams in the league, the A's, Tigers, and Senators.) Eddie and the others did not realize that accepting the bribe money in 1919 left them open to exposure, and even blackmail, in 1920. The gamblers leaned on the players all season and continued making money, while Eddie and the other Black Sox were powerless to stop them.

Eliot Asinof, author of *Eight Men Out*, interviewed Red Faber many years later. Faber told Asinof, "The hoodlums had some of the boys in their pocket all through the 1920 season, too, throwing ball games right up to the last week of the pennant. I could feel it out there when I pitched—Risberg letting an easy ground ball go by, or Happy Felsch letting a runner take an extra base. You want to scream at them but you don't because you can see how scared they are."[14] Yankees shortstop Roger Peckinpaugh said as much to writer Donald Honig. Peckinpaugh said that Nemo Leibold told him before the series in New York, "Something screwy is going on here. I don't know what it is, but it's screwy, all right. You guys bear down and you ought to take all four games."[15]

10

The Walls Close In

> "*I regard reports that the recent series was not on the square as absurd. Cincinnati won because it played the better ball and deserved the victory. Convincing proofs must be presented to me before I would believe any Chicago player failed to give his best efforts.*"—Umpire Billy Evans, January 1920.[1] Evans was one of the four umpires who worked the 1919 World Series.

The story of the Black Sox Scandal might never have come to light without a clumsy attempt to fix a game in the National League. On August 31, 1920, Chicago Cubs president William L. Veeck (father of future White Sox owner Bill Veeck) received six telegrams and two phone calls warning him that the game that afternoon between his Cubs and the last-place Philadelphia Phillies was fixed for the Phillies to win. A suspiciously high number of large bets had been made on the Phillies that morning, and the odds shifted sharply, just as they had done before the 1919 World Series. Veeck ordered his manager to replace the Cubs' starting pitcher, Claude Hendrix, with his ace, Grover Cleveland Alexander, but the Phillies won the game anyway. This news hit the papers a few days later, and by September 8, Chief Justice Charles A. McDonald of Chicago's Criminal Court had ordered a grand jury investigation into the matter.

A few days later, *Collyer's Eye* weighed in again. On September 11, 1920, *Collyer's Eye* told the story that the main Chicago newspapers could not tell—that the Chicago clubhouse was a war zone, and that one faction suspected the other of rank dishonesty.

> Internal dissension, which earlier in the season threatened to shatter the pennant chances of the White Sox, has again broken forth. Bitter recriminations fill the air both on the field and in the club house. The "old guard" who have at all times given their best and who came through the last world's series "clean as a hound's tooth," have arranged to make demands on Comiskey looking to the ousting of the "wrecking crew."
>
> "We went into New York and Boston looking like pennant winners," said one of the

10. The Walls Close In

players, "and came out of the series looking like amateurs. We have a good ball club, but it's a house divided. Just why players should toss off four or five thousand dollars of world's series money is quite beyond me."

"Take Risberg, for instance. Over in Boston he struck out three times without taking his bat off his shoulder. Did you notice that Cicotte failed to win a game at Boston, also in New York? Then as a crowning piece of Merkleism, did you see Felsch get nipped off of second base? All of this may be 'the breaks of the game,' but then there is another name and like murder it 'will out' sooner or later." Over at skull practice Wednesday morning it was said that several of the White Sox players were "interested" in the grand jury probe into the alleged scandal surrounding the Cubs-Philadelphia games. The consensus of opinion seemed to be that Sherry Magee [a focus of the Cubs-Phillies investigation] will have plenty of company and that said company would not be confined to members of the Cubs' playing staff.[2]

The article was written by "Joe LeBlanc," most likely a pseudonym for the paper's publisher, Bert Collyer. Black Sox researchers now believe that Collyer received his inside information from Hugh Fullerton, the disgruntled *Chicago Herald-Examiner* writer whose reporting about the fixed Series was not only ignored, but ridiculed, during the fall of 1919.

This investigation soon morphed into an inquest on baseball gambling in general. With a grand jury in session, the sportswriters were now free to speculate on the honesty of the fall classic, and the Cubs-Phillies game faded into the background. Even the *Chicago Tribune*, the very model of caution regarding the scandal, gave reporter Jim Crusinberry the green light to vent his suspicions. On September 19, Crusinberry devoted his column to a letter, signed by prominent Chicago baseball booster Fred Loomis (but actually composed by Crusinberry himself), demanding that the grand jury investigate the 1919 World Series. Said Loomis (and Crusinberry):

> Widespread circulation has been given to reports from various sources that the World Series of last fall between the Chicago White Sox and the Cincinnati Reds was deliberately and intentionally lost through an alleged conspiracy between certain unnamed members of the Chicago White Sox team and certain gamblers.
>
> I have been startled by these rumors and was inclined in the first place to give no credence to these reports, but where there is so much smoke there must be some fire...
>
> There is a perfectly good grand jury located in this county. The citizens and taxpayers of Illinois are maintaining such an institution for the purpose of investigating any alleged infraction of the law.
>
> Those who possess evidence of any gambling last fall in the World Series should come forward and present it in a manner that may give assurance to the whole country, so that justice will be done in this case where the confidence of the people seems to have been so flagrantly violated.[3]

On September 23, the grand jury received affidavits from two Boston Braves that a pitcher for the New York Giants, Rube Benton, had been tipped off by Hal Chase that the first two games of the World Series had been rigged for the Reds to win. Benton had also been told that the Reds would win the Series itself, and the pitcher used this information to win $3,800 in bets.

On that same day, the grand jury heard testimony from Veeck, Charles Comiskey, and Ban Johnson, who was quoted in the *Tribune* as stating that he had "heard statements that the White Sox would not dare to win the 1920 pennant because the managers of a gambling syndicate, alleged to have certain players in their power, had forbidden it."[4] The assistant state's attorney, Hartley Replogle, would not reveal what was said in the closed hearing room, but he made a stunning pronouncement. "The last World Series between the Chicago White Sox and the Cincinnati Reds was not on the square," said Replogle. "Five to seven players on the White Sox team are involved."[5] This bold assertion put the grand jury hearings on the front pages of the country's newspapers.

Time was running out on Eddie Cicotte. He won his 20th game of the season on September 21 against the last-place Philadelphia A's, 9–2, the sixth game of a seven-game winning streak that kept the White Sox close to the Indians. But Tris Speaker's Cleveland club refused to lose, winning seven in a row at the same time, and the White Sox remained in second place with a three-game set in Cleveland coming up.

On Thursday, September 23, the White Sox won the first game in Cleveland by a 10–3 score behind Kerr, but lost the next day, 2–0, when Indians rookie Duster Mails shut down the Sox on three hits. This loss dropped Chicago a game and a half out of the lead with six games to play. Back in Chicago, the grand jury investigating the baseball scandals called Rube Benton, the pitcher named in the affidavits, to the stand. This was the same Rube Benton who defeated Eddie Cicotte in the third game of the 1917 World Series.

Benton's testimony, while mostly hearsay, was devastating. The Giants pitcher repeated to the grand jury what a Cincinnati gambler named Hahn had told him—that five White Sox had accepted $100,000 in cash from a coterie of Pittsburgh gamblers to lose the 1919 World Series. Benton named four of them—Eddie Cicotte, Chick Gandil, Happy Felsch, and Lefty Williams. Benton also detailed how his New York teammates, Hal Chase and Heinie Zimmerman, had offered him a bribe to throw a game in 1919, but the World Series accusations knocked the Chase matter off the front pages. For the first time, the names of the crooked White Sox were out in the open.

The news was so sensational that it made the afternoon editions of America's newspapers that very day. Eddie was in big trouble now, especially as Benton told the grand jury that, as the papers said, "he was sure Cicotte could name the Pittsburgh gamblers and would be glad to give the information to the Grand Jury."[6] The papers further reported Ban Johnson's claim that the White Sox did not try to win the 1920 pennant, because the gamblers had threatened to expose the 1919 fix if they did.

10. The Walls Close In

Eddie made an attempt at damage control on Saturday. He spoke by phone from Cleveland to several Chicago sportswriters and insisted that he knew nothing about the scandal. That afternoon, Lefty Williams, who was also named by Benton, pitched a 5–1 win over the Indians to pull the Sox to within half a game of the lead. This game ended the season series against Cleveland, and now the White Sox needed to keep winning and pray for the Indians to stumble.

The Sox returned to Chicago on Sunday for a game against the Tigers, and Eddie Cicotte pitched one of his best games of 1920. He gave up a run in the first inning but cruised the rest of the way, allowing only seven hits in an 8–1 win. Eddie also belted two hits and drove in a run himself. It was his 21st win of the season and the 209th of his major league career.

It was also his last.

James T. Farrell, the future novelist, was at the game that day. Farrell was 19 years old, and reported that the mood at Comiskey Park was a strange one, especially as it surrounded a team in the middle of an exciting pennant fight:

> It was a muggy, sunless day. I went to the park early and watched the players take their hitting and fielding practice. It looked the same as always. They took their turns at the plate. They took their turns on the field. They seemed calm, no different than they had been on other days before the scandal talk had broken. The crowd was friendly to them and some cheered. But a subtle gloom hung over the fans. The atmosphere of the park was like the muggy weather. The game began. Cicotte pitched. The suspected players got a hand when they came to bat. The White Sox won easily. Cicotte was master of the Detroit Tigers that day. One could only wish that he had pitched as well in the 1919 Series.[7]

The next set of damaging revelations in the case came not from Chicago, but from Philadelphia. On Monday, September 27, the *Philadelphia North American* printed an interview with Billy Maharg, the ex-boxer and confederate of Sleepy Bill Burns and Abe Attell. Maharg, one of the biggest losers in the fix, laid out the timeline from the Burns-Attell perspective and claimed that Cicotte was the man who set the whole sordid series of events in motion. After discussing an upcoming hunting trip with Sox pitcher Bill James, Maharg said,

> Cicotte came in and started to talk in a low voice to Burns. I heard enough to know that he said that a group of prominent players of the White Sox would be winning to "throw" the coming world's series if a syndicate of gamblers would give them $100,000 on the morning of the first game.[8]

Maharg's story, like Benton's, appeared that same day in the evening papers all over the country. The 1919 World Series scandal was suddenly a national sensation, sharing the front page with the League of Nations and the upcoming presidential election.

Eddie, now outed as not only a participant, but a ringleader of the scheme, made a desperate attempt to distance himself from his accusers. "I wouldn't know Maharg if I saw him," he said on Monday night. "I do not recall ever having met him. He might have been introduced to me the same as any other fan, but I do not remember him. Bill Burns called at the Ansonia Hotel in New York. He did not talk to me alone, but conversed with other members of the team. While I was with him he was making arrangements for a hunting trip with Bill James. The talk of the World Series being fixed is all a joke. I know nothing of it."[9]

Cicotte's denials convinced no one, and it had to be apparent to him that the jig was up. His guilty knowledge had ground away at his emotions all season. Cicotte family lore says that the pitcher sought guidance from his parish priest on the matter, and some of his teammates later said that Eddie was drinking much more than usual during the summer of 1920. Eddie was usually an outgoing and friendly type, but in 1920 he kept to himself more than ever.

The White Sox remained half a game behind Cleveland after a 2–0 win over Detroit on Monday (Kerr's 20th win of the season[10]), but when the afternoon papers hit the stands, the pennant race hardly mattered. All that remained on the schedule was a three-game set in St. Louis against the Browns the next weekend. This gave the White Sox three days off with nothing to distract them from the never-ending stream of bad news. The pressure on the suspected players kept building.

By Tuesday morning, September 28, Eddie had reached the end of his endurance. He could no longer live with his guilty knowledge, and he knew that even more damaging revelations would emerge soon enough. The house of cards was falling, and it was falling on Eddie and his teammates. It was time to put an end to the uncertainty. It was time to tell the truth.

Jim Crusinberry of the *Chicago Tribune* was close to both Charles Comiskey and Kid Gleason, and he had known about the fix for nearly a year. He could not write about it without solid proof, fearing a lawsuit for libel, but he saw how the scandal weighed so heavily on Eddie Cicotte throughout the 1920 season. Now, with the dam about to burst, Crusinberry knew that if anyone was likely to break down and confess, Cicotte was the one.

If Crusinberry's later recollections are to be believed, he said that Cicotte's hands shook and his face was pale as he read the account of Maharg's accusations on Monday night. The pitcher made a show of defiance, but looked like he hadn't had a good night's sleep in a while. Eddie was ready to crack.

In Crusinberry's telling, Kid Gleason had also fingered Eddie as the player most likely to confess. Gleason visited Comiskey on Tuesday morning, September 28, and offered to break the stalemate. "Cicotte will break down, boss," said the manager. "A confession is the only way to clean it up. I've been

10. The Walls Close In

working on him all summer. I know he's the weak one. He's ready to break down. Shall I get him?"[11]

Comiskey agreed, and Harry Grabiner called Eddie and ordered him to report to the office of Comiskey's attorney, Alfred Austrian. When Eddie arrived, nervous and groggy from lack of sleep, a receptionist seated him in the foyer. After 20 anxious minutes, the receptionist led the pitcher to another room, which was empty. There Eddie waited for another 20 minutes, though he could hear Gleason, Comiskey, and Austrian talking in muffled tones and moving from office to office. If all the waiting was designed to increase the pressure on Eddie, it worked. By the time the three men finally entered the room, Eddie was a nervous wreck.

The room was silent for a while before Eddie, in tears, spoke up. "I know what you want," Cicotte told the team owner. "I was crooked, Mr. Comiskey. I took money to throw games. I—"

"Tell it to the grand jury,"[12] replied Comiskey, and the Black Sox Scandal was finally out in the open. Comiskey's year-long cover-up had failed, and with more revelations of the scandal breaking out in all directions, Comiskey decided that he would control the flow of information as best he could. The White Sox owner would feed the players to the grand jury and not wait for Ban Johnson to do so.

Eddie gave a deposition in Comiskey's office in which he named all eight of the players involved in the fix. Afterward, Austrian escorted Eddie to the courthouse, where they met with assistant state's attorney Hartley Replogle. Austrian and Replogle told Eddie, in reassuring tones, that the State was after the gamblers, not the players, and if Eddie would come clean, they would "take care" of him. Austrian and Replogle, who would be questioning Eddie in the grand jury room, steered him into the office of Judge Charles McDonald.

Judge McDonald was a good friend of Ban Johnson, and Johnson was pushing McDonald's candidacy for a seat on baseball's National Commission. McDonald wanted to make a splash in the press by exposing the gamblers and the players both, and he expected the pitcher to provide him with that information. Eddie again gave up the names of the eight players, but when he failed to name any of the fixers, McDonald grew irritated. He accused Eddie of holding out on him. As Eddie described the meeting in his later testimony, he insisted to McDonald that he had told all he knew, and McDonald ordered Replogle to indict him. Eddie protested that Austrian and Replogle had promised to protect him.

It never occurred to Eddie to engage legal representation of his own. He followed the advice of a lawyer, but that lawyer was Austrian, who represented Comiskey's interests and not those of the ballplayers. After a bit more bullying by the ambitious judge, Austrian led Eddie to the grand jury room.

In a 1944 interview, Judge McDonald gave a different interpretation of the meeting. "While the investigation was in progress, Edward Cicotte, the pitcher, walked into my chambers," Judge McDonald recalled. "Of his own free will he told of the deals with the gamblers. I warned him he did not have to testify, that he couldn't be compelled to give evidence against himself. He said he wanted to tell the truth."[13]

Eddie sat down to testify, and Replogle presented him with an immunity waiver. This document, the 1920 version of the present-day Miranda warning, stated that Eddie was aware that his testimony might be used against him. It read:

> Chicago, Illinois, September 28, 1920. I, Edward Cicotte, the undersigned, of my own free will make this my voluntary statement and be willing to testify and do testify before the Grand Jury with full knowledge of all the facts and of my legal rights, knowing full well that any testimony I may give might incriminate me and might be used against me in any case of prosecution or connected with the subject matter of my testimony, and now having been fully advised as to my legal rights, I hereby with said full knowledge waive all immunity that I might claim by reason of my appearing before the Grand Jury and giving testimony concerning certain crimes of which I have knowledge.

The poorly-educated pitcher certainly did not understand it, but signed it anyway.

Eddie testified for a little more than two hours. Unfortunately, as Black Sox researchers William F. Lamb and Jacob Pomrenke have pointed out, Eddie's testimony has not survived intact. Several newspapers reported their own versions of what he said in the closed grand jury room, most of which added a healthy dose of melodrama, with a sobbing pitcher on the stand admitting to throwing the Series for "the wife and kiddies." One report posted by the *Associated Press* and made available to hundreds of newspapers across the nation stated that Eddie said, "I wasn't putting anything on the ball. You could read the trademark on it when I lobbed it to the plate."[14]

Though this account of Eddie's testimony has been the widely accepted one for nearly 100 years, mostly due to the quotes directly attributed to Cicotte in the *New York Times*, the *Chicago Tribune*, and many other papers, his real testimony was not nearly so histrionic. Pieces of his testimony can be gleaned from two sources—a synopsis created during the grand jury session, and the excerpts that were read into the trial record four years later, when Joe Jackson sued Charles Comiskey for breach of contract. The available text shows that Eddie, despite his nervous state, shed some tears, but was otherwise remarkably composed throughout. In direct contrast to the incriminating quotes that appeared in the national media, Eddie firmly denied throwing any games, and insisted that despite accepting the $10,000 in cash, he played to win in all three of his World Series appearances.

On the stand, Cicotte claimed no authorship of the scheme; instead, he

FIX THESE FACES IN YOUR MEMORY

"CHICK" GANDIL

"HAP" FELSCH

JOE JACKSON

EDDIE CICOTTE

CLAUDE WILLIAMS

FRED McMULLIN

RISBERG

"BUCK" WEAVER

EIGHT MEN CHARGED WITH SELLING OUT BASEBALL

The eight suspected players in *The Sporting News*, October 7, 1920 (author's collection).

stated that Chick Gandil and Fred McMullin presented the idea to him at the Ansonia in New York. He attended a meeting there with seven of the eight Black Sox, with only Felsch missing.[15] Eddie quoted either Gandil or McMullin—he didn't remember which—as saying, "We ain't getting a divil [sic] of a lot of money and it looks like we could make a big thing if we threw these games to Cincinnati."[16] Asked his price, Cicotte replied, "Either Gandil or McMullin asked me what I would take to throw the series and I said I would not do anything like that for less than $10,000. And they said, well, we can get together and fix it up. That's all there was to that conference."[17]

At a second meeting three days before the Series, at the Warner Hotel in Chicago, six players were present, with Jackson and Risberg absent. This, Eddie told the grand jury, was when he told the group, "There is so much double crossing stuff, if I went in [on] the series [fix] I wanted the money put in my hand."[18] Several hours later, Cicotte returned to his hotel room and found $10,000 under his pillow.

At the start of Game One, Eddie admitted, he was supposed to either walk or hit the first batter, Morrie Rath, as a signal to the fixers. "Well. I went into the first game and tried to walk Roth [sic] and I hit him." Replogle asked, "So you wanted him to get on base?" Eddie replied, "Yes. But after he passed, after he was on there, I don't know. I guess I tried too hard. I didn't care, they could have had my heart and soul, that is the way I felt about it after I had taken that money. I guess everybody is not perfect."[19] That evening, after the loss in the first game, Cicotte said he was "sick all night" and said to his roommate Felsch, "Happy, it will never be done again."[20]

Cicotte also declared that he pitched his best in the fourth game, despite his pair of fielding gaffes. "I tried to make good but I made two errors. I was very anxious to get the ball but [we] didn't make any runs. If we could have made four or five runs, I would have won that game." When asked why he would do so after taking money from fixers, he replied, "Well, because I didn't care whether or not I got shot out there the next minute. I was going to win the ball game and the Series." Although crossing the fixers might be dangerous to him personally, he "was going to take a chance. I wanted to win. I could give [the money] back with interest if they would only win the game that day."[21]

However, though Eddie insisted that he played to win, he did not return the $10,000. He couldn't very well do that, he admitted. Instead, he paid off his $4,000 mortgage and bought animals and supplies for his farm. In the end, Eddie confessed only to accepting the $10,000, but either denied or claimed ignorance of everything else.

Why did Eddie's actual testimony differ so greatly from the accounts that appeared that evening in the press? Perhaps the nation was so shocked by the news of corruption in the national pastime that the papers could not resist exaggerating the admissions made by Cicotte and the players who followed him. In an era of sensationalism in journalism, the Black Sox Scandal represented the perfect opportunity for news outlets—especially in Chicago, which had six functioning daily newspapers—to compete. Maybe the reporters who covered the Sox and knew the situation believed that the core of his testimony—that he took the money but didn't actually throw any games—was self-serving and illogical, so they put more damning words in his mouth. Eddie Cicotte must have been surprised when he read his "quotes" in the evening papers.

After Eddie stepped down from the stand, the jury foreman, Henry Brigham, called the reporters together and announced that the grand jury had voted true bills (indictments) against each of the eight players that

Cicotte named. "This is just the beginning," added Hartley Replogle. "We will have more indictments within a few days and before we get through we will have purged organized baseball of everything crooked and dishonest.... We are going after the gamblers now. There will be indictments within a few days against men in Philadelphia, Indianapolis, St. Louis, Des Moines, Pittsburgh, Cincinnati and other cities. We've got the goods on these men and we are going to the limit."[22]

Replogle then brought Eddie's Chicago landlord, Mrs. Henrietta Kelley, to the stand. The nation's newspapers, which described her as the "mystery woman," reported that she made another sizzling revelation. "I overheard a conversation between Eddie Cicotte and his brother Jack during the world's series," she allegedly said. "It was after one of the games lost because of Eddie's pitching. I heard him say, 'To hell with 'em, I got mine.'"[23] Eddie did not have a brother named Jack, though one of his brothers was with him in Chicago during the Series. Harry Grabiner's diary had stated in 1919 that Mrs. Kelley had heard Eddie say, "To hell with them, I got mine," but other reports state that no sensational revelations came from her on this day. Did Replogle feed the reporters the story from Grabiner, or did Mrs. Kelley make that damning statement before testifying, but refuse to repeat it on the stand? Her appearance added one more confusing incident to the convoluted story of the scandal.

Things picked up again when Joe Jackson heard that Cicotte had spilled the beans. The outfielder panicked and called Judge McDonald at the courthouse. McDonald suggested that Jackson come downtown and tell his side of the story. Jackson may have been drinking, since the White Sox had no game that day, but he straightened himself out as best he could, put on a suit and a bow tie, and made his way to the courthouse, where Austrian met him on the steps outside. Austrian gave him the same assurances as he had given Cicotte. After a talk with Judge McDonald, Jackson entered the grand jury room. There Austrian presented him with a waiver of immunity, the same as Cicotte's. Jackson was illiterate, and so had no idea what he was signing, but Jackson signed and began his testimony.

Jackson knew little of the inner workings of the fix, but he admitted that he accepted money to throw the Series. He was questioned by Hartley Replogle.

> Q. Were you present at a meeting at the Ansonia Hotel in New York about two or three weeks before? A conference there with a number of ball players?
> A. I was not, no, sir.
> Q. Did anybody pay you any money to help throw that series in favor of Cincinnati?
> A. They did.
> Q. How much did they pay?

A. They promised me $20,000 and paid me five.
Q. Who promised you the 20,000?
A. Chick Gandil.
Q. Who is Chick Gandil?
A. He was their first baseman on the White Sox club.
Q. Who paid you the $5,000?
A. Lefty Williams brought it in my room and threw it down.[24]

Jackson insisted, however, that he played his best during the Series. The *Associated Press* reported that Jackson admitted that "throughout the Series, [he] either struck out or hit easy fly balls when hits would mean runs."[25] This is patently untrue, as seen in the transcript of Jackson's testimony, which has survived intact and can be found easily online.

Q. Do you recall the fourth game that Cicotte pitched?
A. Yes, sir.
Q. Did you see any fake plays made by yourself or anybody on that game, that would help throw the game?
A. Only the wildness of Cicotte.
Q. What was that?
A. Hitting a batter, that is the only thing that told me they were going through with it.
Q. Did you make any intentional errors yourself that day?
A. No, sir, not during the whole series.
Q. Did you play to win?
A. Yes.
Q. And run the bases to win?
A. Yes, sir.
Q. And fielded the balls at the outfield to win?
A. I did.
Q. Did you ever hear anyone accusing Cicotte of crossing the signals that were given to him by Schalk?
A. No, sir, I did not.
Q. Do you know whether or not any of those signals were crossed by Cicotte?
A. No, sir, I couldn't say.[26]

To the disappointment of Judge McDonald, Jackson could tell the court almost nothing about anything but his own involvement. All he knew is that he was promised $20,000 and received 5,000. He neither knew, nor cared, where it came from.

Lefty Williams testified the next day, but he knew no more than Jackson. He took no part in planning the fix either. He was questioned by Alfred Austrian:

Q. Did you ever talk to any of the other ballplayers?
A. I never talked to no one.
Q. I mean about it.
A. I never talked to no one.

10. The Walls Close In

Q. Did any of the other ballplayers talk to you about it?
A. They never mentioned it to me.
Q. Do you know how much Weaver got?
A. I could not say.
Q. Did he tell you how much he got?
A. He never did.
Q. Or Felsch?
A. None of the boys ever told me a word of what they got—whether they got a penny or not.
Q. Did you know what games the Sox were to lose for all this money they were getting?
A. Why, they were supposed to lose the first two to Cincinnati, and I never did hear whether they were to lose or win the one with Kerr.
Q: Now, is that all you know about the whole thing?
A: That is all I know.[27]

He did, however, tell the court that he and Cicotte, both disillusioned with the whole mess, talked after Game Six.

> On the second trip to Cincinnati, for the sixth and seventh games Cicotte and I had a conference. I told him we were double crossed and I was going out to win if there was any possible chance. Cicotte said he was the same way. Gandil had informed me in Cincinnati [before the Series began] that Bill Burns and Abe Attell was also fixing where we would get one hundred thousand dollars making twenty thousand dollars more. That I never received.[28]

Oddly enough, Replogle failed to confront Cicotte and Jackson about the glaring inconsistency in their testimonies; specifically, how both men could receive a large sum of money for their participation in the fix, but nonetheless claim to have played the games honestly. As Black Sox researcher and author William F. Lamb explains, "An experienced prosecutor would have immediately confronted Jackson with the irreconcilability of the two and required Jackson to explain, if he could, just how he could have done two mutually exclusive things at the same time."[29] But Replogle, a recent hire of the state's attorney office with little trial experience, failed to do so, which seriously weakened the state's case against the players. Instead, Replogle became the go-to source of quotes for the newspapermen; he even urged Congress "to make it a felony by anyone to offer a bribe to any baseball player to play our national game other than on the merits, also making it a felony for any player to accept a bribe. Let Congress act,"[30] the assistant state's attorney declared.

An enterprising reporter for the *Chicago American*, Harry Reutlinger, tracked down Happy Felsch at the outfielder's apartment. Carrying a bottle of Scotch, Reutlinger convinced Felsch to tell his side of the story. Said Felsch, "Cicotte's story is true in every detail. I don't blame him for telling." He also paid the pitcher a compliment. When asked how Cicotte received his payment before he pitched, he said, "Because he was wise enough to stand pat for it, that's all. Cicotte had brains. The rest of us roundheads just took their word for the proposition that we were going to get an even split on the $100,000 [the total they were promised]." The center fielder also stated,

> Well, the beans are all spilled and I think that I am through with baseball. I got my $5,000 and I suppose the others got theirs too. If you say anything about me, don't make it appear that I'm trying to put up an alibi. I'm not. I'm as guilty as the rest of them. We were in it alike.... I'm not saying that I double crossed the gamblers, but I had nothing to do with the loss of the world's series. The breaks just came so that I was not given a chance to do anything toward throwing the game. The records show that I played a pretty good game. I know I missed one terrible fly but, you can believe me or not, I was trying to catch that ball...
>
> I got $5,000. I could have got just about that much by being on the level if the Sox had won the series. And now I'm out of baseball—the only profession I know anything about, and a lot of gamblers have gotten rich. The joke seems to be on us.[31]

If the state was really going after the gamblers, Eddie and the other players certainly didn't help them much. Eddie was canny enough to remain close-lipped about the mechanics of the scheme, though he and Gandil were, by most accounts, the main organizers, and neither Jackson, nor Williams, nor Felsch knew enough to shed any light on it. Nonetheless, Eddie had named himself and seven other White Sox as participants in the fix. All except Weaver had received money to throw games, and Weaver had been present at some of the meetings. The three who testified—Cicotte, Jackson, and Williams—and Felsch all denied that they played to lose, but their actions on the field told a different story.

The public, for its part, cared much more about the players than the gamblers. The gamblers, in the public eye, were a predictable collection of lowlifes, but the players were their athletic heroes who had sold out. The fans were furious and reacted favorably to the indictments against the eight players, with promises of more to come. The eight were indicted on the nebulous charge of "conspiring to commit an illegal act." The indictment, returned on October 29, 1920, was titled "People of the State of Illinois v. Edward V. Cicotte, et al." Eddie's name came first in the alphabet among the eight men, now identified in the papers as the Black Sox, so his name appeared in the title.

The question must be asked—what if Eddie had kept his mouth shut, as any lawyer looking out for his interests would have told him to do? Benton's testimony, sensational as it was, was merely hearsay (a recollection of what a Cincinnati gambler told him) and Maharg's interview in the Philadelphia paper was not conducted under oath. Maharg's charges were damaging, but a smart lawyer would make the case that Burns and Maharg were small-time losers who were miffed about losing their shirts in a betting scheme gone wrong. The grand jury could not break the case open unless somebody cracked, and that somebody turned out to be Eddie Cicotte. Joe Jackson and Lefty Williams only rushed to the courthouse to testify after they heard that Cicotte had told his story, and Felsch's interview with Harry Reutlinger occurred after the revelations—exaggerated though they were—from all three men had appeared in the papers.

Charles Comiskey's investigators had pieced the story together, but they had no concrete proof that they could put before a judge. Comiskey said as much in an interview he gave in 1930, the year before he died, in which he stated, "I hired detectives and sent them all over the country that winter [of 1919] but I was unable to obtain facts that would bring about a conviction."[32] The story of the Black Sox Scandal might have dribbled out, little by little, for years, but nothing could have been proven against the eight players had they formed a united front of silence. Chick Gandil might have enforced such an information embargo had he still been on the team, but he was playing ball in Bakersfield, California, more than 2,000 miles from Chicago. Eddie Cicotte's testimony broke the case open. The man who, with Gandil, created the scheme is the one who exposed it.

The late author Gene Carney, a leading authority on the Black Sox Scandal and its participants, once gave writer Todd Schulz his take on what motivated Cicotte to come clean. "He had the keenest conscience," said Carney. "This really bothered him. He was a Catholic and he talked to his priest and other friends about it. If he doesn't go to the grand jury this really could have been slipped under the rug. There was no real evidence that anything had happened. But when a player confesses he took money, that ended the cover-up."[33]

After Cicotte and Jackson testified, Charles Comiskey sent a letter to each of the seven accused players on his team.

> Chicago, Sept 26. [with the 6 crossed out in pencil and replaced by an 8]
> To Charles Risberg, Fred McMullin, Joe Jackson, Oscar Felsch, George Weaver, C. P. Williams and E. V. Cicotte:
> You and each of you are hereby notified of your indefinite suspension as a member of the Chicago American Base-Ball Club. Your suspension is brought about by information which has just come to me directly involving you and each of you in the baseball scandal resulting from the world's series of 1919.
> If you are innocent of any wrongdoing you and each of you will be reinstated; if you are guilty you will be retired from organized base-ball for the rest of your lives, if I can accomplish it. Until there is a finality to this investigation it is due to the public that I take this action, even though it costs Chicago the pennant.
> CHICAGO AMERICAN BASEBALL CLUB
> By CHARLES A. COMISKEY[34]

Either the original date on the letter was typed wrong, or Comiskey actually did compose it two days before Cicotte's testimony. Bill Burns had named five of the players, but Comiskey and Grabiner had known all eight names for nearly a year.

If Comiskey steered Eddie Cicotte and the rest to the grand jury in an attempt to promote himself as the Savior of Baseball, his plan worked. An outpouring of affection for the Chicago owner filled the newspapers, especially in Chicago, and offers of help for his decimated team came from all corners of the league. The most generous proposal came from the New York Yankees co-owners, Colonel Jacob Ruppert and Colonel T. L. Huston. Their Yankees had been eliminated from pennant contention a few days before, so they sent a telegram to Comiskey that read,

> Your action in suspending players under suspicion, while it wrecks your entire organization and perhaps your cherished life work, not only challenges our admiration, but excites our sympathy and demands our practical assistance. You are making a terrible sacrifice to preserve the integrity of the game. So grave and unforeseen an emergency requires unusual remedies.
>
> Therefore in order that you may play out your schedule, and if necessary, the world series, our entire club is placed at your disposal. We are confident that Cleveland sportsmanship will not permit you to lose by default and will welcome the arrangement. We are equally certain that any technicalities in carrying it out can be readily overcome by action of the National Commission.[35]

Harry Grabiner was touched by the offer. "Of course it is impossible," said the White Sox secretary, "but the offer will bring tears to the old man's eyes."[36]

Now that the story was out, the "Clean Sox," as the papers now called them, were finally able to express their frustrations and disappointments. Red Faber told a reporter, "The playing of the Sox on the Eastern trip made some of the others believe that something was crooked. It looks like we were double-crossed in the World Series last year and in the pennant race this year."[37] Shano Collins agreed. "We suspected some of them in the World Series," he told the *Cleveland Plain Dealer*, "and we suspected them again because of the way of their play on the last eastern trip. Some of them not only didn't try, but really acted as though they didn't want to win."[38]

All seven of the suspended players came in for their share of criticism, but several of the remaining Sox called out Eddie Cicotte by name. As Shano Collins told the *Boston Post*,

> We fought a losing battle all this year. We had a fine team and we seldom were defeated by any wide margin. We had the strength to stay up there to win if everything had been right, and yet at the critical moment something would always happen....
>
> You may remember our last visit this year to Boston. Just before we came there the Red Sox had started a spurt and were beating all comers. This allowed us to creep up to the top, or very near it, for we had been fattening at Cleveland's and New York's expense. And we reached the Hub with a splendid chance to go away out in front.

> Well, we lost all three games; Cicotte was batted out of the box. Our men were hopeless at the bat. The big stickers fell down miserably. I have heard a lot about certain players watching the score board while playing in the Hub and not trying as hard as they might. Well, I'm not going to discuss that. I only know that we lost three straight to the Red Sox, that our defeat put the Indians in first place and that we left Boston with every hope blasted.[39]

It also appeared that some of the Sox were suspiciously interested in the out-of-town scoreboard. If Cleveland and Chicago were both playing at home, or if the Indians played in the East and Chicago in the West, the Cleveland game would be well along before the White Sox began their contest. It seemed to Eddie Collins and others that if the Indians won their game, the Sox would feel free to win theirs, but if Cleveland was behind, the crooked White Sox would contrive to lose. As Byrd Lynn said at season's end, "We lost the pennant because certain players—they are among the eight indicted by the Cook Grand jury—didn't want us to win.... We soon noticed how carefully they studied the scoreboard—more than even the average player does in a pennant race—and that they always made errors which lost us the game when Cleveland and New York were losing. If Cleveland won—we won. If Cleveland lost—we lost. The idea was to keep up the betting odds, but not to let us win the pennant."[40]

Black Sox researcher Bruce S. Allerdice studied Lynn's accusation and found that the backup catcher may well have been correct. Between September 3 and September 27, 1920, the day before the scandal broke, Cleveland and Chicago played on the same day 18 times, not counting the three games they played against each other. On 15 of those dates, Allerdice found, the Indians and White Sox either both won or both lost.[41]

One unidentified Sox player, who may or may not have been Eddie Collins, expressed no sympathy for Cicotte in an interview with *The Sporting News*:

> When we started on our last trip east we had every reason to believe we were on the way to win a pennant.... Then Cicotte and Williams seemed to go bad without reason; Jackson, Felsch and Risberg began dumping the ball to the infield every time we had a chance to score runs. Some of us always had believed we were sold out in the [1919] World Series. When the [crooked] players showed they meant to beat us out of getting in on this one we decided to act. Cicotte was told that he would have to win a certain game or he would be mobbed on the field by the honest players on the team—he won it.... Between double crossing his gambler partners and taking a licking from his team mates he decided, naturally, to double cross.[42]

Even an umpire got into the act. Brick Owens, who umpired the questionable Boston series in early September, said that "Eddie Cicotte laid down in the series with Boston a month ago.... Cicotte would put lots of stuff on the ball up to the third strike ... then he would send over a grooved fast ball without a thing on it. His work could scarcely be detected from the stands, but there was a lot of comment among the players."[43]

In the midst of all this controversy, the now-decimated White Sox still fought for the pennant and had three more games to play in St. Louis. Kid Gleason had to replace two of his starting pitchers (both 20-game winners), the left side of his infield, two power-hitting outfielders, and his key substitute, McMullin. No other major league team has ever had so much of its core ripped out all at once.[44] It was as if a plane crash wiped out most of a club's key performers and the rest had to carry on. Because the Indians won two weekday games while the Sox were idle, the Chicago club stood one and a half games behind the Indians entering the final weekend, and needed to sweep the Browns and hope that Cleveland lost at least two of its four games to the last-place Tigers.

For the first game in St. Louis, played on Friday, October 1, Gleason patched together a lineup with reserves Hervey McClellan at short, Amos Strunk in left, and Eddie Murphy at third. The manager shifted Nemo Leibold to center and installed Bibb Falk, a Texan making his first major league start, in right. Gleason decided to start Faber on Friday and Kerr on Saturday; if a win was still needed in the third contest on Sunday, he would be forced to bring back Faber on one day's rest.

The papers speculated on how the patchwork White Sox would fare in the World Series if they somehow pulled out a pennant, but Red Faber lasted only three innings on Friday, losing to the Browns, 8–6. The Indians gained at least a tie when they split a doubleheader in Detroit that day to keep the clubs two games apart with two to play. Dickey Kerr, once again called upon in the clutch, delivered a 10–7 win on Saturday, but the Indians won in Detroit to clinch the 1920 pennant, their first in the American League. The White Sox sent rookie Joe Kiefer to the mound on Sunday and closed their season with a 16–7 loss. It was a dispiriting end to the most tumultuous campaign in major league history.

When the White Sox returned to Chicago from St. Louis, Comiskey had a surprise for the ten honest players who were with the team in 1919. He gave each man a letter that read,

> As one of the honest ball players of the White Sox team of 1919, I feel that you are deprived of the winner's share of the World Series receipts, through no fault of yours. I do not intend that you, as an honest ball player, should be penalized for your honesty or by reason of the dishonesty of others, and therefore take pleasure in handing you $1,500, this being the difference between the winner's and the loser's share.[45]

Actually, the difference between the winning and losing shares was $1,952.71, but the players appreciated the gesture. They composed a statement as follows:

To the Fans of Chicago:

We, the undersigned players of the White Sox, want the world to know the generosity of our employer, who of his own free will has reimbursed each and every member of our team the difference between the winning and losing share of last year's World Series, amounting to approximately $1,500 each.[46]

The statement was signed by Ray Schalk, Red Faber, Eddie Collins, Shano Collins, Nemo Leibold, Dickey Kerr, Eddie Murphy, Roy Wilkinson, Hervey McClellan, and Byrd Lynn.

11

The Trial

> *One thing that's overlooked in the whole mess is that we could have beat them no matter what the circumstances! Sure, the 1919 White Sox were good. But the 1919 Cincinnati Reds were better. I'll believe that till my dying day.*—Edd Roush, Cincinnati center fielder, 1964[1]

In December of 1920, two months after news of the scandal broke, Kid Gleason talked to reporter Joe Vila of the manager's hometown paper, the *Philadelphia Inquirer*. Vila reminded Gleason that the manager had said after Game One of the Series, "I tell you something was the matter out there.... Certain players aroused my suspicions and I intend to call them down hard." Vila could not print these statements at the time, but now that Gleason's instincts were proven true, the manager faced the daunting task of assembling the 1921 White Sox from the wreckage of the scandal. Said Gleason,

> I don't care to have any of those indicted players remain under my management. They must not be allowed to wear White Sox uniforms or play with any other club in Organized Baseball...
>
> The indicted Chicago players were fools, pure and simple. They fell for a bunch of sure thing gamblers and barred themselves from the game that made them prosperous and would have maintained them handsomely for some time to come.
>
> I had the greatest ball club ever put together when those pinheads went wrong because they couldn't withstand tempting offers to play dishonestly. Yet it was a hard task to obtain proof of their guilt until Cicotte squealed to the grand jury.[2]

Umpire Billy Evans, who wrote a nationally syndicated newspaper column, was especially saddened by Eddie Cicotte's involvement.

> When I heard that Eddie Cicotte was in the frame-up. I could have felt no worse had it been my brother. Cicotte's fall was a blow to me. It was almost enough to destroy one's faith in humanity, for I always regarded Eddie Cicotte as a man worth while.
>
> Cicotte had a remarkable temperament. He never fussed with umpires or players. He was always congenial. Often some Chicago player would start to protest a decision, only to have Cicotte remark that the umpire was right. No matter how many errors his teammates made behind him, he always had a word of cheer for them. Cicotte

11. The Trial

has done so many good things in baseball that I hate to think of his one fatal error."[3]

Though baseball people felt genuine sadness at the fall of Eddie Cicotte, the public made jokes about him. In one gag, an astronomy professor asked his students to name three fixed stars. One eager pupil raised his hand and said, "Cicotte, Jackson, and Williams!" The *Philadelphia Inquirer* called Eddie "the inventor of the self-registering and fast calculating hotel pillow."[4] But when a fan wrote to the *Chicago Tribune* to ask how Cicotte's name was pronounced, the paper replied tersely, "It is not pronounced any more."[5] Or, as a Wisconsin paper put it, "most people would pronounce him a rotten double-crossing crook whose actions would make those of Judas look like those of the Good Samaritan."[6]

No wonder Eddie hid out in Detroit. After his testimony, he abandoned Chicago and secluded himself at home so quickly and completely that one paper asked in a headline, "Has Eddie Cicotte Committed Suicide?"[7] Other articles told of how the young fans and amateur clubs in Detroit returned the trophies and souvenirs Eddie had given them over the years, including the first ball pitched in the 1919 Series, and how his 14-year-old daughter was "in angry tears" over the revelations. One reporter even grabbed a quote from Eddie's wife. Rose Cicotte made it clear that she stood by her husband. "I don't believe a word of all this talk about him,"[8] she said. The man himself, however, kept silent and let his attorney handle things.

Buck Weaver took a different tack. When the grand jury made the indictments public on September 28, the third baseman made a beeline for Comiskey's office to plead his innocence. He remained in Chicago after his suspension, and when a reporter asked if he would testify in front of the grand jury, Weaver grinned. "Not as these other fools have done," he said. "I have been wrongfully accused and I intend to fight. I shall be in major league baseball next year … if not with the White Sox then with some other team. They have nothing on me. I am going to hire the best lawyer in Chicago to defend me and I'm going to be cleared."[9]

While the Black Sox Scandal monopolized the headlines during the fall of 1920, a fierce battle played out in baseball's boardrooms. The three-man National Commission, which had ruled the sport since the American and National leagues made peace in 1903, was on its last legs. Its utter failure to stem the sport's serious gambling problem culminated in the 1919 World Series fiasco, and many club owners demanded the creation of a new Commission to govern all of professional baseball.

Ban Johnson had dominated the National Commission since its formation, and many of the 16 owners were sick of him. The entire National League opposed the increasingly erratic and unpredictable Johnson, and three American League teams—the Yankees, Red Sox, and Comiskey's White Sox—were prepared to join them. Rumor had it that the 11 teams that opposed Johnson were ready to form their own league and leave the other five American League franchises to fend for themselves. These 11 teams demanded a new Commission of three members, all drawn from outside the sport. The names of former President William Howard Taft, General John J. Pershing, and assorted judges and politicians were floated as candidates for the new governing body.

The strongest candidate of all was a colorful, headline-grabbing federal judge from Chicago. Kenesaw Mountain Landis, a 54-year-old jurist, was appointed to the federal bench in 1905 by President Theodore Roosevelt. Landis gained his initial fame by slapping a $29 million fine on the Standard Oil Company in an antitrust case. The fine was rescinded on appeal, but the trial made Landis a national figure. He stayed in the headlines by handing out long sentences to draft evaders during the war years. His shock of white hair, theatrical manner, and instinct for the grand gesture put him in the spotlight, and in the wake of the Black Sox Scandal, Landis emerged as the man whom both the owners and the fans could trust to clean up the game. He was an enthusiastic Chicago Cubs fan, too, a frequent attendee at Wrigley Field. As Landis' friend, humorist Will Rogers, put it, "Somebody said, 'Get that old boy who sits behind first base all the time. He's out there every day anyhow.'"[10]

Johnson tried his best to save the National Commission, which had been his power base for 17 years. With a majority of the major league owners opposing him, he turned to the minor leagues for support. Finding none there, he finally admitted defeat, paving the way for a new Commission. Before long, the owners agreed to make the Commission a one-man

Judge Kenesaw Mountain Landis in 1907. He became the first Commissioner of Baseball in 1920 (Library of Congress).

11. The Trial

governing body. As National League President John Heydler explained, "We want a man as chairman who will rule with an iron hand.... Baseball has lacked a hand like that for years. It needs it now worse than ever. Therefore, it is our object to appoint a big man to lead the new commission."[11] That "big man" was Kenesaw Mountain Landis.

On November 12, 1920, Landis accepted the post as sole Commissioner of Baseball at a salary of $42,500 per year. Though Landis remained on the federal bench for two more years, he now wielded almost dictatorial power over all of professional baseball. His first order of business was to rid the sport of gambling and corruption, and he immediately set to work. On January 30, 1921, Landis gave a speech in which he said, "Now that I am in baseball, just watch the game I play. If I catch any crook in baseball, the rest of his life is going to be a pretty hot one. I'll go to any means and to anything possible to see that he gets a real penalty for his offense."[12]

The case against the Black Sox proceeded slowly. Eddie Cicotte and the other seven Black Sox had been indicted by the Cook County grand jury the previous October, but the state attorney's office changed hands in the 1920 fall elections. The new prosecutor, Robert Crowe, had to start the investigation from scratch because the defeated incumbent, Maclay Hoyne, took all his staff with him. The new prosecutor needed time to assemble his case, but the changeover had disrupted the office, and the files were in disarray. Most notably, the testimonies of Cicotte, Williams, and Jackson, along with their waivers of immunity, were missing. The prosecutor could reconstruct the testimonies from the stenographer's notes, but the waivers, which the three players had signed, could not be replaced.

Hoyne was no help and may have tried to sabotage the investigation. Soon after his defeat at the ballot box, Hoyne left Chicago for a vacation and made himself unavailable to consult with Crowe and his staff. Perhaps Hoyne was simply not interested in the Black Sox case from the beginning; in a city sinking under the weight of organized crime and political corruption, Hoyne may have considered the baseball scandal too minor to demand his attention. He had only investigated the possible fixed game between the Cubs and the Phillies due to pressure from the newspapers, and he assigned the case to Hartley Replogle, the least experienced member of his staff. The immunity waivers disappeared during Hoyne's vacation, and either Hoyne "lost" them to make Crowe's job harder, or someone in Hoyne's office stole them at the behest of parties unknown.

Both Hoyne and Crowe faced a major obstacle to an effective prosecution—the fact that there was, at the time, no law on the books in the state of Illinois that made the fixing of a sporting event a crime. The indictment charged Eddie Cicotte and his teammates with "conspiracy to commit an illegal act," but such a vague charge would probably not stand up to legal scrutiny. Crowe and his assistants would have to strengthen the indictment if they hoped to succeed at trial.

During this time, Eddie Cicotte holed up in his hometown. He hired a lawyer, a Detroit friend named Daniel P. Cassidy, who advised the pitcher to lay low and stay out of the newspapers. When Hoyne, the outgoing state's attorney, floated the possibility in mid-November of 1920 that Eddie might be awarded immunity from prosecution if he agreed to testify against his teammates, Cassidy quickly shot that idea down. Eddie would stick with his story—that he accepted the bribe money, but played the games honestly after hitting Morrie Rath with his second pitch of Game One.

The eight players and five gamblers, among them Abe Attell, Bill Burns, Hal Chase, and Sport Sullivan, were arraigned in Chicago on February 14, 1921. Eddie and all the other Black Sox—even Chick Gandil and Swede Risberg, both of whom traveled from California—were present, but the gamblers made themselves scarce. The presiding judge, William Dever, scheduled the start of the trial for March 12, but Crowe could not assemble his case in time. The prosecutor asked the court to dismiss the indictments. He then impaneled a new grand jury, which voted new indictments on March 26. Crowe added five more gamblers to the list of defendants, with the trial slated to begin that summer.

The court issued arrest warrants for all the defendants, but Eddie Cicotte returned to Chicago voluntarily to post bond. He put up $5,000 worth of Liberty Bonds to secure his release. Chick Gandil, by contrast, was arrested in Los Angeles and spent a night in jail before the state sent him by train to Chicago. He, too, posted bond. However, though the state secured the presence of seven of the eight ballplayers, some of the gamblers slipped through the net. Sport Sullivan simply disappeared, and both Hal Chase (who defiantly told the papers, "If they want me, let 'em extradite me"[13]) and Abe Attell successfully defeated extradition requests in California and New York respectively. This reduced the number of defendants to eight players and eight gamblers.

That number dropped by one when Fred McMullin, working as a carpenter in California, told the prosecutor's office that he could not afford to post bond, and that the state of Illinois would have to pay his way to Chicago. The prosecutors denied his request and issued a warrant for his arrest, but California refused to extradite him, and the prosecutors dropped the former utility infielder from the case. McMullin had batted only twice in the World Series, belting a single in Game One and grounding out in Game Two, and did not play at all in the field. He was the least important of the eight players, so Crowe and his staff decided to postpone his case.

The new Commissioner, Judge Landis, faced a problem. The players awaited trial, but had not been convicted, nor would they be for at least

11. The Trial

White Sox owner Charles Comiskey (left) and American League president Ban Johnson around 1912. By 1919, the two men were bitter enemies (Library of Congress).

several months. Were the seven Black Sox (less the retired Chick Gandil) eligible to play in 1921? How could Eddie Cicotte and the others return to the White Sox and resume their careers as if nothing had happened? Even if Charles Comiskey had wanted to get rid of them, what other team would take them on? Landis solved the dilemma by ruling Eddie and his teammates ineligible for the 1921 campaign. "I deeply regret the postponement of these cases," said the new Commissioner. "However, baseball is not powerless to protect itself. All of the indicted players have today been placed on the ineligible list."[14] A few days later, Charles Comiskey released all seven of the Black Sox unconditionally.

Ban Johnson had, by this time, taken over the investigation, using American League funds to gather evidence and hire detectives. Johnson was more determined than ever to punish the errant ballplayers, and during the spring of 1921, he and George Gorman, the new assistant state's attorney, decided that they needed one of the players to turn on the others. They wanted one of the Black Sox to describe the inner workings of the plot to implicate his teammates, so they decided to "build some fires" around Eddie Cicotte, the first man to confess the previous fall. Perhaps, they suggested, Johnson's detectives should "hound" Eddie until he agreed to cooperate. However, Daniel Cassidy, who had rejected a similar proposal from Maclay Hoyne, put up a barrier between Eddie and the outside world. Cassidy made sure that the pitcher cut himself off from friends, reporters, and former teammates so completely that no one could penetrate the bubble. As Detroit Tigers owner Frank Navin, a good friend of both Cassidy and Ban Johnson, advised the league president, "I cannot see how a detective would have a chance to get in touch with Cicotte."[15] Eddie remained out of sight until the start of the trial.

Johnson and Gorman gave up on turning one of the ballplayers, so they focused their efforts on bringing Sleepy Bill Burns to their side. Burns had fled Chicago for western Texas, and when Billy Maharg offered to find the pitcher turned fixer, Johnson took him up on it. Johnson and Maharg traveled to Texas, where Maharg, after a series of false leads, located Burns in a remote fishing village near the Rio Grande. He brought Burns to a meeting with Johnson in Del Rio, where the American League president offered to drop the charges against him if Burns would testify for the prosecution. Burns agreed and returned with Johnson to Chicago, where Gorman grilled him extensively. Burns, as Gorman discovered, was "not a talkative man and requires a lot of coaching,"[16] but the effort to woo Burns was a successful one. Now the prosecution team had what it wanted—an insider ready to spill the beans.

Once the trial began, Eddie and the other ex–White Sox were required to stay in Chicago, so they rented apartments and settled in for a long summer. There was nothing much to do aside from conferring with their attorneys, and the former players suffered from boredom as the weeks dragged by. Joe Jackson owned an interest in a pool room on the city's south side, so Eddie and the others spent a lot of time there, playing pool and discussing the trial. Eddie's wife, Rose, and their children visited from Detroit whenever they could, but for the most part the ex-pitcher was alone with his thoughts for much of the spring and summer. He also faced another problem. In November of 1920, the Bureau of Internal Revenue informed Eddie that the $10,000 payoff he admitted to taking in his testimony was subject to the federal income tax. Eddie now owed a tax bill of at least $2,000. He also faced a possible indictment for tax evasion.

The trial finally began on June 27, 1921, during the hottest summer ever recorded in Chicago up to that time, with jury selection, preliminary motions, and the like. Seven of the eight accused ballplayers, excepting Fred McMullin, were there, but only four minor gamblers stood in the dock with them. None of the main fixers were present, as Arnold Rothstein was never indicted, Abe Attell and Hal Chase had escaped extradition, Burns and Maharg joined the prosecution, and Ban Johnson could not build enough of a case against Sport Sullivan to bother pursuing him. That left four gamblers, all mere small fry in the scheme of things, and the seven players, who would be sure to draw most of the attention. The judge was the 38-year-old Hugo Friend, who had been

11. The Trial

appointed by the governor of Illinois to the Cook County Circuit Court only nine months before.

Daniel Cassidy wisely allowed Benedict Short, a former state's attorney who also represented Williams and Jackson, to handle the bulk of Eddie's defense, but Cassidy earned his fee during the early stages of the trial. The prosecution intended to call several of the Clean Sox, including Eddie Collins, Ray Schalk, and Kid Gleason, to the stand, most likely to detail instances of crooked ballplaying. Their testimony would have been highly damaging to the defense, so Cassidy decided to tell his friend Frank Navin a story that Eddie Cicotte had related to him. On June 30, Cassidy informed Navin that Collins, Schalk, and others were themselves guilty of some shady dealings during the championship season of 1917. Specifically, all the Chicago players, Clean Sox and Black Sox alike, had contributed to a fund to pay off the Detroit Tigers "as a reward for Detroit not playing their best against them in the final games of the season."[17]

The games to which Cassidy referred occurred on Labor Day weekend in 1917. The Tigers played two doubleheaders against the White Sox in Chicago on Sunday, September 2, and Monday, September 3, losing all four games, with Eddie winning two of them. The four wins gave the White Sox a commanding lead over the second-place Red Sox in the pennant race, increasing their margin from three and a half games to six and a half in only two days. A few weeks later, said Cassidy, the White Sox paid $45 apiece into a fund, which was collected by Chick Gandil and handed over to Tigers pitcher Bill James for distribution to the Detroit players.

Navin informed Ban Johnson of this potentially embarrassing development, though neither the Tigers owner nor the league president believed it. Just to be safe, Johnson interviewed Eddie Collins and asked him about the story. "It was my conviction," wrote Johnson in a letter to Navin, "[that Collins] would register an unqualified denial."[18] Instead, to Johnson's amazement, Collins admitted that a "pot" had been collected and given to the Tigers, but insisted that it not a bribe. It was, instead, intended to reward the Detroit club for beating Boston three times in mid–September, virtually knocking the Red Sox out of the race. The state's attorney called in Ray Schalk and Kid Gleason, who corroborated Collins' account. The players claimed that handing gifts to other teams that helped them, a practice called "tipping," was commonplace in baseball at the time.

Obviously, it was now too risky to put the Clean Sox on the stand, where the defense would bring up the 1917 incident during cross-examination, smearing the good name of baseball with yet another scandal. This little bit of legal blackmail, carried out by Eddie Cicotte and Daniel Cassidy, forced the prosecution to drop the idea of using the honest White Sox to tar their former teammates. It also enraged Ban Johnson, who discovered that Ray Schalk had apprised Commissioner Landis of the episode five months earlier. Landis had not bothered to share that information with Johnson, who did not find out about it until the trial was under way.

Jury selection proceeded at a snail's pace. Both prosecution and defense were allowed up to 120 preemptory challenges to the 600 members of the jury pool, and after two weeks of challenges and dismissals, Judge Friend ordered the two sides to speed it up. He threatened to schedule court sessions on nights and weekends if necessary to finish the process, and this threat worked. On July 16, the jury of 12 men, all white and mostly from the working class, was impaneled. After Judge Friend issued rulings on another flurry of motions from the defense team, the trial began in earnest.

It only took one day for Eddie to grow frustrated with the lawyers and court officials who constantly mispronounced his name. During a heated verbal battle between defense lawyers and prosecutors over the confessions of Jackson, Cicotte, and Williams, Eddie suddenly stood up and asked for attention. "I beg your honor's pardon," he said, "but would you please have it entered in the court record that my name is Edward V. Cicotte pronounced 'See-kott,' with the accent on the 'See.'"

"Let it be so entered," agreed the judge after a burst of laughter in the courtroom.[19]

Sleepy Bill Burns, the state's star witness, testified for three days, exuding confidence throughout. He wore a green checkered suit with a lavender shirt and a bow tie. He repeatedly wiped his forehead with a handkerchief, as the courtroom was brutally hot, but his self-assurance never wavered. Burns, examined by assistant state's attorney Edward Prindiville, described the scene at the Sinton Hotel in Cincinnati on the day before Game One of the Series.

> Q. [What players were there at the meeting]?
> A. There was Gandil, Fred McMullin, Lefty Williams, Happy Felsch, Eddie Cicotte, Swede Risberg, and Buck Weaver.
> Q. How about Jackson?
> A. I didn't see him there.
> Q. Did you have any conversation with them?
> A. I told them I had the $100,000 to handle the throwing of the World Series. I also told them that I had the names of the men who were going to finance it.
> Q. Who were the financiers?
> A. They were Rothstein, Attell, and Bennett.
> Q. Did the players themselves make any statements concerning the order of the games to be thrown?
> A. Gandil and Cicotte said the first two games should be thrown. He said, however, that it didn't matter to the players. They would throw them in any order that the financiers desired.
> Q. [What else was said?]
> A. Gandil and Cicotte said they'd throw the first and second games. Cicotte said

11. The Trial

he'd throw the first game if had to throw the baseball clear out of the Cincinnati park.[20]

Judge Friend ruled that, since Burns had testified to the existence of a conspiracy, the prosecution could question Burns about the meeting at the Ansonia in mid–September. Burns revealed that Chick Gandil and Eddie Cicotte had presented the game-fixing proposition to him; the players, not the gamblers, had initiated the scheme. When Burns finally stepped down, having done damage to the defense of several ballplayers, especially Gandil and Cicotte, the state tried to enter the grand jury testimony from the previous October into evidence. The defense immediately objected, because the prosecutors could not produce the original transcripts and, more importantly, the signed waivers of immunity from Cicotte, Jackson, and Williams.

This is where the myth of the "signed confessions" began. The newspapers claimed that the signed confessions of the three players (actually, the record of their testimonies) and their waivers of immunity had been pilfered by parties unknown, and this idea forms one of the main dramatic incidents of Eliot Asinof's *Eight Men Out*, and in the movie of Asinof's book. Chicago was a wildly corrupt city in the Roaring Twenties, and it seemed possible to the casual observer that some interested party, perhaps Arnold Rothstein, or other characters stole the documents to derail the trial.

The truth is that there were no "signed confessions." When the players testified, their words were taken down by court reporters in shorthand and transcribed later. Witnesses do not sign their testimonies and probably never see the paper copies. The prosecutors could, and did, re-create the grand jury testimonies from the shorthand notes, which they still had. In 2013, Leland's auction house issued a public offer of $1,000,000 for the missing signed confessions; thanks to the research of Jacob Pomrenke, William F. Lamb, and others in the Society of American Baseball Research, we now know that such documents never existed.

A bigger problem for the prosecutors was the absence of the waivers of immunity, which had been signed by Cicotte, Jackson, and Williams. Without them, the state could not prove that they made their testimonies voluntarily, nor could they prove that they knew their rights at the time. Judge Friend decided to inquire about the waivers directly. With the jury out of the room, Hartley Replogle, the former state's attorney, testified that the waivers were signed voluntarily and with no promises of immunity. Judge Friend then called Eddie Cicotte to the stand.

Eddie told the court that he met Replogle in Alfred Austrian's office, and that Austrian told him,

> Replogle has the goods on you, Eddie. You know this will be a long trial, you don't want your wife and babies here then. Now come clean with Replogle and he'll take

care of you. They took me to Judge McDonald. He asked me if I couldn't tell him more about the gamblers. I told him I couldn't and McDonald then said, "go ahead and indict him."

I said to Replogle on my way to the grand jury room, "Don't this go, about what you and Replogle promised me?" He said "Sure it does." Then I went before the grand jury.[21]

Prosecutor George Gorman, who claimed that Cicotte confessed because he was "panic-stricken" at Billy Maharg's revelations in the *Philadelphia North American*, took over the questioning.

Q. Didn't you tell Austrian the whole story?
A. Yes, I did.
Q. Didn't you sign a statement there?
A. No.
Q. Didn't a stenographer take your statement?
A. I don't remember.
Q. Did you cry bitterly in Judge McDonald's office?
A. There were tears in my eyes. I cried plenty of times, but not bitterly.
Q. In the grand jury room an immunity waiver was read to you?
A. Yes.
Q. You signed it?
A. I signed something; I don't know what it was.

Gorman read the text of the waiver to the pitcher.

Q. Didn't Replogle tell you what you said could be used against you and read the waiver?
A. I don't remember.
Q. Didn't Replogle read something to you and didn't you sign it?
A. Yes, sir. When I told Judge McDonald I didn't know any more than I told him he got sore and said, "What are you trying to do, bull me?" I told him Austrian and Replogle had promised to take care of me and then they took me into the wash room while they talked. Austrian had told me I would not be imprisoned or have to pay a fine.
Q. Didn't you tell Judge McDonald that you threw the 1919 World Series and got $10,000 for it?[22]

A flurry of objections to that question ended Eddie's testimony, but not before Gorman proclaimed that Eddie was "perjuring himself when he says he is telling us everything about this conversation with Judge McDonald."[23] Joe Jackson later told a similar story; he, too, did not understand what he was signing, and he trusted Austrian and Replogle to look after his interests.

In the end, the prosecution won a partial victory. The judge allowed the confessions to be used against the three players; however, all references to other players and defendants would have to be redacted. This brought a halt to the trial, as Eddie's grand jury testimony had to be scrubbed of all mentions of Weaver, Felsch, Risberg, and the rest. The names of the other players

11. The Trial

were replaced by "Mr. Blank" to keep them from being identified. It took several days of meticulous editing to make Eddie's testimony acceptable to the judge and the defense. Finally, the text was read into the trial record by Special Prosecutor Edward Prindiville and the court stenographer. This process took a while as the defendants, lawyers, and spectators wilted in the heat.

The case against Eddie Cicotte was the strongest of all the defendants, as Eddie had admitted to performing an act that was part of the conspiracy; specifically, hitting Morrie Rath as a signal that the fix was on. Jackson and Williams, like Cicotte, confessed to receiving bribe money, but insisted that they played to win anyway, as Eddie claimed to do after hitting Rath. The other players and gamblers appeared to be in the clear, as the redacted testimony could not tie them to the scheme at all (coupled with their understandable reluctance to take the stand and incriminate themselves). Indeed, Judge Friend declared that he would not let a conviction stand against Weaver, Felsch, and one of the gamblers.

But the possibility of conviction and jail time still loomed over Eddie Cicotte, and the prosecutors, in their closing arguments, hammered away at him. Said Edward Prindiville:

> He said he'd throw the ball over the fence if necessary to lose the first game. And what happened in the first game? Cicotte, the American League's greatest pitcher, hurling with a heavy heart—by his own confession—and a pocket made heavy by $10,000 in graft, was beaten 9 to 1. No wonder he lost. The pocket loaded with filth for which he sold his soul and his friends was too much. It overbalanced him and he lost.[24]
>
> I say, gentlemen, that the evidence shows that a swindle and con game has been worked on the American public. The crime in this case warrants the most severe punishment of the law. The crime strikes at the heart of every red blooded citizen and every kid who plays on a sand lot. This county is for sending criminals to the penitentiary whether they are idols of the ball diamond or gangsters guilty of robbery with a gun. The state is asking in this case a verdict of five years in the penitentiary and a fine of $2,000 for each defendant.[25]

George Gorman followed Prindiville. He asked the jury to remember the fans:

> In his confession Cicotte tells how the games were fixed. Then we have the spectacle of the public going to the game believing it was on the square. Thousands of men throughout the chilly hours of the night, crouched in line waiting for the opening of the first World Series game. All morning they waited, eating a sandwich perhaps, never daring to leave their places for a moment. There they waited to see the great Cicotte pitch a ballgame. Gentlemen, they went to see a ballgame. But all they saw was a con game![26]

Defense attorney Benedict Short replied that "there may have been an agreement entered into by the defendants to take the money offered by scheming gamblers, but it has not been shown that the players had any intention of defrauding the public or of bringing the game into ill repute. They believed, we contend, any arrangement they may have made was a secret one and would, therefore, reflect no discredit on the national pastime as it would never be disclosed."[27] Defense attorney A. Morgan Frumberg, who represented two of the gamblers, reminded the jurors that Arnold Rothstein was not in the courtroom. "Why was [Rothstein] not indicted? ... Why were these underpaid ballplayers, these penny-ante gamblers from Des Moines and St. Louis who bet a few nickels perhaps on the World Series, brought here to be the goats in this case? Ask the powers in baseball. Ask Ban Johnson who pulled the strings in this case. Ask him who saved Arnold Rothstein."[28]

On August 2, when final arguments were complete, the defense won its biggest victory of the trial when Judge Friend ruled that the fact that the players had thrown games for money was not sufficient reason to convict them. He required the jurors to find that the players and gamblers did so with the intent to defraud the public and harm Charles Comiskey's business. As the White Sox enjoyed record attendance in 1920—they drew more than 10,000 fans per game through the gates of Comiskey Park for the first time that year—Comiskey could hardly claim that he was harmed or that the fans felt defrauded. If anyone was still in danger of conviction after this ruling, it was Eddie Cicotte, who had performed an act to further the conspiracy, but now even Cicotte appeared to be safe. It was clear to all that Eddie did not throw two World Series games to harm Comiskey or defraud the fans. He did it because he needed the money.

The prosecutors probably knew they were destined to lose as the jurors left to deliberate the fate of the defendants. A little more than two and a half hours later, at about 11:30 at night, the jurors returned with their verdicts. They declared all the players and gamblers not guilty on all counts. They had taken only one ballot.

The gallery exploded with cheers. When the final not guilty verdict was announced, the defendants rushed in a mass toward the jury to shake their hands. Eddie was the first to reach the jury box and enthusiastically pumped the hands of every juror he could reach. He shouted at the jury foreman, "Thanks! I knew you'd do it!" It was hard to hear anything in the hubbub of voices and cheers, but one juror said to the pitcher, "Eddie, we were talking the other night about you, and I want you to know that every man on this jury hopes that the next time he sees you you'll be in the center of the diamond putting over strikes."[29]

Joe Jackson told the assembled reporters, "The jury could not have returned a fairer verdict, but I don't want to go back to organized baseball. I am through with it." Buck Weaver said, "I had nothing to do with this so-called conspiracy; I believe that I should get my old position back. I cannot express my contempt for Bill Burns." Lefty Williams asked, "How could the verdict

11. The Trial

Eddie, in bow tie, shakes hands with the jurors after his acquittal on August 2, 1921. Buck Weaver is in the center of the picture, and Happy Felsch is at right (author's collection).

have been anything else?" Gandil blamed "those two liars, Bill Burns and Billy Maharg."[30]

Eddie Cicotte was happy with the outcome, but had little to add. "All I want to do is to get to Detroit. Talk, you say? I talked once in this building, never again," he said.[31] Eddie rushed to a Western Union office and sent a two-word telegram to his wife in Detroit. The message said "Not guilty" and was signed "Daddy."[32] It was past midnight by this time, but the players and jurors adjourned to a nearby Italian restaurant and celebrated into the wee hours.

State's Attorney Robert E. Crowe announced that there would be no further prosecution of the players. "The State's through," he said. Three years later, Crowe would face off against Clarence Darrow in one of the most famous murder trials of the 20th century, the Loeb and Leopold case.

American League President Ban Johnson issued a statement that read,

> The trial of the indicted players, which closed yesterday, uncovered the greatest crime that it was possible to commit in baseball. The fact that the outfit was freed by the Cook County jury does not alter the conditions one iota, or minimize the magnitude of the offense.

> The players are as odious to a clean, right thinking public as the crooks and the thieves they dealt with. The energetic prosecution by the State clearly indicates that crimes of this character will not be permitted to go unchallenged.
>
> Failure to obtain convictions is disappointing, but a lesson has been taught.[33]

Charles Comiskey was relieved. He had hinted in the past that he might take at least some of the Black Sox back, but the trial had disabused him of that notion. Now he would not object if they continued their careers, but he did not want to rehire any of them, especially not Eddie Cicotte. Said Comiskey,

> I have no comment to offer on the outcome of the baseball trial. However, Cicotte confessed to me that he helped "throw" the world's series of 1919 and also implicated the other seven players. Until such time as Cicotte can explain to me that confession I will have nothing to do with him or with them.
>
> I do not believe the White Sox fans want to see the players back. It is my duty to do what they want. That's the way I make my living.
>
> I have nothing against the players and would like to see them back into the game. They might get with another team in the league. I am glad they were freed.[34]

If Comiskey's statement offered hope to Eddie Cicotte and the other defendants, Judge Landis quickly dashed it. He had already decided that no matter how the trial came out, the eight Black Sox had to go. He issued a statement that read,

> Regardless of the verdict of juries, no player that throws a ball game, no player that entertains proposals or promises to throw a game, no player that sits in a conference with a bunch of crooked players and gamblers where the ways and means of throwing games are discussed, and does not promptly tell his club about it, will ever again play professional baseball.
>
> Of course, I don't know if any of these men will apply for reinstatement, but if they do, the above are at least a few of the rules that will be enforced. Just keep in mind, regardless of the verdict of juries, baseball is entirely competent to protect itself against crooks, both inside and outside the game.[35]

12

Outlaw Ball

Cicotte, the poor boy doing the best he could
On a pair of knees so knocked they couldn't betray a pitch.
The French-Canadian family man who couldn't say Yes, and couldn't say No.
And so he woke the morning after
In someone else's room at the Warner Hotel
With Rothstein G's under his pillow
And a new saying for Americans on his lips,
"I did it for the wife and kids."
—"The Swede Is a Hard Guy," poem by Nelson Algren, 1942[1]

If Eddie and his teammates thought their acquittals would clear a path back to major league baseball, their hopes were quickly dashed by Commissioner Landis. Eddie and the other Black Sox were now faced with the reality that their professional baseball careers were over. Baseball was all they knew. None had gained much education—Eddie had quit school at 12, while Jackson was illiterate—so they had to keep playing ball. They would have to make their own way on the fringes of the game. During and after the trial, the Black Sox set up games to play on the weekends in and around Chicago and in neighboring states. Despite, or perhaps because of, their notoriety, people were willing to pay to see them play. The players discovered that passing the hat at the games brought in much more money than settling for a set fee beforehand, so they played, collected the money, and divided it among themselves.

Eddie stood aloof, at least for a while. "I'll never throw another ball unless it is in a major league,"[2] he told a reporter in late July as the trial dragged on. But his family's need for money outweighed his reservations. The papers said that the Black Sox earned as much as $100 to $200 per man for a single Sunday game, so Eddie put on his old White Sox uniform and joined his teammates on the diamond once more.

The fields that he played on, with all-dirt infields, bumpy outfields, and no clubhouse, were a huge step down in quality from Comiskey Park, but it was baseball, and Eddie was determined to play, one way or another. He spent a few days at home in Detroit after the trial and then was eager to hit the road. "If I am not reinstated by Judge Landis," he told the press a few days after his acquittal, "I will join the 'boys' in a tour through the country. If they don't go I will play independent ball, but I'll play this summer, you can tell the world that."[3] He claimed to have received 42 offers to pitch for independent teams.

A few days after the conclusion of the trial, Eddie and three other Black Sox headed to Oklahoma for a two-week tour of the state. A promoter named J. C. Hunt from Oilton, a recently settled oil boom town northeast of Oklahoma City, had wired an offer to Buck Weaver in July. Weaver turned it down, but Eddie, Chick Gandil, Swede Risberg, and Joe Jackson took him up on it. They traveled to Oklahoma in mid–August for a series of games in Duncan, Ada, El Reno, and Lawton, among other cities.

Black Sox researcher Ron Coleman, who wrote an article on the tour for the Society for American Baseball Research Black Sox newsletter in 2018, found that the four Black Sox played at least 11 games in Oklahoma and won all of them for which records could be found. Eddie Cicotte pitched in every game, and only a few of the contests were close ones. The people of Oklahoma, a state that had joined the Union only 14 years before, would now see the real major leaguers that they read about in the papers, and the promoter expected large crowds. Predictably, some objected to the presence of the recently acquitted Black Sox, but the *El Reno Daily Democrat* gave them a hearty thumbs-up:

> Every man, woman and child who wants to see Cicotte, Jackson, Felsch and company perform at Legion park is requested to appear at the mayor's office at the city hall tomorrow morning and make their opinions known. These men have been exonerated by the courts and we must respect the law.... Let's revere the law and go out and see Cicotte, Jackson, Felsch and Co. perform at Legion park next Tuesday.[4]

The *Wichita Daily Times* saw it differently:

> Despite the fact that the Chicago Black Sox are generally regarded as guilty as they were before their recent trial, and despite the fact that it was thought that no fans who called himself a real fan would ever turn out to see them play, Duncan promoters have decided to take a chance and have arranged a game for them with the Duncan club to be held in the near future.
>
> Yes, the Black Sox are among us or will be in a few days. Jackson, Felsch, Risberg, Gandil, Cicotte and Williams will all be in Duncan soon to give the fans the horse laugh as they did in Chicago when "acquitted" by a jury of "12 tried and true men."
>
> The players know that they cannot play in the larger cities and have evidently turned their attention to the smaller ones. Real fans have black-balled them.[5]

The Black Sox also had Judge Landis on their tail. Landis and J. H. Farrell, president of the National Association (minor leagues), wrote the promoters to remind them that Cicotte and company were banned from all professional ballparks. Eddie responded by offering to pitch a game in Oklahoma City, the state capital, for free. When reports emerged that the attendance at the opening games in Duncan failed to meet expectations, Cicotte breezily assured a reporter from El Reno, the next stop on the tour, that "six thousand fans jammed in the park to watch them play at Duncan, the largest crowd that ever attended a baseball game in Southern Oklahoma." Eddie and the Black Sox demolished their opponents at El Reno in a 17–2 win, and the local paper reported that Eddie struck out every man in El Reno's lineup save one at least once.[6]

Despite Eddie's air of confidence, the crowds were not as big as the promoter hoped, and public resistance to the Black Sox built by the day. Oklahoma City's main paper, the *Daily Oklahoman*, was especially rough on Eddie Cicotte, stating that the former White Sox pitcher "came into our midst to capitalize your notorious reputation as a crook." The writer continued, "Chances are Oklahoma will remember you—with deep humiliation and regret—long after the ill-gotten dollars you have carried out of this state have gone the same route as that bundle of bills you said you found under your pillow after that game you admitted you purposely lost."[7]

By August 27, even the *El Reno Daily Democrat* had turned on them in an article titled, "A Man Is Known by the Company He Keeps."

> Soon there will be nothing but bandits playing the baseball profession in this state. El Reno is besmirched by affiliating with the "Black Sox" and hence will carry the contagion to our sister city, Yukon. Incidentally, Duncan, Hobart, Lawton, Oilton, Guthrie, Ponca City, and a host of other municipalities are infected by associating with Ed Cicotte and are unfit to play with. Verily, it would seem that if Judge Landis persists in his contempt for the courts, baseball will be unable to recruit its ranks from [Oklahoma].[8]

The tour concluded with a Labor Day contest in Guthrie, in which Eddie spun a 6–0 shutout of the locals. The moment the Oklahoma trip was finished, Eddie and two other Black Sox hurried to McDonough County, Illinois, a farming and mining area in the western part of the state. The two small towns of Colchester (population 1,400 at the time) and the county seat of Macomb (population 6,700) were locked in a fierce baseball rivalry. The teams had played four times during the summer of 1921, with Colchester winning twice and Macomb twice. Now, on Sunday, September 11, the two teams squared off for the final game of the year. This game would decide the McDonough County championship.

Both teams had used "ringers" that summer, usually players with minor-league experience who could be counted on to dominate the locals. This time, a Colchester booster named Henry "Kelly" Wagle, a businessman and bootlegger who ran rum between Chicago and Kansas City, went all out. Wagle figured that if he could hire a ringer or two to bolster his hometown team, why not hire the best? Why not hire a pitcher who won 209 major league games and a hitter with a career batting average of .356? And why not add one of baseball's slickest-fielding shortstops?

Eddie Cicotte, Swede Risberg, and Joe Jackson signed one-day contracts—most likely for a few hundred dollars apiece, paid in advance—to play for Colchester. Wagle insisted that the signing remain a secret until game day, so the three Black Sox did not arrive in Macomb, the site of the contest, until just before game time. Many fans recognized the three when they stepped onto the field, and the rest found out when the umpire announced Cicotte as the starting pitcher. The local paper called it "the surprise of a lifetime, as no one could conceive of the bigness of the deal, not thinking Colchester was able to handle a deal of this magnitude."[9]

The Macomb fans jeered the Black Sox lustily (though their club had tried, and failed, to land Lefty Williams for the afternoon), and the Macomb team promoter, a man named Thompson, complained that the game should not be played with the "blackest of the Black Sox." One fan pointed to the red, white, and blue stockings that Cicotte wore, probably left over from the 1917 World Series, and shouted, "You've got a lot of guts to wear those colors."[10] Others razzed Jackson for his decision to play ball in the shipyards during the war. The Black Sox were used to such comments. They ignored the heckling and buckled down to the task at hand.

The Macomb club had no chance that afternoon. Eddie toyed with them, allowing only four hits and striking out 11 batters. Eddie walked no one and banged out two hits himself in a 4–0 win. It was just another Sunday for the Black Sox, though the Macomb newspaper expressed its displeasure in its pages. "Colchester won a ballgame yesterday and Macomb lost one," the paper said, "but both teams lost something that means a lot more than winning or losing…. It is not 'sport' to engage or play these men who have sold out their clubs and their friends. If the 'Black Sox' are 'out in the sticks to get the money,' as one player put it, the [paper] won't give any of its space to help them do it."[11]

Swede Risberg, the strong-armed shortstop, played outlaw ball with Eddie in 1921 and 1922 (author's collection).

Eddie then separated from the other Black Sox and chased one-game offers from teams near and far, but Commissioner Landis was not yet through with him. When the Saginaw club of the Michigan-Ontario League tried to hire Eddie to pitch on a Sunday in late September, Landis sent the club a bluntly-worded missive, threatening to permanently ban from professional baseball anyone who played with or against any of the former Black Sox, including Eddie Cicotte. Saginaw quickly rescinded its offer. In Bellefontaine, Ohio, on October 2, Eddie was "hooted from the field" by the local fans, who objected to his presence. He was slated to pitch against Zanesville for the championship of Logan County, but the players on both teams were afraid of Judge Landis, and the umpire threatened to cancel the contest if Cicotte took the mound.[12]

He even found trouble in his home state of Michigan. In mid–September, a club in Lansing, the state capital, dropped its offer to Eddie after fans and players raised objections to his participation in a Sunday contest. Two weeks earlier, he pitched for a team in Northville, outside of Detroit, but the manager neither introduced him to his teammates nor announced his name to the fans. Eddie won the game, collected his fee of $100, and left before anyone recognized him.

Undeterred, Eddie put his uniform on again in the spring of 1922. This time, he joined Swede Risberg on a team called the Ex-Major League All Stars. Their business manager was a theater executive from Chicago named David Meek, who had formed his own entertainment agency with the Black Sox as one of his first clients. Meek and his agency allowed Risberg and Cicotte to find players to fill the roster, and the first two who signed on were Happy Felsch and Buck Weaver. The rest of the team was comprised of amateurs and semi-pros who agreed to a salary of $100 a week, with the Black Sox and Meek splitting the rest.

Business was slow at first. Risberg and Meek sent out postcards advertising the team and looking for games, but some small-town teams resisted the notorious Black Sox. As one manager from Ironwood, Michigan, put it, "We don't care how much money it would mean to us to have a game with players of this kind. We are willing to sacrifice a hundred dollars or so to keep our clean name in the national pastime."[13] Other teams avoided the Ex-Major League All Stars because they expected severe criticism if they took the field against Risberg, Cicotte, and the other banned players. As spring turned to summer, Meek found opportunities in the small communities of northern Wisconsin. Eddie Cicotte, two years removed from big league competition, was still good enough to mow down the locals, and the strong-armed Risberg took turns on the mound with equal success. The Ex-Major League All Stars, playing on dusty fields with patchy grass and rickety benches, won almost all their games against teams from Hurley, Stevens Point, and other Wisconsin towns.

The Black Sox were winning, but trouble was never far away. In the middle of the tour, Risberg and Cicotte signed to play a game for Appleton, Wisconsin, of the Fox River Valley League on June 11. Not only did the two Black Sox arrive late, after the game was already out of hand, but the other league teams were so angry at the signing that they threatened to kick Appleton out of the league. After two weeks of argument, the league allowed Appleton to keep its franchise.

Commissioner Landis posed another problem for the Ex-Major League All Stars. He had not only banned the eight Black Sox, but also threatened to ban anyone who played with or against them. Landis' edict was most likely unconstitutional; he had total control of organized professional baseball, but the Fox River Valley League was an independent circuit not subject to the commissioner's rule. His attempt to assert dominance over independent teams and leagues might have been successfully challenged in court had Landis suspended a player for something that happened outside his purview. Still, this edict was a direct threat to college stars and semipros with professional aspirations. No one who dreamed of a baseball future wanted to risk it by playing with or against the Black Sox. This made finding games immensely more difficult for Cicotte, Risberg, and the rest.

The tour began to falter after the Appleton controversy. Though the Black Sox drew as many as 3,000 people for some of the games, lodging and transportation costs were higher than expected, and bad weather washed out some potentially profitable contests. Cicotte and the other former major leaguers were upset at the small amounts of money they received. By late June, Eddie was tired of the travel and wanted to go home. He begged off pitching a game in Merrill, Wisconsin, on June 23 and was replaced by Ray Cannon, a Milwaukee attorney who was then representing four of the Black Sox (not including Cicotte) in a pending suit against Comiskey. Cannon, a former semipro hurler, kept the locals at bay until Eddie took the mound in the eighth inning and saved the game.

Risberg and Meek made plans to play 20 more games in the Mesabi iron ore region of Minnesota, but Eddie was not interested. On a sidewalk in front of a tavern in Merrill that evening, Eddie demanded that Risberg pay him in advance for the Mesabi trip, just as he had pressed for that $10,000 payment before the first game of the 1919 World Series.

Risberg, a man of few words, replied with a right cross to Eddie's jaw.

A young man named Leonard Schmitt, a college student who later became an attorney, was an eyewitness.

> Risberg figured Cicotte was running out on him which he was, and started the fight. Risberg took Cicotte down in the gutter right on the corner and I remember Cicotte had his arms over his face. Risberg was the bum of the bunch. Anyway, Felsch, who really was just a big kid, pulled Risberg off and threw him halfway across the sidewalk

and back to the tavern. Risberg then challenged Moore [the catcher who was] sitting in a chair in the corner. Risberg asked him where he was going. I remember that Moore picked up a bat, laid it across his knee, and said, 'I'm staying right here.'"[14]

The fight cost Eddie two of his teeth and made headlines in the nation's newspapers, giving even more bad publicity to men who didn't need it. Lefty Williams replaced Eddie on the Black Sox nine, but the left-hander was out of shape and battling a drinking problem. Though Williams was still dominant enough to strike out 19 batters in one game, he complained of a sore arm, so Risberg became the team's main pitcher. Risberg and Felsch also drank a lot in the mornings while fishing, and showed up impaired to many of their games. Inattention and pitching woes caused the Black Sox to lose most of their games in Minnesota. The tour ended early due to money problems, and the former major leaguers received only about $100 apiece for their two months of work.

Eddie left Wisconsin and went home to Michigan. He spent the rest of the summer of 1922 pitching a few semipro games near Detroit, and in late August, while visiting his brother in Michigan's Upper Peninsula, he took the mound for Newberry against Marquette and struck out 17 men in a 17-inning contest. He could still pitch, and one could only wonder how he, at age 38, would have fared in the American League.

In April of 1923, Eddie made the newspapers once again when he took a job as a game warden with the State of Michigan. This position paid only $3.50 per day, a salary that drew much derisive comment in the sporting press. Francis Richter spoke for many when he stated in *The Sporting News*, "This is an awful fall for one who drew as high as $12,000 per season from baseball—and what applies to Cicotte applies to nearly all of the White Sox crooks who now all are hard put to make a decent living. Truly in baseball, as in all other matters, it pays to be honest."[15]

Perhaps the job as a game warden did not pay enough, because in May of that year the 39-year-old pitcher headed South to Bastrop, Louisiana, to join a new semipro team put together by Joe Jackson. To avoid the problems caused by Landis' threats against those who played with or against the Black Sox, Jackson took the last name of Johnson, while Cicotte called himself Moore.

This tour was a success for a while. Fans who had never seen major league players, as there were no big league teams in the South in those days, marveled at the feats of the left-handed slugger Johnson and the stocky junkball pitcher Moore. "The team has been cleaning up in Morehouse Parish," said one local newspaper, "and has walloped almost every club it has met in north Louisiana and south Arkansas."[16] The good times did not last. The fans and reporters quickly figured out that Johnson was Joe Jackson and Moore was Eddie Cicotte. Once again, Eddie's attempt at continuing his baseball career was cut short by controversy. "Semi-pro ball clubs in this section naturally ducked Bastrop and refused to play the north Louisiana club with Jackson a member of it," said the *New Orleans States* in July. "Now Jackson is spotted in the vicinity of Albany, Ga."[17] When Jackson left the Bastrop club in mid–June, Eddie did the same. Jackson joined a team in Americus, Georgia, under his real name, and led his club to the championship of the South Georgia League. Eddie Cicotte went home to Detroit. He never played with his fellow Black Sox again.

The fallout of the scandal was not yet over, as Joe Jackson, Happy Felsch, Buck Weaver, and Swede Risberg all hired lawyers and filed civil suits against the Chicago White Sox for breach of contract and back pay. Eddie Cicotte declined to join his former teammates, and though his banishment from baseball cost him his $10,000 annual salary, the former pitcher was content to leave well enough alone. As he told investigator John R. Hunter, "I am not suing Comiskey myself. He paid every nickel I was entitled to … and I have no ill feelings against him."[18] Surprisingly, when Comiskey's defense team contacted Eddie about testifying in support of the White Sox, Eddie at first appeared willing to "tell all the facts surrounding the conspiracy and the final result."[19] But his lawyer, Daniel P. Cassidy, put an end to that idea. Cassidy informed Comiskey's team that Eddie had changed his mind and would not cooperate. The pitcher preferred to stay out of it.

However, Jackson's lawyers, led by Ray Cannon, sought depositions from all the principals of the 1921 trial, and on February 23, 1923, Cannon and his assistants came to Detroit to depose Eddie. They may as well have saved themselves the trip, because they learned nothing of substance from the one-time pitching ace. Eddie, at Cassidy's direction, took an approach that was, at the time, a new gambit in legal circles. Eddie simply declined to answer any questions, invoking his constitutional right to remain silent lest he incriminate himself, as guaranteed by the Fifth Amendment. The tactic worked, though a sharp lawyer would have recognized that Eddie's Fifth Amendment claim was irrelevant to the case at hand. Eddie's acquittal in the Black Sox trial immunized him from further prosecution, so he could not possibly incriminate himself due to the Constitution's protection against double jeopardy. But Cannon, caught unprepared by this novel legal strategy, did not challenge him on it, and went away empty-handed.

George Hudnall, lead attorney for the White Sox, was more successful when he and Comiskey's legal team deposed Eddie on January 14, 1924, in Detroit. Hudnall simply waved away Eddie's stab at invoking the Fifth Amendment and grilled the pitcher on his testimony before the original grand jury in 1920. Eddie could not refute or recant his previous testimony lest he put himself in danger of a perjury charge, so the pitcher reluctantly admitted to Hudnall, "what I told the grand jury is the truth."[20] This statement was a blow to Jackson's case, as Eddie had placed the outfielder at the first meeting of the players at the Ansonia in New York. Jackson would now find it difficult to support his claim that he knew nothing about the fix until it was already well under way.

Eddie's decision to not sue the White Sox turned out to be the correct one, as Joe Jackson's suit was a disaster for the ex-outfielder. Jackson's suit for back pay took place in Milwaukee (because the White Sox were incorporated in Wisconsin, not Illinois) in January of 1924. Jackson's testimony in Milwaukee directly contradicted the story he told to the Chicago grand jury in

Buck Weaver, error-prone shortstop turned star third baseman (author's collection).

October of 1920, and when the jury members retired to their deliberations, the judge ordered Jackson and Happy Felsch, who testified on Jackson's behalf, jailed for perjury. The two Black Sox spent a few hours in jail before they posted bail, and when the jury returned with a verdict in Jackson's favor, the judge overturned it and dismissed the case. Comiskey offered Shoeless Joe a small settlement to bring an end to the whole unhappy mess, and Jackson took it and went home to his native South. The man with the .356 career batting average plied his trade in semipro and outlaw leagues on dusty fields in his home state of South Carolina for years afterward. Jackson applied several times to Commissioner Landis for reinstatement, but none of his attempts succeeded.

As the years passed, and Eddie and the other Black Sox faded from the spotlight, the question remained—why? Why would Eddie Cicotte, a popular pitcher with a successful career and no apparent enemies in the baseball world, agree to participate in a crooked enterprise that had every chance of going spectacularly wrong? Eddie, unlike Swede Risberg and Chick Gandil, harbored no blazing hatred of Eddie Collins, nor of Charles Comiskey. He got along with both factions on the club, and was friendly and accommodating to the sportswriters. Why would he violate the trust of three men—Comiskey, who rescued him from career oblivion with the Red Sox in 1912, Kid Gleason, who worked with him tirelessly during his early years with the White Sox, and Ray Schalk, who caught all of Eddie's trick pitches and played a major role in his rise to stardom?

Eliot Asinof, in *Eight Men Out*, tried to explain the pitcher's state of mind.

> [Cicotte] had grown up believing it was talent that made a man big. If you were good enough, and dedicated yourself, you could get to the top. Wasn't that enough of a reward? But when he got there, he had found otherwise. They all fed off him, the men who ran the show and pulled the strings that kept it working. They used him and used him and when they had used him up, they would dump him. In the few years he had been up, they had always praised him and made him feel like a hero to the people of America. But all the time they paid him peanuts. The newspapermen who came to watch him pitch and wrote stories about him made more money than he did. Meanwhile, Comiskey made a half million dollars a year on Cicotte's right arm.[21]

Asinof's book presented a Cicotte filled with bitterness at Charles Comiskey's cheapness, but thanks to the research of Bob Hoie and others, we now know that Eddie was the second-highest-paid pitcher in the American League at the time of the 1919 World Series. Comiskey may have been a cheapskate, but so were all the major league owners during that era. Eddie's $8,000 salary in 1919, augmented by a losing Series share of $3,254, was a much higher income than most Americans earned 100 years ago.[22] Eddie Cicotte, who quit school at age 12, was fortunate indeed that his baseball skills provided such a good living for him and his family.

Besides, Comiskey certainly did not make "a half million dollars a year" from Cicotte's labor. According to the testimony of team secretary Harry Grabiner at the Black Sox trial in 1921, the Chicago club's average annual net profit for the 1915 through 1920 seasons was just over $68,000. The club made a profit of $409,337 during that six-year period, with more than half of it ($225,913) earned in 1920. The club finished the 1919 season with a profit of $110,015, but the war-shortened 1918 season showed a loss of $51,678.[23] Charles Comiskey was a successful baseball entrepreneur, but he was no millionaire. He did not light his cigars with $100 bills.

Nelson Algren, the Chicago-based novelist (his most famous work was *The Man with the Golden Arm*) and baseball fan, saw Eddie Cicotte in a different light. Algren drew a portrait of Eddie as a man who knew that the good times and high salaries would end someday, probably soon.

> Eddie Cicotte, the French-Canadian family man, was a worrier. He worried about the debt still owed on his Michigan farm. He worried about sending his daughters to a reputable college. But mostly he worried because he'd been pitching winning baseball for fourteen years and yet had nothing to fall back on should his knuckle-ball fail him for a single season. He worried because one bad season would drop him back into the

bushes, pitching for whoever would have him. He was thirty-five years old and all he could do was throw a knuckle-ball better than anyone else in the world.[24]

In the end, it was not about bitterness, or revenge, or a lack of appreciation. It was all about the money. Eddie Cicotte needed money, so he, Sport Sullivan, and Chick Gandil hatched a scheme to fix the nation's biggest annual sporting event. Perhaps it did not seem like such a big deal to them, as Hal Chase had thrown games for years without facing any serious consequences, and the stands at Fenway Park in Boston (and several other ballparks as well) were crowded with gamblers placing bets. Sullivan's breezy proclamation, "It's been pulled before and it can be again," must have sounded perfectly reasonable to the aging pitcher's ears. At no time did Eddie consider what would happen to him if his role in the fix were ever exposed. Such was the temptation of an easy $10,000 to the financially strapped Cicotte.

Though Jackson, Weaver, and other Black Sox kept playing well into the 1930s, Eddie, nearing his 40th birthday, was done with life as an itinerant ballplayer for hire. He pitched a few semipro games during the next few years, but he could not play baseball forever. It was time to find a job.

13

Later Life

> *The honest ball player need have no fear of any gambler. There are thousands and thousands of honest ball players. There is another small group—they were ball players once—to be immured in the Chamber of Oblivion. There let them rest.—* John B. Foster, 1921[1]

While Eddie Cicotte built a new life in Detroit, two more baseball scandals exploded in 1926, one of which directly involved him. At the conclusion of the 1926 season, Ty Cobb and Tris Speaker, two of the biggest stars in the game, resigned their positions as player-managers in Detroit and Cleveland respectively. Not long afterward, the news came out that the two superstars were forced out of baseball by Ban Johnson. Dutch Leonard, a former Detroit pitcher who held a grudge against both Cobb and Speaker, had given the American League president copies of two letters written in 1919, one by Cobb and one by Cicotte's old Boston teammate, Joe Wood. In those letters, it appeared that Cobb, Speaker, Wood, and Leonard had fixed a game between the Tigers and Indians on September 25, 1919, and bet on the outcome. Johnson bought the evidence from Leonard for $20,000, presented Cobb and Speaker with his findings, and arranged their resignations.

Johnson tried to keep the Cobb-Speaker scandal a secret, but the story hit the papers in due time and caused a national outcry. The two stars hired lawyers and fought for reinstatement, and the controversy wound up in the lap of Commissioner Landis. Landis held a hearing and grilled Cobb, Speaker, and Wood about their actions on that day; their defense was that they placed bets on the game (which was not illegal at the time) but that it was not fixed for Detroit to win. Though the Tigers won, 9–5, Cobb had only one hit that day, while Speaker, whose Indians were supposed to lose, belted three hits, including two triples. Leonard refused to attend the hearing, fearing retaliation from the outraged Cobb, and in the end, lacking solid proof of game-fixing, the commissioner overruled Johnson and reinstated Cobb and Speaker.

In the midst of the Cobb-Speaker affair, Swede Risberg resurfaced and

13. Later Life

made some sensational charges of his own. On December 30, 1926, the *Chicago Tribune* carried an interview with the former shortstop, who now worked on a dairy farm in Minnesota. Risberg claimed that on Labor Day weekend in 1917, the White Sox bribed the Detroit Tigers to lose two doubleheaders in Chicago. The White Sox were battling the Red Sox for the pennant at the time, and were only three and a half games in the lead entering the season's final month. The White Sox won all four games and increased their lead to six and a half games, giving them a boost to the pennant. A few weeks later, the Sox, charged Risberg, raised $45 per man to pay off the Tigers. Chick Gandil collected the money and gave Bill James, a Tigers pitcher who played for the White Sox two years later, $1,100 to distribute among his teammates. Risberg said that manager Pants Rowland and such "Clean Sox" as Ray Schalk and Eddie Collins took part in this scheme.

This was the "tipping" scandal that Eddie Cicotte and his attorney, Daniel Cassidy, had threatened to expose at the 1921 Black Sox trial. This piece of what Eddie Collins' biographer Rick Huhn called "blackmail-lite" had kept the prosecution from putting Schalk, Collins, and other Clean Sox on the stand to impugn the character of Eddie and his fellow defendants. Everyone—Commissioner Landis, Ban Johnson, Charles Comiskey, and the players involved—thought the matter was safely buried, never to see the light of day. Now, six years later, Swede Risberg had blasted it all over the front pages. What's more, the shortstop charged that the White Sox did the Tigers a favor by "sloughing off" their last two games of the season in 1919 to help Detroit clinch third place. "I know I played out of position [in those games]," said Risberg, "and Jackson, Gandil and Felsch also played out of position."[2]

Risberg's hatred of Eddie Collins burned as brightly as ever. "They pushed Ty Cobb and Tris Speaker out on a piker bet," he said. "I think it's only fair that the 'white lilies' get the same treatment."[3] His assertion that Collins had not only participated in the 1917 fix, but also contributed to the payoff, stunned the average fan as much as the allegations against Cobb and Speaker. "I can give baseball's bosses information that will implicate twenty big leaguers who never before have been mentioned in connection with crookedness," said the ex-shortstop. "Landis and the big bosses of baseball don't want to know the facts. This is a challenge to the commissioner. Let's see what he'll do about it."[4]

Landis was incensed at the news of another scandal, though he and everyone inside baseball knew about it. Ray Schalk had discussed the matter with the Commissioner in 1921, and it appeared in the trial that same year when attorney Benedict Short asked Charles Comiskey, "Didn't you and Clarence Rowland, your former manager, get into some trouble about the last series with Detroit in 1917?"[5] This quote appeared in the *Chicago Tribune* and other papers, but the public paid no attention, and it made no waves during the trial in 1921. Now, six years later, the story was out, and Landis complained, rather disingenuously, to an associate, "Won't these God damn things that happened before I came into baseball ever stop coming up?"[6]

Landis invited more than 30 former and current Tigers and White Sox to Chicago for a hearing on January 3, 1927. At the hearing, Collins, Schalk, Rowland, Kid Gleason, and others denied paying the Tigers to lose four games; instead, they testified that the $45 per man was meant to reward the Detroit club for beating Boston three times in a row on September 20 and 21, 1917. This practice of "tipping" was common at the time, insisted Collins with the backing of almost everyone else present. The anger in the crowded hearing room toward Risberg was palpable, with ex–Tiger Bernie Boland sneering at the former shortstop, "You're still a pig." Landis managed to control the hearing, and though Chick Gandil traveled all the way from Arizona to support his old teammate, Risberg was outnumbered. Gandil was the only player who corroborated Risberg's account, while 33 others testified to the contrary. Buck Weaver, who was expected to support Risberg, surprised everyone when he took the stand and stated that he did not contribute to any fund—he was injured and not with the team on that Labor Day weekend—and then brought the hearing to a standstill by pleading with Landis for reinstatement.

Did Risberg tell the truth? And, if so, could Eddie Cicotte have corroborated his claims?

Cicotte was the winning pitcher in two of the four games on Labor Day weekend in 1917. In the first game on Sunday, September 3, Eddie pitched a complete game for his 21st win of season, beating the Tigers, 7–2. The White Sox jumped into the lead with four runs in the first inning, but the Tigers were probably not going to beat Cicotte that day anyway. Game Two on Sunday was a much tighter affair, as Sox starter Reb Russell pitched eight strong innings but collapsed in the ninth, as Detroit scored four runs to take a 5–3 lead. The Sox scored twice in the ninth, and Lefty Williams kept the Tigers off the board in the tenth. The Sox won it in the bottom of the 10th when Eddie Collins walked, stole second and third, and scored on Joe Jackson's single.

Red Faber started the first game of Monday's doubleheader and failed to finish the fifth inning as the Tigers took a 5–2 lead. Dave Danforth and Lefty Williams shut out the Tigers the rest of the way as Chicago's offense came to life, scoring five times for a 7–5 victory. Pants Rowland sent Faber out to pitch the second game, and the spitballer was even worse this time. The White Sox scored four runs in the first inning, but the Tigers drove Faber to the sidelines with four runs in the second. Danforth and Williams allowed three more, and the Tigers went ahead, 7–5. Rowland sent Eddie out to pitch the fourth inning, and he threw the last six innings, allowing only one run and four hits. A three-run homer by Ray Schalk, a two-run pinch single by Eddie Murphy, and an array of other run-scoring hits gave the Sox a 14–8 win.

13. Later Life

The White Sox certainly expended a lot of effort in winning games that were supposed to be fixed. The Tigers held the lead at some point in three of the four games. Even the last contest, which the White Sox won by six runs, was close until Eddie Cicotte slammed the door with six stellar relief innings. On the other hand, Chicago ran wild on the bases, with 22 steals in four games. Detroit catcher Oscar Stanage denied letting them steal—he drew laughter in the hearing room when he "sheepishly admitted" that such a thing had happened to him before—but perhaps the Tiger pitchers were not holding the runners close.

Chick Gandil, first baseman of the White Sox from 1917 to 1919. In 1927, he confronted Commissioner Landis and demanded to know why he had been banned from baseball (author's collection).

The two "sloughed off" games in 1919 were more problematic, but still not obviously thrown. The Tigers beat the White Sox on Saturday, September 27, 1919, 7–5, but this was an extra-inning affair, pitched by second-stringers Win Noyes and Erskine Mayer. The Sox had clinched the pennant three days before, and it was not unusual for a manager to fill the lineup with scrubs while resting the regulars for the World Series. On Sunday, Eddie Cicotte started the last game of the season and threw only two innings in a tune-up for the Series (though he could have won his 30th game had he stayed in). Roy Wilkinson pitched the final seven innings, allowed nine runs, and took the loss.

Most of the 1917 White Sox, including some who were thrown out of baseball in the World Series scandal, attended the hearing at Commissioner Landis' request. Eddie, however, ignored the invitation, though the hearing in Chicago was a relatively short train ride from Detroit. Instead, Eddie put out a statement through his attorney in which he claimed he did not remember any of the games in question. The ex-pitcher, wary of the spotlight, was happy to put this painful part of his past behind him. "Organized baseball is a closed book in my life," he said. "I do not care to take part in any of its squabbles."[7]

In the end, Landis condemned and banned the practice of tipping, which he called "an act of impropriety, reprehensible and censurable, but not corrupt," but took no action against Collins, Schalk, and the other "white lilies." Landis denied Weaver's bid for reinstatement, and when an embittered Chick Gandil demanded to know why he had been blacklisted, Landis reminded him that he had admitted playing out of position to allow Detroit to win two games in 1919. That, said Landis, is reason enough for a lifetime ban. Comedian and columnist Will Rogers, a baseball fan, offered his take on Risberg's motive. Rogers suggested, "It was just that bottled up hate against everything that made [Risberg] think he hadn't had a square deal in the game, and he exaggerated the incident."[8]

This embarrassing episode led Landis to set fixed punishments for gambling and betting transgressions. He decreed that tipping, or offering any kind of reward to another player or team, would result in a one-year suspension, as would betting on any game in which a player was not involved. He set a lifetime ban for "betting any sum whatsoever upon any ball game in connection with which the bettor has any duty to perform." This is the rule used by a later commissioner, A. Bartlett Giamatti, to ban Cincinnati Reds manager Pete Rose for life in 1989. Landis also declared a statute of limitations on all offenses committed before he assumed the commissioner's post in 1920. Officially, the era was now off-limits to further investigations.

Eddie, now in his 40s, was done with baseball, and though he enjoyed being outdoors in his job as a game warden, it did not pay nearly enough to support his family. Fortunately for the Cicottes, in 1924 he found a job at the Ford Motor Company plant in Highland Park, an independent city within the boundaries of Detroit. He took a position with the Ford Service Department, which was run by Henry Ford's right-hand man, Harry Bennett.

Harry Bennett was, to put it simply, a thug in a suit and tie. Hired by Henry Ford in 1916, after one of Ford's associates was impressed by Bennett's performance in a street fight, Bennett soon became Ford's most trusted confidant. Bennett's job, as defined by Henry Ford, was to keep the workers in line, by threats, intimidation, and violence whenever necessary. Bennett's Service Department, despite its benign-sounding name, was Henry Ford's own private police force. It ruled the assembly plants with an iron fist and was responsible to no one but Bennett. "Harry Bennett did whatever he was told, and he did it very efficiently and very fast," said Ford historian and University of Michigan professor David Lewis. "So he did a good deal of Henry Ford's dirty work."[9] Some of that dirty work involved covering up Ford's extramarital affairs, and intimidating jurors and witnesses in lawsuits against the company. People referred to Bennett as "Henry Ford's brass knuckles."

Bennett filled the Service Department with the most intimidating men that he could find, including ex-boxers, ex-wrestlers, former football players, and goons from the Detroit mob. After Ford used his political clout to place Bennett on Michigan's Parole Board, Bennett hired ex-cons and parolees too. A disgraced ex-ballplayer like Eddie fit right in. These rough characters were there to keep the assembly lines running, even as Ford secretly ordered the lines speeded up, driving his workers beyond their breaking point. The Service Department, which the *New York Times* called "the largest quasi-military organization in the world,"[10] controlled a network of spies and informants, with undercover operatives among the working men. They recorded every complaint, or, worse yet, any desire to unionize. Union activity, real or suspected, could result in a severe beating from the Service Department men.

Henry Ford hated the very idea of unions, and during the 1930s the Service Department stepped up its anti-union activities. One of its worst excesses occurred on March 7, 1932, when a march of unemployed workers on Ford's plant in River Rouge was quelled by the Service Department and Dearborn police, who opened fire on the marchers and killed four of them. Bennett himself fired at the crowd from the safety of his car. We don't know if Eddie Cicotte was involved.

In 1935, Bennett made Eddie the director of the Service Department at Highland Park. We don't know how much strong-arm activity he personally took part in, as Eddie was in his fifties by this time and was never a big, intimidating presence. He certainly would have kept reports on the workers and perhaps directed Henry Ford's spy network at the plant. Because Bennett loved baseball—he was a close friend of Tigers catcher and manager Mickey Cochrane—he appointed Eddie as manager of the company's sandlot baseball team.

The worst incident of Harry Bennett's career occurred at the "Battle of the Overpass" on May 26, 1937. As United Auto Workers union organizers led by Walter Reuther passed out leaflets near the River Rouge plant that day, they were set upon by about 40 men from the Ford Service Department. As newspaper photographers recorded the scene, Reuther and the UAW people were savagely beaten, kicked, stomped, and thrown down several flights of concrete steps. No one was killed, but 16 people were injured in the attack, including seven women. The brazen brutality of the scene shocked the nation when the photos were published in the *Detroit News* the next day. The incident gained nationwide sympathy for the union movement and turned the public against Henry Ford, who finally signed an agreement with the UAW four years later. It was a classic case of Ford and Bennett winning a battle but losing the war.

Was Eddie Cicotte present, and was he one of the thugs who beat up the UAW organizers? Photographic evidence is inconclusive. Eddie was nearly 53 years old in 1937, and though some say that they saw him there, most of the men in the photos look younger than him. Still, Eddie was a high-ranking official of this violent organization, reporting directly to Bennett, and that, along with the Black Sox Scandal, is a black mark on the record of his life.

Eddie retired in 1944 at age 60 after 20 years in the Ford Service Department. One year later, Henry Ford II, the 28-year-old grandson of the founder, took the reins of the company. On his first day in charge, the junior Ford fired Harry Bennett.

It is possible that Bennett hired Eddie not because of his fighting skill, but because of his status as a local athlete. Eddie, despite his expulsion from baseball, maintained a degree of popularity in his hometown, and as memories of the Black Sox Scandal faded, he was asked about it less and less. Perhaps Bennett used Eddie's baseball fame to put a friendly face on the excesses of the Service Department. We'll never know, because neither Eddie nor Bennett, who lived until 1979, talked much about their Ford careers during their later lives. Also, when Bennett was fired, he burned all his files before he left the company for the last time.

Eddie Cicotte, though banned from baseball for life, stepped on a major league field one more time in 1938. On Opening Day that year, the Detroit Tigers staged a pre-game parade for the team down Lafayette Avenue and Trumbull Avenue to the ballpark. Honored guests that day included 19 old-time local ballplayers such as infielder Bobby Lowe, outfielder Davy Jones, catcher Oscar Stanage, outfielder Bobby Veach, and other ex–Tigers from the Ty Cobb era. Also invited to participate was Eddie Cicotte, who pitched three games for the team in September of 1905. As the *Detroit Free Press* said that day, these men were "a pretty good ball club if you ask your old dad."[11] When the procession arrived at the newly renovated Briggs Stadium (the former Navin Field), 54,000 fans watched as Eddie and the others marched to the flagpole in deepest center field for the pregame ceremony. Also present was Nemo Leibold, a native Detroiter who was Eddie's Chicago teammate and one of the "Clean Sox" of 1919.[12]

American League President Ban Johnson had declared all the Black Sox *persona non grata* in the circuit's ballparks, and in 1926 he had Sport Sullivan, the fixer of 1919, removed from his seat at a World Series game in New York and ejected from the stadium. But in 1938, Johnson had been dead for seven years. Kenesaw Mountain Landis, who banned the eight players after they were acquitted at trial in 1921, was still the Commissioner of Baseball, but Landis registered no protest at Eddie's participation. He probably never knew about it until afterward, if he ever did at all. Despite his banishment, Eddie was a member in good standing of Detroit's Old Time Baseball Players Association and remained so for the rest of his life.

While Eddie raised strawberries and tomatoes on his farm outside of Detroit, his great-nephew Al Cicotte pursued a baseball career of his own. Al Cicotte, the grandson of Eddie's older brother Alva, was a talented pitcher

13. Later Life

Eddie with members of Detroit's Old Time Baseball Players Association, January 29, 1938. Left to right: Eddie Cicotte, Oscar Stanage, Lew "Sport" McAllister, Fred "Frank" Scheibeck, Bobby Veach, Bernie Boland, and Davy Jones (courtesy Ernie Harwell Sports Collection, Detroit Public Library).

who dominated the prep school scene in Detroit, posting a 29–1 record in high school. Signed by the New York Yankees in 1948, he finally reached the major leagues in 1957 after six years in the minors and two stretches of service in the United States Air Force. Like Eddie, Al was obliged to spend much time and effort correcting people who mispronounced his name.

Al Cicotte bore little resemblance to his famous relative and was a totally different kind of pitcher. Al was tall and thin, while Eddie was much shorter and stockier. Al, unlike Eddie, had an outstanding fastball, but suffered from streaks of wildness. Al pitched for six major league teams from 1957 to 1962, and while he enjoyed success in the minors (he won the Most Valuable Player Award for Toronto of the International League in 1960) he could never establish himself in the majors. Al Cicotte quit the game when his final team, the expansion Houston Colt .45s, demoted him to the minors during the 1962 campaign.

In an interview with *The Sporting News* in 1953, Al Cicotte, then a prized prospect with the Yankees, talked about the advice he received from his great-uncle. "Work on control, boy," said Eddie Cicotte. "This is a good game.

Always was, but it's better now because if you make good, there's no telling how far you can go." Then in an afterthought he added, "Watch yourself, but watch your companions more. Stay away from gamblers. Stay away from wrong people."[13]

Did Al ever ask his great-uncle about the scandal? "I never wanted to talk to him about it," Al said. "I never knew how much he wanted to talk about it. I didn't want to push it." However, Al said that Eddie told his family the story of how Charles Comiskey had reneged on a promise of a $5,000 bonus for winning 30 games in 1919. Eddie said something else that resonated with his young relative. "I live here in Farmington," said Eddie, "but my home is really in Chicago."[14]

During the 1950s, the aging Black Sox began to pass from the scene. Joe Jackson was the first, dying of heart failure in Greenville, South Carolina, his hometown, in December of 1951. During his final years, Shoeless Joe gave several interviews in which he insisted that he played his best in the 1919 World Series. He had applied for reinstatement to professional ball several times, but was turned down on each occasion. "I positively can't say that I recall anything out of the way in the [1919] Series," recalled Jackson in a 1949 interview. "I mean, anything that might have turned the tide. There was just one thing that doesn't seem quite right, now that I think back over it. Cicotte seemed to let up on a pitch to Pat Duncan, and Pat hit it over my head. Duncan didn't have enough power to hit the ball that far, particularly if Cicotte had been bearing down."[15]

Fred McMullin, the most obscure of the eight banned players, died in 1952, and in 1956 Buck Weaver collapsed of a heart attack on a Chicago street and died soon afterward. Ray Schalk was one of his pallbearers. Weaver, too, had petitioned for reinstatement, but three Commissioners of Baseball—Kenesaw Mountain Landis, A. B. "Happy" Chandler, and Ford Frick—rejected his entreaties. Lefty Williams, who lived in near-total obscurity and worked in a series of menial jobs after his banishment, died in November of 1959. His death came a month after the Chicago White Sox won their first American League pennant since 1919 and lost the World Series in six games to the Los Angeles Dodgers.

After Weaver's death, Chick Gandil broke his silence. In September of 1956, *Sports Illustrated* printed an article, written by Melvin Durslag, in which Gandil outlined the planning of the fix, with himself and Eddie Cicotte as the ringleaders and Sport Sullivan as the instigator. In the article, Gandil, a 68-year-old retired plumber, made the astounding claim that the Series was honestly played after all, and that he and the Sox changed their minds about throwing the Series and played to win. The former first baseman suggested that the poor play and fielding errors were caused by nervousness, as all the fix rumors put the Sox under intense pressure. "When we trotted out on the field that day for the opener," he said, "we were still a tense bunch of ballplayers. And, as if things weren't bad enough, some joker in the stands yelled to Cicotte, 'Be careful, Eddie. There's a guy looking for you with a rifle.'"[16]

Gandil claimed that he dealt with Arnold Rothstein directly, and Rothstein gave him ten $1,000 bills that were turned over to Cicotte. Though Rothstein promised each player $10,000, no one other than Cicotte received any money. Said Gandil,

> I never did get any part of Rothstein's $10,000 and I don't know who did. Since Rothstein probably won his bets anyway, he never gave us any trouble. Naturally, I would have liked to have had my share of that ten grand, but with all the excitement at the Series' end and with Comiskey's investigation, I was frankly frightened stiff. Besides, I had the crazy notion that my not touching any of that money would exonerate me from my guilt in the conspiracy. I give you my solemn word I don't know to this day what happened to the cash.[17]

He blamed Cicotte for exposing the fix, believing that if Eddie had never talked, the scandal might never have been exposed. Gandil did, however, exonerate Cicotte for his errors in Game Four of the Series.

> One [error] was probably my fault. Eddie fielded an easy roller and threw wide to first, permitting the runner to move to second. When the next batter singled to left center, and Jackson threw to the plate to try to cut off a run, I yelled to Cicotte to intercept the throw. I felt we had no chance to get the man at home but could nail the batter now trying to reach second. Cicotte juggled the ball and all hands were safe. The next man then doubled, and Cincy had both its runs.[18]

Gandil's article, self-serving as it was—did he really expect anyone to believe that he received no money?—made national headlines and brought new attention to the scandal. A Chicago reporter called Eddie at his home in Detroit for his reaction. Eddie said only that "I've taken my medicine. I've forgotten about it. All I can say is that it is Gandil's story, but what he is telling isn't the truth."[19]

At the same time, Buck Weaver's death led political columnist Westbrook Pegler to revisit the 1919 World Series, which he had covered as a young reporter. Pegler visited Happy Felsch in Milwaukee, where the former outfielder worked as a crane operator. He had owned a tavern for a while, but gave it up when too many drunks wanted to argue with him about the scandal. During their conversation, Felsch gave his version of Eddie's second misplay in Game Four against the Reds. "The runner had the throw beat," claimed Felsch, "and I heard Schalk yell to Cicotte to take it and catch the hitter trying for second."

Pegler relayed this statement to Ray Schalk, who still lived in Chicago and dismissed Felsch's opinion of the play. "How could Felsch, over 100 yards away, know what I said to Cicotte with the crowd yelling?" asked the old catcher. "But I am not going to argue. Let it go."[20]

Pegler did not locate Lefty Williams, but he did contact Swede Risberg by phone from California. Risberg said nothing about the fix, but had plenty of opinions about modern baseball. Like many old players, he disparaged the modern major leaguers, especially the hitters. The old shortstop complained that Ted Williams and Mickey Mantle pulled all their hits, even when the defense played a shift on them. "I would like to see Eddie Cicotte against these fellows," he told Pegler. "He could give you eight or nine hits and beat you. He could put three on base and strike three out…. He could throw the wet one, too, and do pretty good tricks with mud. He threw a knuckleball and used to claim he invented it. Maybe he did."

Risberg also had no use for the slider. "Girls can throw that one," he said. "Cicotte didn't have a slider but he had something that no one else had. He had that knock-kneed motion. The first thing you knew it was on top of you. You would start swinging just when you heard the ball hit the mitt. He didn't have so much speed, either, but he could burn your letters with a strike. He owned every inch of that strike zone and used it all."[21]

Finally, Pegler visited Eddie Cicotte at his home in Farmington, outside of Detroit. Eddie, at age 72, and his wife Rose survived on small stipends from Social Security, $76 a month for Eddie and $36 a month for Rose. Eddie also received a pension from Ford Motor Company. The first thing Eddie did was correct Pegler's pronunciation of his name. "It is not Sy-cott," he said. "It is a French name. It is pronounced See-cott in Detroit and Sy-cott everywhere else. My great-great-grandfather came here with Cadillac."[22] Eddie then had to explain to Pegler who Cadillac, the founder of Detroit, was.

"The grip of his hand was startling," wrote Pegler. "His fingers, which pitched with marvelous control and did tricks on the hide of a baseball with emery and mud, are talons of crushing strength at 72 years. I let my hand fold in. He could have mashed my knuckles."[23]

Eddie, whose son Eddie Junior lived next door and worked for Ford, explained that he farmed on five acres and helped his neighbors. He was in good health and needed little prodding to tell stories of the old days. "I had control," he said. "I could throw it through a curtain ring all afternoon." He still denied the existence of the shine ball. "Oh, heck, there wasn't any shine ball…. I used to rub it on my pants but it was shiny already. I didn't have anything on my pants but sweat."[24]

At the end of the interview, Eddie addressed the scandal.

> We done wrong and we deserved to get punished but not for a life sentence. That was too rough. I could have earned a living coaching later but they wouldn't let me. I wasn't paid so bad. I got $10,000, but Lefty Williams and I won over 80 games between us in a couple of years and he only got about $2,500. Ed Walsh won over 40 games for Comiskey one year [1908] and the most he ever got was $3,200.[25]

13. Later Life

Eddie was open and accommodating to Pegler, but he turned down all interview requests for the next nine years. When Eliot Asinof contacted Eddie in 1961 to question him for the book *Eight Men Out*, the old pitcher politely declined, as did Chick Gandil and Swede Risberg. Asinof spoke at length to Happy Felsch, who was his main source for information on the scandal. Cicotte, however, was not interested in rehashing the events of 1919. His wife Rose had died in 1958, and the widowed Eddie preferred to spend his remaining years on his farm, free of prying questions about his younger days.

Epilogue

For a good many years, I held a deep resentment against Cicotte for his initial confession. I felt I would never forgive the guy, but I think I have by now. Still, I don't believe we would have ever been caught if he hadn't gabbed. —Chick Gandil, 1956[1]

Joe Falls was a veteran sportswriter for the *Detroit Free Press*. He had interviewed dozens, if not hundreds of old ballplayers during his career, but this one was different.

Falls drove from downtown Detroit to a farmhouse outside the city one evening in November of 1965. Living in that house was an 81-year-old former baseball player who was, a half-century before, one of the most celebrated and popular men in the sport. This right-handed pitcher won more than 200 major league games, threw a no-hitter, won a World Series in 1917, and may have invented the knuckleball. At the peak of his fame, in 1919, he won 29 games for the pennant-winning Chicago White Sox. His name was Eddie Cicotte, and he was on a path that may well have led to the Baseball Hall of Fame.

That all ended on October 1, 1919, when Eddie accepted a $10,000 bribe from a cabal of gamblers to lose the World Series. The truth did not surface for nearly a year, but when it did, Eddie's baseball career came to a screeching halt. Suspended for life from the game he loved, branded as one of the "Black Sox" in the national press, his reputation was ruined for all time. After his expulsion, Eddie almost totally disappeared from the public eye. Falls entered the farmhouse to find an octogenarian who kept busy by growing strawberries and selling them at a roadside stand. Eddie greeted the reporter with a smile and a firm handshake.

The elderly man made small talk with the sportswriter, telling stories about Ty Cobb and Babe Ruth. Eddie smiled when he related how Ruth, the game's greatest slugger, never hit a home run off him. But both men knew why Falls was there. After a while, Eddie's guest cleared his throat and gingerly asked about the events of 1919. Do people still bring up the scandal, Eddie? What do you say to them?

The old ballplayer stopped smiling and looked intently at Falls.

> I admit I did wrong, but I've paid for it the last 45 years. Sure, they asked me about being a crooked ball player. But I've become calloused to it. I figure if I was crooked in baseball, they were crooked in something else.
>
> I don't know of anyone who ever went through life without making a mistake. Everybody that has ever lived has committed sins of their own. I've tried to make up for it by living as clean a life as I could. I'm proud of the way I've lived and I think my family is, too.[2]

The smile returned shortly, and Joe Falls left the farmhouse with another firm handshake and a batch of strawberries. He had conducted Eddie Cicotte's final interview.

Eddie had been diagnosed with bladder cancer in 1964 and was already fighting a losing battle with the disease at the time of the interview. He remained busy on his farm, driving his tractor during the summer and plowing snow for his neighbors in the winter, but as his health declined, he was forced to give up hunting and fishing. He spent a lot of time watching his first major league team, the Detroit Tigers, on television. "Oh, he still loved baseball," said his son, Eddie Junior. "It was his life. Later on, after games were on TV, I'd visit him and he'd be watching a game. He wouldn't want to be interrupted while he was watching a game."[3]

However, Eddie's friends could never convince him to attend a game at Tiger Stadium (the former Navin Field, where he had battled the Tigers many times) in person. Eddie had not been there since the parade on Opening Day in 1938. Billy Rogell, who played shortstop for Detroit's pennant-winning teams in 1934 and 1935, was a friend of Eddie's. Rogell retired from baseball in 1940 and then served a 38-year stint on Detroit's City Council. "I'd invite him [to the ballpark], but he'd never go," said Rogell. "I guess he wasn't allowed to." Though Rogell grew up in Chicago as a White Sox fan at the time of the scandal, he and Eddie never talked about it. "Was he sorry about what he did? Well, what the hell, I never asked him. Listen, he was my friend. I liked the guy. We never talked about it. I didn't look at him as an old Black Sock. I liked the guy, that's all."[4] Eddie Junior also said that, while his father loved talking about baseball, he never mentioned the 1919 Series.

In 1967, the Chicago White Sox reached out to Eddie. The club had decided to stage an old-timers celebration, and planned to recognize all six of the living pitchers who had thrown no-hitters for the team. Eddie, who pitched his no-hitter 50 years before, was the oldest of the six and was invited to appear between games of a doubleheader against the Boston Red Sox on August 27 of that year. Eddie had not set foot in White Sox Park (formerly called Comiskey Park) since he pitched the last game of his career there in

September of 1920, two days before his confession broke open the 1919 World Series scandal.

The Comiskey family no longer owned the team. Charles Comiskey died in 1931, and the club passed down to his son and then to his grandchildren. Bill Veeck bought controlling interest in the White Sox in 1959, and Charles Comiskey II, the grandson of the original owner, sold his remaining stock in 1962, severing the Comiskey connection with the team. The new owners renamed the old stadium White Sox Park. With the Comiskeys gone, perhaps there was no one left to object to Eddie Cicotte's return to the scene of the tragic events of 1919. Or perhaps nobody gave it a thought, though the publication of Eliot Asinof's best-seller *Eight Men Out* had revived interest in the Black Sox Scandal, nearly half a century after it happened.

We will never know how the Chicago fans would have received Eddie, because the elderly pitcher was too ill to make the trip. The older fans certainly remembered him and recalled how the Black Sox Scandal tore the team apart and plunged the White Sox into a 40-year pennant drought. It would have been interesting to find out if Eddie's introduction to the fans drew cheers, boos, or some combination of the two.

Eddie Cicotte died of pneumonia and heart failure in Detroit's Henry Ford Hospital on May 8, 1969, at the age of 84. His death certificate listed his occupation neither as a farmer nor as a retiree from the Ford Motor Company, but as a baseball player. His employer, as shown on the certificate, was the Chicago White Sox. He had outlived all but two of his fellow Black Sox, as only Chick Gandil and Swede Risberg now remained. He was survived by his three children, one grandchild, and one great-grandchild. His funeral was a small one, attended by family, neighbors, and attorney Daniel Cassidy, who defended him at the trial in Chicago 48 years before.[5]

Ray Schalk, still an active presence on the Chicago sports scene at age 76 (as was another of the "Clean Sox," the 81-year-old Red Faber), paid tribute to Cicotte's pitching skill. "He had command of every type of pitch," said Eddie's old catcher. "That includes the knuckler, the fadeaway, the slider, the spitter, the screwball, and emery ball."[6] However, Schalk, still deeply wounded by the betrayals of Eddie and his disgraced teammates, always refused to talk about the scandal. "Gandil? Risberg? I don't know where they are and couldn't care less," said Schalk in August of that year. "You can ask me anything in the world except about the Black Sox scandal and I'll give you an answer. I have my personal feelings about it all. It's one of the saddest things that ever happened. There were a few players I felt sorry for and always will—Weaver, Jackson, Felsch, Williams. I know one thing. If it hadn't happened it's no telling how far that great team would have gone. It was the greatest ever."[7]

Not everyone was so reluctant to share their feelings on the fixed World Series. Eddie's old Boston teammate, Joe Wood, had once been a friend, but

Wood's disgust for the scandal and its participants soured his memory of Eddie Cicotte. Wood lived to be 95 years old, and in one late-in-life interview, Wood cut loose on the Black Sox. "Chick Gandil was the ringleader of the whole thing," said Wood. "He always was a louse. Everyone knew he was a louse." Cicotte, said the old pitcher, "was on the same order, only not so openly ... [with] the sailer ball ... the only thing that made Cicotte a great pitcher." Wood also said that Eddie was a joker, but his jokes weren't funny.[8]

If Eddie Cicotte had been honest, would he have been elected to the Baseball Hall of Fame?

Had Eddie refused the offer of $10,000 (or had Red Faber been healthy, or had the White Sox kept Jack Quinn), the Black Sox Scandal might never have happened. Without the scandal, Eddie and the White Sox stood a good chance of winning the 1919 World Series. Switching two losses to wins—one from Eddie and one from Lefty Williams—would have given Chicago the title. The Sox would then defend their championship in 1920, and without the gamblers pressuring the players to throw games in that season, the Sox likely would have won the pennant again and entered the 1920 World Series as the favorite. Chicago, with the best starting pitching in baseball and Hall of Fame–level players like Joe Jackson and Eddie Collins, and the New York Yankees, led by Babe Ruth, would have battled for American League supremacy during the first half of the decade.

Cicotte, given the financial pressures facing his family, would have played for a few more years. He turned 37 years old during the middle of the 1921 season, so he would probably have already begun his decline phase. Many of the tricks he used to reach stardom, including the shine ball, disappeared in 1920, though he would have continued throwing the spitter and the knuckleball. If Eddie played a few years longer and compiled a .500 record—say, 40 wins and 40 losses—on his way out, his career win-loss total would be 249–188, well within the range in which pitchers have been elected to the Hall. His record would have been a bit better than those of his teammate Red Faber (254–213) and a later White Sox star, Ted Lyons (260–230). Faber and Lyons, both of whom pitched well into their 40s, have plaques in Cooperstown. Eddie played on a World Series winner in 1917,[9] and one or two more titles would have further strengthened his candidacy.

Instead, Eddie Cicotte's expulsion ended his career in the most embarrassing manner possible, and he was extremely lucky that his participation in the scandal did not land him in prison. No one has ever mounted a public campaign for his reinstatement; that is reserved for Joe Jackson, who received some of the bribe money but batted .375 in the Series, and Buck Weaver, who took no money at all but knew about the plot. Eddie Cicotte, by contrast, helped plan the scheme, took twice as much money as Jackson, and played so poorly in two games that there is little doubt that he threw them, despite his later denials. By all accounts, Eddie was a good man, a fine husband and father with many friends in the baseball world—Billy Rogell called him "one of the nicest guys God put on this earth"[10]—but one could make the case that his guilt in the 1919 World Series scandal is the greatest of the eight players involved.

During Eddie's grand jury appearance, the pitcher did his best to minimize his role in the scandal. He stubbornly claimed that he played to win after hitting Morrie Rath with his second pitch of Game One, even after accepting a large bribe from the fixers. Given the poor quality of his play in both Games One and Four, this assertion makes no logical sense. Kid Gleason, Ray Schalk, and other honest White Sox could tell almost immediately that Eddie and his co-conspirators were throwing the Series. Many of the Clean Sox called Eddie out by name after the scandal broke a year later, and almost all accounts of the fix say that Eddie played a key role in its planning. There is simply too much evidence that points to Eddie's guilt, not only in losing the 1919 World Series but also in the stunning collapse of the White Sox in August and September of 1920.

In 1904, Sport Sullivan presented a game-fixing proposition to Cy Young, the star pitcher of the Boston Americans. Sullivan offered Young a substantial amount of money, larger than the pitcher's annual salary, to lose a game. Young did not hesitate. He punched Sullivan in the jaw and booted him out of the room.

That's what Eddie Cicotte should have done.

Because he accepted the easy payday, Eddie Cicotte lived the last half-century of his life under a cloud. The Black Sox Scandal, in which he was a pivotal figure, destroyed Eddie's reputation both inside and outside of baseball. Because his moral compass failed at a key moment in his life, he would forever best be known not as a 29-game winner or as a pioneer of the knuckleball, but as one of the Eight Men Out. The role he willingly played in the fixed World Series of 1919 made him infamous, and in the end, Eddie Cicotte must have realized that no amount of money could possibly be worth it.

In the popular movie *Field of Dreams*, released in 1989, a reclusive writer named Terrence Mann (portrayed by James Earl Jones) convinces a farmer named Ray Kinsella (played by Kevin Costner) that people will gladly pay to watch baseball in a remote Iowa cornfield. "They'll pass over the money without even thinking about it," says Mann to Kinsella. "For it is money they have and peace they lack."

This line sums up the tragedy of Eddie Cicotte.

He took the money and found no peace.

Appendix A: Indictment

This is the three-count indictment that was filed against Eddie Cicotte and the rest of the defendants in their trial, which took place in July and August of 1921.

in the Case of State of Illinois v Edward Cicotte, et al.

(February 1921)

STATE OF ILLINOIS)

) SS:

COUNTY OF COOK)

IN THE CRIMINAL COURT OF COOK COUNTY:

THE PEOPLE OF THE STATE OF ILLINOIS)

vs.

Indictment No. 23912

EDWARD V. CICOTTE, et al.)

Bill of Particulars as to Count 1, Count 2, and Count 3, of Indictment No. 23912, filled in conformity to rule entered July 5th, 1921, by his Honor Judge Hugo Friend, one of the Judges of the Criminal Court of Cook County.

The defendants in the above entitled cause, and each of them, are hereby notified that the State will offer evidence tending to show that the defendants, Edward V. Cicotte, Claude Williams, Joe Jackson, Fred McMullin, Arnold Gandil, George Weaver, Oscar Felsch and Charles Risberg, in September and October of 1919 were engaged as base ball players and were members of a base ball club known as the American League Base Ball Club of Chicago, a corporation;

That said American League Base Ball Club of Chicago was engaged to play in competition with a certain other base ball club known as the National League Base Ball Club of Cincinnati, Ohio, a certain series of games of base ball; some of the games of said series to be played in Chicago and other games of said series to be played in Cincinnati, Ohio;

That the defendants, William Burns and Hal Chase were at various times connected with base ball as professional base ball players but were not participants in any of the games of the above mentioned series;

That the defendants, Joseph J. Sullivan, Rachael Brown, Abe Attell, Carl Zork, Ben Franklin, Ben Levi, Louis Levi, and David Zelzer were not connected with base ball as players, but were reputed to be gamblers or prize fighters and interested in the promotion of gambling enterprises and sporting events of questionable character;

That considerable public interest was manifested in the outcome of said series of games and each game of said series;

That each of said games was publicly regarded as an important sporting event and that the spectators of said games and each to them was required to pay an admission fee to the field where said games were played;

That the defendants participating in said games as players conspired, confederated and agreed together with the defendants not participating therein to so conduct themselves throughout the said games and each of said games and so manipulate their playing in each of said games as to make certain in advance of the playing of said games the outcome thereof and the winner thereof, and so as to make certain in advance of the playing of all of the games of said series the outcome of the majority of the games of said series and the winner of the majority of said series of games;

And the defendants not participating in said games, as base ball players, conspired, confederated and agree together and with the defendants participating in said games to operate among the spectators of said games and others and the general public to procure divers large sums of money by means of and by use of the confidence game.

That one Charles C. Nims, a resident of Chicago, Illinois, was unlawfully, fraudulently and feloniously swindled out of the sum of $250.00 by the defendant, Joseph J. Sullivan, who was then and there engaged in carrying out the conspiracy aforesaid and who did then and there obtain from the said Charles C. Nims the sum of $250.00 by means and by use of the confidence game contrary to the Statute in such cases made and provided.

And further particulars, the defendants are respectfully referred to the first, second, and third counts of said indictment.

Signed: Robert E. Crowe
State's Attorney of Cook County, Illinois
Signed: Geo E Gorman
Assistant State's Attorney

Appendix B:
Eddie Cicotte's Statistics

See table on following two pages.

Appendix B

Year	Team	Games	Starts	Complete Games	Shut-outs	Saves	Innings Pitched	Hits
1905	DET A	3	1	1	0	0	18	25
1908	BOS A	39	24	17	2	2	207.1	198
1909	BOS A	27	17	10	1	1	162.1	117
1910	BOS A	36	30	20	3	0	250	213
1911	BOS A	35	25	16	1	0	220	236
1912	BOS A	9	6	2	0	0	46	58
1912	CHI A	20	18	13	1	0	152	159
1912	TOT	29	24	15	1	0	198	217
1913	CHI A	41	30	18	3	1	268	224
1914	CHI A	45	30	15	4	3	269.1	220
1915	CHI A	39	26	15	1	3	223.1	216
1916	CHI A	44	19	11	2	5	187	138
1917	CHI A	49	35	29	7	4	346.2	246
1918	CHI A	38	30	24	1	2	266	275
1919	CHI A	40	35	30	5	1	306.2	256
1920	CHI A	37	35	28	4	2	303.1	316
Total		502	361	249	35	24	3226	2897

Statistics courtesy of Retrosheet (www.retrosheet.org).

Eddie Cicotte's Statistics

Home Runs	Runs	Earned Runs	Walks	Strike-outs	Wins	Losses	ERA
0	8	7	5	6	1	1	3.50
0	77	56	59	95	11	12	2.43
3	63	35	56	82	14	5	1.94
4	94	76	86	104	15	11	2.74
2	121	69	73	106	11	15	2.82
0	34	29	15	20	1	3	5.67
3	63	48	37	70	9	7	2.84
3	97	77	52	90	10	10	3.50
2	77	47	73	121	18	11	1.58
0	96	61	72	122	11	16	2.04
2	89	75	48	106	13	12	3.02
1	56	37	70	91	15	7	1.78
2	76	59	70	150	28	12	1.53
2	102	82	40	104	12	19	2.77
5	77	62	49	110	29	7	1.82
6	128	110	74	87	21	10	3.26
32	1161	853	827	1374	209	148	2.38

Chapter Notes

Introduction

1. *Chicago Tribune*, September 14, 1956.
2. *The Sporting News*, October 7, 1920, 2.

Chapter 1

1. Her first name is also rendered as Archangel. It is spelled Archangel on her gravestone.
2. Friend Palmer, *Early Days in Detroit* (Detroit: Hunt and June, 1906), 633.
3. *Detroit Free Press*, June 23, 1894.
4. *Detroit Free Press*, March 30, 1905, 10.
5. *Detroit Free Press*, March 28, 1905, 10.
6. *Detroit Free Press*, April 20, 1905. Some references list this game as a no-hitter, but both the *Free Press* and *The Sporting News* say that Savannah got one hit.
7. *Detroit Free Press*, June 22, 1905, 10.
8. Ty Cobb, *My Twenty Years in Baseball* (New York: Dover, 2009), 26. This book is a collection of articles Cobb wrote for the *New York Evening Journal* in 1925.
9. *Detroit Free Press*, September 6, 1905.
10. "Twirlers Show How It Is Done," *Washington Evening Star*, April 19, 1908, 60.
11. *Washington Post*, March 8, 1908.
12. *Indianapolis News*, May 10, 1906, 14.
13. *Indianapolis News*, March 31, 1908.
14. Ibid.
15. Lawrence Ritter, *The Glory of Their Times*, the enlarged edition (New York: William Morrow, 1984), 56.
16. *Washington Evening Star*, November 10, 1924, 25.
17. *Nebraska State Journal*, April 7, 1907, 22.
18. *Des Moines Tribune*, April 26, 1907, 6.
19. *Nebraska State Journal*, July 28, 1907, 23.
20. *Boston Globe*, August 24, 1907, 4.
21. James C. Mills, "The Finger-Nail Ball," *Baseball Magazine*, July 1908.
22. Bill James and Rob Neyer, *The Neyer/James Guide to Pitchers: An Historical Compendium of Pitching, Pitchers, and Pitches* (New York: Simon and Schuster, 2004), 40.

Chapter 2

1. Francis C. Richter, editor, *The Reach Official American League Base Ball Guide for 1906* (Philadelphia: A. J. Reach, 1906), 29.
2. *Detroit Free Press*, March 22, 1908, 18.
3. *Detroit Times*, August 3, 1908, 2.
4. Ibid.
5. *Boston Globe*, February 17, 1909, 4.
6. Ibid.
7. *Boston Globe*, February 19, 1909, 4.
8. *Boston Globe*, March 4, 1910, 5.
9. *Boston Globe*, April 29, 1910. President Taft started the tradition of throwing out the first ball a few weeks before at Washington's home opener.
10. *Milwaukee Sentinel*, December 28, 1912.
11. *Boston Globe*, January 20, 1911.
12. Bill Nowlin, *The Great Red Sox Spring Training Tour of 1911: Sixty-Three Games, Coast to Coast* (Jefferson, NC: McFarland, 2010), 21.
13. *Boston Globe*, April 4, 1911, 8.
14. *Boston Globe*, April 5, 1911, 8.
15. *Sporting Life*, June 17, 1911, 11.
16. Ibid.
17. *Boston Globe*, May 9, 1911, 8.
18. *Detroit Times*, February 8, 1912.
19. *Sporting Life*, February 3, 1912, 2.
20. *Washington Times*, April 25, 1912, 14.
21. *Boston Herald*, June 5, 1912.

22. *Baltimore Sun*, December 29, 1912, 14.

Chapter 3

1. John J. Ward, "The American League's Premier Catcher," *Baseball Magazine*, November 1916, 33.
2. Dan Lindner, "Kid Gleason," biography at SABR Bioproject web site, https://sabr.org/bioproj.
3. Charles Fountain, *The Betrayal: The 1919 World Series and the Birth of Modern Baseball* (New York: Oxford University Press, 2016), 77.
4. *Lake County Times* (Hammond, IN), July 20, 1912, 2.
5. *Chicago Tribune*, October 20, 1912, 29.
6. *Washington Times*, March 15, 1913, 11.
7. Martin Kohout, "Hal Chase," SABR Bioproject, https://sabr.org/bioproj.
8. *Dayton Herald*, June 2, 1913, 9.
9. *The Sporting News*, June 12, 1913, 1.
10. *Chicago Tribune*, February 21, 1914, 15.
11. *Toledo News-Bee*, September 2, 1914.
12. Rick Huhn, *Eddie Collins: A Baseball Biography* (Jefferson, NC: McFarland, 2008), 118.
13. Charles A. Comiskey, "Why I Bought Eddie Collins," *Baseball Magazine*, March 1915, 16.
14. *Chicago Tribune*, December 19, 1914, 8.
15. *Reading (PA) Times*, January 7, 1915, 7.
16. *Pittsburgh Post-Gazette*, February 7, 1915, 18.

Chapter 4

1. Eddie Cicotte, "The Secrets of Successful Pitching," *Baseball Magazine*, July 1918, 26.
2. *The Sporting News*, August 28, 1915.
3. *Louisville Courier*, August 7, 1915.
4. *Washington Post*, September 18, 1917, 8.
5. Eddie Cicotte, "The Shine Ball, and Other Things," *Baseball Magazine*, December 1917.
6. *Baseball Digest*, April 1948, quoted in Bill James and Rob Neyer, *The Neyer/James Guide to Pitchers: An Historical Compendium of Pitching, Pitchers, and Pitches* (New York: Simon and Schuster, 2004), 164.
7. Dave Lewis, "Once Over Lightly," *The Long Beach Independent*, July 25, 1953.
8. Joe Vila, "Gamblers Have Been Active in Baseball for Many Years," *Philadelphia Inquirer*, October 16, 1920.
9. "Nationals, 100 to 1. Price Boston Gambler Lays Against Flag Chances," *Washington Post*, February 24, 1911.
10. Ring Lardner, "Awake with the News," *Chicago Tribune*, October 13, 1915.
11. *Boston Traveler*, April 21, 1949.

Chapter 5

1. *The Sporting News*, May 2, 1918.
2. *Chicago Tribune*, March 2, 1917.
3. *Washington Post*, March 27, 1951.
4. Chick Gandil and Melvin Durslag, "This Is My Story of the Black Sox Scandal," *Sports Illustrated*, September 17, 1956.
5. *Washington Times*, September 27, 1917, quoted in Risberg's biography, written by Kelly Bayer Sagert and Rod Nelson, on the SABR BioProject website, http://sabr.org/bioproj.
6. *Chicago Tribune*, April 8, 1917, 17.
7. *St. Louis Post-Dispatch*, April 15, 1917.
8. Eddie Cicotte search at Baseball History Daily website, https://baseballhistorydaily.com/tag/ed-cicotte/.
9. Ibid.
10. *Day Book*, May 31, 1917.
11. Ty Cobb, *My Twenty Years in Baseball* (New York: Dover, 2009), 59, 62.
12. *Washington Post*, August 30, 1917, 8. Griffith, a star pitcher for Cap Anson's Chicago Colts of the 1890s, was famous for doctoring the ball. He even banged the baseball against his spikes to gouge holes in the cover.
13. *Buffalo Times*, March 20, 1925.
14. *New York American*, July 31, 1917.
15. *New York Tribune*, August 26, 1917.
16. *Chicago Tribune*, September 9, 1917, 18.
17. *Chicago Tribune*, June 17, 1917, 17.
18. *The Sporting News*, June 21, 1917, 1.
19. Jacob Pomrenke, "Call the Game! The 1917 Fenway Park Gamblers Riot," at https://jacobpomrenke.com.
20. *Philadelphia Evening Bulletin*, October 6, 1917.
21. *Detroit Free Press*, October 5, 1917.
22. *Chicago Tribune*, October 7, 1917.

23. Charles Einstein, *The Third Fireside Book of Baseball* (New York: Simon and Schuster, 1968), 490.
24. *New York Tribune*, October 14, 1917.
25. *Chicago Tribune*, October 16, 1917.
26. Brian E. Cooper, *Ray Schalk: A Baseball Biography* (Jefferson, NC: McFarland, 2009), 115.
27. *Ibid.*

Chapter 6

1. Eddie Cicotte, "The Shine Ball, and Other Things," *Baseball Magazine*, December 1917.
2. *Chicago Herald*, October 15, 1917.
3. Cicotte, "The Shine Ball, and Other Things."
4. *Ibid.*
5. During the Spanish-American War of 1898, exactly one player left his team and entered military service: Arlie Pond, a Baltimore Orioles pitcher who had recently earned his medical degree.
6. *Chicago Tribune*, March 21, 1918, 16.
7. Rick Huhn, *Eddie Collins: A Baseball Biography* (Jefferson, NC: McFarland, 2008), 144.
8. *Ibid.*
9. In fact, Quinn's ERA was the lowest ever posted in the PCL during its years as a AA-class league (1912 to 1945).
10. *Washington Post*, February 6, 1919.
11. *Baseball Magazine*, April 1919.
12. *New York Herald*, February 6, 1919.
13. *The Sporting News*, August 22, 1918.
14. Martin Kohout, "Hal Chase," biography on the Society for American Baseball Research (SABR) Bioproject web site, https://sabr.org/bioproj.

Chapter 7

1. G. W. Axelson, *Commy: The Life Story of Charles A. Comiskey* (Chicago: Reilly and Lee, 1919), 318.
2. *The Sporting News*, December 4, 1965, 23.
3. Ty Cobb and Al Stump, *My Life in Baseball: The True Record* (New York: Doubleday, 1961), 82–83.
4. "Kid Gleason Appointed Manager of the White Sox," *Chicago Tribune*, January 1, 1919.
5. *The Sporting News*, August 30, 1969, 29.
6. Charles Einstein, *The Fireside Book of Baseball* (New York: Simon and Schuster, 1987), 490.
7. Warren Brown, *The Chicago White Sox* (New York: G. P. Putnam's Sons, 1952), 118.
8. *The Sporting News*, April 24, 1919, 1.
9. *Chicago Tribune*, May 15, 1919, 19.
10. Jacob Pomrenke, editor, *Scandal on the South Side: The 1919 Chicago White Sox* (Phoenix: Society for American Baseball Research, 2015), 103–104.
11. *Chicago Tribune*, June 1, 1919, 17.
12. *Philadelphia North American*, September 17, 1919.
13. Chick Gandil and Melvin Durslag, "This Is My Story of the Black Sox Scandal," *Sports Illustrated*, September 17, 1956.
14. Sullivan may have been responsible for some underhanded dealings in the 1914 Series too. The Philadelphia A's, managed by Connie Mack and starring Eddie Collins, were prohibitive favorites against the upstart Boston National League club, the "Miracle Braves" who rose from last place in mid–July to the National League pennant. Somehow, the Braves swept the Series in four straight, and George M. Cohan, the famous song and dance man, won a bundle betting on the Braves. Sport Sullivan was the man who handled his bets.
15. This comes from the deposition that Eddie Cicotte gave in Charles Comiskey's office before he appeared before the grand jury in Chicago on September 28, 1920. The first part of the existing transcript, which contains this paragraph, can be seen at the Shoeless Joe Jackson Virtual Hall of Fame web site, at http://www.blackbetsy.com.
16. Gandil and Durslag, "This Is My Story of the Black Sox Scandal."
17. *Ibid.* Gandil stated that Joe Jackson was at this meeting, but Jackson later insisted that he did not attend any of the pre–Series fix meetings. Jackson said that Gandil discussed the fix with him privately.
18. The Sox played the Yankees in New York on September 17 (a doubleheader after the game of September 16 was rained out) and 18. By this account, Burns made his pitch to Gandil and the rest before Sullivan did. If so, Sullivan approached Gandil and Cicotte while Burns was busily trying to line up financing.
19. Many previous writers have assumed

the name Maharg is an alias, as it is Graham spelled backwards, but it actually was his name. Maharg is a real Scotch-Irish surname, and appears on the ex-boxer's birth certificate, as detailed by William F. Lamb in Maharg's biography on SABR.org.

20. Maharg also played for the Tigers in one game in 1912, when the Tigers players went on strike to support the suspended Ty Cobb. The Detroit club was set to play the Athletics in Philadelphia and recruited a motley group of local athletes, including Maharg, to fill in for one day. The pseudo–Tigers lost that day, 24-2.

21. When Eddie's grand-nephew Al Cicotte, a future major league pitcher, was interviewed by *The Sporting News* in 1953, he said that Eddie told Al's father the story of Comiskey and the bonus. Al Cicotte said that the bonus was for $5,000, and that Kid Gleason told Eddie that they were resting him for the upcoming World Series. *The Sporting News*, March 18, 1953, 15.

Chapter 8

1. *Boston Globe*, October 1, 1919.
2. *Brooklyn Eagle*, October 1, 1919, 20.
3. This quote comes from a synopsis of Eddie Cicotte's testimony before the Chicago grand jury in 1920. The quote appears in William F. Lamb, *Black Sox in the Courtroom: The Grand Jury, Criminal Trial and Civil Litigation* (Jefferson, NC: McFarland, 2013), 51.
4. This quote came from an interview with Eddie Collins by Joe Williams in the *New York World-Telegram*, July 10, 1943.
5. *Brooklyn Eagle*, October 2, 1919, 18.
6. *Boston Post*, October 2, 1919.
7. Charles Fountain, *The Betrayal: The 1919 World Series and the Birth of Modern Baseball* (New York: Oxford University Press, 2016), 99.
8. *Ibid.*
9. Eliot Asinof, *Eight Men Out: The Black Sox and the 1919 World Series* (New York: Henry Holt, 1963), 88.
10. *The St. Louis Star and Times*, December 13, 1930, 10.
11. *New York Times*, October 3, 1919, 11.
12. *The Sporting News*, February 25, 1937, 5.
13. Donald Honig, *Baseball America: The Heroes of the Game and the Times of Their Glory* (New York: Simon and Schuster, 1985), 109–110.
14. *The Sporting News*, February 25, 1937, 5.
15. Gene Carney, *Burying the Black Sox: How Baseball's Cover-Up of the 1919 World Series Fix Almost Succeeded* (Dulles, VA: Potomac Books, 2006), 198.
16. Victor Luhrs, *The Great Baseball Mystery* (New York: A. S. Barnes, 1966), 248.
17. *Chicago Tribune*, October 5, 1919.
18. *Boston Post*, October 5, 1919.
19. *Chicago Tribune*, October 6, 1919, 23.
20. *Ibid.*
21. *Chicago Tribune*, October 7, 1919, 21–22.
22. *Chicago Tribune*, October 7, 1919, 22.
23. *Ibid.*
24. This legend apparently began with Eliot Asinof, who created a character named "Harry F." who threatened Williams in *Eight Men Out* before Game Eight. Asinof later said he created this fictional character to thwart potential plagiarists. However, Eddie Cicotte's family says that Eddie was threatened during the Series.
25. *Chicago Tribune*, October 10, 1919, 19.

Chapter 9

1. *The Sporting News*, February 19, 1920, 6.
2. *Morning Call* (Allentown, PA), October 11, 1919, 1.
3. Hugh S. Fullerton, "Is Big League Baseball Being Run for Gamblers, with Players in the Deal?" *New York Evening World*, December 15, 1919, 3, 20.
4. *New York Evening World*, Dec. 16, 1919, 10.
5. Harold Seymour and Dorothy Seymour Mills, *Baseball: The Golden Age* (New York: Oxford University Press, 1971), 295–297.
6. *Collyer's Eye*, November 1, 1919, 1.
7. *Chattanooga News*, February 7, 1920, 9.
8. *The Sporting News*, February 12, 1920, 6.
9. *Ibid.*
10. I. E. Sanborn, "Ruth-less Yankees Mop Up Sox, 3–0, for Record Mob," *Chicago Tribune*, August 29, 1920.
11. *Chicago Tribune*, September 2, 1920.

12. Rick Huhn, *Eddie Collins: A Baseball Biography* (Jefferson, NC: McFarland, 2008), 172.
13. Lawrence Ritter, *The Glory of Their Times*, audiotape edition (St. Paul, MN: HighBridge Company, 1998). Wood's interviews were recorded in 1963 and 1965.
14. Eliot Asinof, *Bleeding Between the Lines* (New York: Holt, Rinehart & Winston, 1979), 93.
15. Donald Honig, *The Man in the Dugout: Fifteen Big League Managers Speak Their Minds* (Lincoln: University of Nebraska Press, 1977), 216.

Chapter 10

1. Gary Webster, *Tris Speaker and the 1920 Indians: Tragedy to Glory* (Jefferson, NC: McFarland, 2012), 32.
2. *Collyer's Eye*, September 11, 1920.
3. *Chicago Tribune*, September 19, 1920.
4. *Chicago Tribune*, September 23, 1920.
5. *Chicago Tribune*, September 23, 1920.
6. *Brooklyn Eagle*, September 24, 1920.
7. James T. Farrell, quoted by Eliot Asinof in *Eight Men Out: The Black Sox and the 1919 World Series* (New York: Henry Holt, 1963), 184.
8. *Philadelphia North American*, September 27, 1920.
9. *Brooklyn Eagle*, September 28, 1920, 1.
10. Kerr's 20th win made the White Sox the first major league team in history with four 20-game winners (Cicotte, Williams, Faber, and Kerr). The 1971 Baltimore Orioles are the only other team to match the feat.
11. *St. Louis Globe-Democrat*, February 21, 1933. This article was the last of ten in which Crusinberry related his memories of the scandal.
12. *Ibid.*
13. *Chicago Tribune*, March 6, 1951, 18.
14. *Los Angeles Times*, September 29, 1920, 2.
15. As noted before, Jackson always insisted that he was not at this meeting or any others concerning the fix.
16. William F. Lamb, *Black Sox in the Courtroom: The Grand Jury, Criminal Trial and Civil Litigation* (Jefferson, NC: McFarland, 2013), 51. The excerpts quoted here come from the testimony that was read into the official record in Joe Jackson's civil suit against Charles Comiskey for breach of contract in January of 1924. This and the grand jury synopsis made after the three ballplayers testified are the best sources for what Eddie actually said to the grand jury. Contemporary newspaper accounts, which were highly sensationalized, should be taken with a very large grain of salt.
17. Charles Fountain, *The Betrayal: The 1919 World Series and the Birth of Modern Baseball* (New York: Oxford University Press, 2016), 78.
18. Lamb, 51.
19. Gene Carney, *Burying the Black Sox: How Baseball's Cover-Up of the 1919 World Series Fix Almost Succeeded* (Dulles, VA: Potomac Books, 2006), 184.
20. Lamb, 51.
21. *Ibid.*
22. *Los Angeles Times*, September 29, 1920, 12.
23. *Evening Review* (East Liverpool, OH), September 28, 1920, 2.
24. Jackson's grand jury testimony, made on September 28, 1920, can be found on the Baseball Almanac web site, https://www.baseball-almanac.com/articles/joejackson.shtml.
25. *Los Angeles Times*, September 29, 1920, 2.
26. Jackson's grand jury testimony, Baseball Almanac.
27. "Statement of Claude 'Lefty' Williams (Excerpts)," from the Famous Trials web site, https://www.famous-trials.com/blacksox.
28. *Ibid.*
29. William F. Lamb, "Grand Jury Prosecutor Hartley Replogle and Public Exposure of the Black Sox Scandal," *The Inside Game*, SABR Deadball Era Committee Newsletter, June 2019, 22.
30. *Richmond Times-Dispatch*, October 1, 1920, 1.
31. *Chicago Evening American*, September 30, 1920.
32. *St. Louis Star and Times*, December 13, 1930, 10.
33. Richard Bak, *Detroitland: A Collection of Movers, Shakers, Lost Souls, and History Makers from Detroit's Past* (Detroit: Wayne State University Press, 2011), 238.
34. This letter can be seen on the Shoeless Joe Jackson Virtual Hall of Fame web site, http://www.blackbetsy.com.
35. *Boston Globe*, September 29, 1920, 9.
36. *St. Louis Globe-Democrat*, September 29, 1920, 9.

37. *Washington Times*, September 30, 1920.
38. *Cleveland Plain Dealer*, September 29, 1920.
39. *Boston Post*, November 27, 1920.
40. *New York Times*, October 4, 1920.
41. Bruce S. Allardice, "'Playing Rotten, It Ain't That Hard to Do': How the Black Sox Threw the 1920 Pennant," *Baseball Research Journal*, Spring 2016.
42. *The Sporting News*, October 7, 1920.
43. *Washington Times*, September 30, 1920.
44. In mid-season of 1902, manager John McGraw and several key players quit the Baltimore Orioles and jumped without warning to the New York Giants of the National League. That might be the only similar situation in baseball history.
45. *New York Times*, October 5, 1920, 3.
46. *Ibid.*

Chapter 11

1. Lawrence Ritter, *The Glory of Their Times, the enlarged edition* (New York: William Morrow, 1984), 222.
2. *Philadelphia Inquirer*, December 20, 1920, 14.
3. *Louisville Courier-Journal*, December 5, 1920.
4. *Philadelphia Inquirer*, November 12, 1920, 12.
5. *Chicago Tribune*, December 18, 1920, 19.
6. *Wisconsin State Journal*, March 29, 1921, 11.
7. *Kane (PA) Republican*, October 1, 1920, 1.
8. *Ottawa Citizen*, October 1, 1920, 14.
9. *Boston Globe*, October 2, 1920, 4.
10. Daniel Okrent, *Nine Innings: The Anatomy of a Baseball Game* (New York: Houghton Mifflin, 1995), 154.
11. Robert C. Cottrell, *Blackball, the Black Sox, and the Babe*, 239–240.
12. *Ibid.*, 251.
13. Charles Fountain, *The Betrayal: The 1919 World Series and the Birth of Modern Baseball* (New York: Oxford University Press, 2016), 204.
14. *Chicago Tribune*, March 13, 1921, 17.
15. Fountain, 200.
16. Fountain, 201.
17. Rick Huhn, *Eddie Collins: A Baseball Biography* (Jefferson, NC: McFarland, 2008), 191.
18. *Ibid.* This letter from Ban Johnson to Frank Navin, dated July 9, 1921, is found in the Black Sox Scandal file (American League records, 1914–1969) at the National Baseball Library, Cooperstown, New York.
19. *Des Moines Register*, July 18, 1921, 3.
20. *Chicago Tribune*, July 20, 1921, 2.
21. *Boston Globe*, July 25, 1921, 2.
22. *Ibid.*
23. *Ibid.*
24. *Los Angeles Times*, July 30, 1921.
25. *Chicago Tribune*, July 31, 1921.
26. *Chicago Tribune*, August 3, 1921, 2.
27. *Chicago Tribune*, August 1, 1921, 12.
28. *New York Times*, August 2, 1921.
29. *Washington Times*, August 4, 1921.
30. *Grand Forks (ND) Herald*, August 3, 1921, 8.
31. *Chicago Tribune*, August 3, 1921.
32. *New York Daily News*, August 3, 1921, 22.
33. *Washington Times*, August 4, 1921.
34. *Ibid.*
35. David Pietrusza, *Judge and Jury: The Life and Times of Judge Kenesaw Mountain Landis* (South Bend, IN: Diamond Communications, 1998), 187.

Chapter 12

1. Nelson Algren, "The Swede is a Hard Guy," *Southern Review* 7, no. 4 (Spring 1942): 873–879.
2. *Brooklyn Eagle*, July 24, 1921.
3. *New Castle (PA) News*, 8/4/21, 2.
4. *El Reno Daily Democrat*, August 19, 1921, 1.
5. *Wichita Daily Times*, August 18, 1921, 8.
6. *El Reno Daily Democrat*, August 17, 1921. The information on the Oklahoma tour comes from Ron Coleman's article, "The 1921 Black Sox Tour of Oklahoma," in the SABR Black Sox Scandal Research Committee newsletter, Volume 10, number 1, June 2018.
7. *Daily Oklahoman (Oklahoma City)*, August 27, 1921, 7.
8. *El Reno Daily Democrat*, August 27, 1921.
9. Jacob Pomrenke, "Bringing Home the Bacon: How the Black Sox Got Back into Baseball," *The National Pastime*, Volume 26

(Cleveland: Society for American Baseball Research, 2006), 45–53.
 10. Ibid.
 11. Ibid.
 12. *Dayton Daily News*, October 3, 1921, 12.
 13. Jacob Pomrenke, "Losing teeth, losing games: Eddie Cicotte and Swede Risberg fight on 1922 Black Sox tour," in the Society for American Baseball Research Black Sox Scandal committee newsletter, December 2017.
 14. Bill Haglund, "Fight on Merrill street corner brought an end to the Black Sox," *Wausau Daily Herald*, October 15, 1970.
 15. *The Sporting News*, April 19, 1923, 4.
 16. Richard Bak, "The sad story of Detroiter Eddie Cicotte and the Black Sox scandal" on Detroit Athletic Club website, https://www.detroitathletic.com.
 17. *New Orleans States*, July 18, 1923.
 18. William F. Lamb, *Black Sox in the Courtroom: The Grand Jury, Criminal Trial and Civil Litigation* (Jefferson, NC: McFarland, 2013), 155, quoted from a letter from John R. Hunter to Alfred Austrian.
 19. Ibid.
 20. Lamb, 163.
 21. Eliot Asinof, *Eight Men Out: The Black Sox and the 1919 World Series* (New York: Henry Holt, 1963), 257.
 22. According to the United States Bureau of Labor Statistics, the median income for male industrial workers in 1919 was 56.1 cents per hour, or $1,346 per year based on 2,400 working hours. Source: Paul H. Douglas, "Wages and Hours of Labor in 1919," *Journal of Political Economy* 29, no. 1 (Chicago: University of Chicago Press, 1921), 78.
 23. *St. Louis Post-Dispatch*, July 28, 1921, 1.
 24. Nelson Algren, *The Last Carousel* (New York: G. P. Putman's Sons, 1973), 274.

Chapter 13

 1. John B. Foster, editor, *Spalding's Official Base Ball Guide for 1921* (New York: American Sports Publishing, 1921), 7.
 2. David Pietrusza, *Judge and Jury: The Life and Times of Judge Kenesaw Mountain Landis* (South Bend, IN: Diamond Communications, 1998), 297.
 3. Harold Seymour and Dorothy Seymour Mills, *Baseball: The Golden Age* (New York: Oxford University Press, 1971), 384.
 4. *Washington Evening Star*, December 30, 1926, 30.
 5. *Chicago Tribune*, June 19, 1921, 2.
 6. Pietrusza, 302.
 7. *Albuquerque Journal*, January 3, 1927, 2.
 8. *Indianapolis News*, January 22, 1927.
 9. *Automotive News*, June 16, 2003.
 10. *New York Times*, June 26, 1937.
 11. *Detroit Free Press*, April 22, 1938.
 12. The details of this day come from Jacob Pomrenke's article, "An Opening Day ovation for a Black Sox exile in Detroit," in SABR's Black Sox Committee newsletter, June 2017, at SABR.org.
 13. *The Sporting News*, March 18, 1953, 15.
 14. Ibid.
 15. Furman Bisher, "This Is the Truth," *Sport*, October 1949.
 16. Chick Gandil and Melvin Durslag, "This Is My Story of the Black Sox Scandal," *Sports Illustrated*, September 17, 1956.
 17. Ibid.
 18. Ibid.
 19. *Marion Star*, September 14, 1956.
 20. *Appleton (WI) Post-Crescent*, September 25, 1956.
 21. *Logansport (IN) Press*, September 20, 1956.
 22. *Logansport (IN) Press*, September 18, 1956.
 23. Ibid.
 24. Ibid.
 25. Ibid.

Epilogue

 1. Chick Gandil and Melvin Durslag, "This Is My Story of the Black Sox Scandal," *Sports Illustrated*, September 17, 1956.
 2. Joe Falls, "Eddie Cicotte—at 81, He's Proud of Life He's Led; Family Is, Too," *The Sporting News*, December 6, 1965.
 3. *Los Angeles Times*, AP wire story, November 13, 1988.
 4. Richard Bak, *Cobb Would Have Caught It: The Golden Age of Baseball in Detroit* (Detroit: Wayne State University Press, 1991), 262.
 5. Cassidy, who died in 1984 at the age of 102, was still practicing law in Detroit at age 100.

6. *The Sporting News*, May 24, 1969, 44.
7. *Santa Cruz Sentinel*, August 10, 1969, 12.
8. Gerald C. Wood, *Smoky Joe Wood: The Biography of a Baseball Legend* (Lincoln: University of Nebraska Press, 2013), 318.
9. Eddie won one more championship than such great players as Ty Cobb, Ted Williams, Carl Yastrzemski and Barry Bonds, who played in the Series but never won it. Napoleon Lajoie, Ernie Banks, Rod Carew, and Ken Griffey Junior, among other stars, never appeared in one.
10. Bak, 262.

Bibliography

Books

Alexander, Charles. *John McGraw.* New York: Viking Penguin, 1988.
Asinof, Eliot. *Bleeding Between the Lines.* New York: Holt, Rinehart & Winston, 1979.
_____. *Eight Men Out: The Black Sox and the 1919 World Series.* New York: Henry Holt, 1963.
Axelson, G. W. *Commy: The Life Story of Charles A. Comiskey.* Chicago: Reilly and Lee, 1919.
Bak, Richard. *Cobb Would Have Caught It: The Golden Age of Baseball in Detroit.* Detroit: Wayne State University Press, 1991.
_____. *Detroitland: A Collection of Movers, Shakers, Lost Souls, and History Makers from Detroit's Past.* Detroit: Wayne State University Press, 2011.
Brown, Warren. *The Chicago White Sox.* New York: G. P. Putnam's Sons, 1952.
Burns, Ken, and Geoffrey C. Ward. *Baseball: An Illustrated History.* New York: Alfred A. Knopf, 1994.
Carney, Gene. *Burying the Black Sox: How Baseball's Cover-Up of the 1919 World Series Fix Almost Succeeded.* Dulles, VA: Potomac, 2006.
Cobb, Ty. *My Twenty Years in Baseball.* New York: Dover, 2009.
Cobb, Ty, and Al Stump. *My Life in Baseball: The True Record.* New York: Doubleday, 1961.
Cooper, Brian E. *Ray Schalk: A Baseball Biography.* Jefferson, NC: McFarland, 2009.
Cottrell, Robert C. *Blackball, the Black Sox, and the Babe.* Jefferson, NC: McFarland, 2002.
Einstein, Charles. *The Fireside Book of Baseball.* New York: Simon & Schuster, 1987.
_____. *The Third Fireside Book of Baseball.* New York: Simon & Schuster, 1968.
Foster, John B., editor. *Spalding's Official Base Ball Guide for 1921.* New York: American Sports Publishing, 1921.
Fountain, Charles. *The Betrayal: The 1919 World Series and the Birth of Modern Baseball.* New York: Oxford University Press, 2016.
Honig, Donald. *Baseball America: The Heroes of the Game and the Times of Their Glory.* New York: Simon & Schuster, 1985.
_____. *The Man in the Dugout: Fifteen Big League Managers Speak Their Minds.* Lincoln: University of Nebraska Press, 1977.
Huhn, Rick. *Eddie Collins: A Baseball Biography.* Jefferson, NC: McFarland, 2008.
James, Bill. *The Bill James Historical Baseball Abstract.* New York: Villard, 1987.
James, Bill and Rob Neyer. *The Neyer/James Guide to Pitchers: An Historical Compendium of Pitching, Pitchers, and Pitches.* New York: Simon & Schuster, 2004.
Johnson, Lloyd, editor. *The Encyclopedia of Minor League Baseball: The Official Record of Minor League Baseball.* Durham, NC: Baseball America, 1997.
Lamb, William F. *Black Sox in the Courtroom: The Grand Jury, Criminal Trial and Civil Litigation.* Jefferson, NC: McFarland, 2013.

Luhrs, Victor. *The Great Baseball Mystery*. New York: A. S. Barnes, 1966.
Nowlin, Bill. *The Great Red Sox Spring Training Tour of 1911: Sixty-Three Games, Coast to Coast*. Jefferson, NC: McFarland, 2010.
Okrent, Daniel. *Nine Innings: The Anatomy of a Baseball Game*. Boston: Houghton Mifflin, 1995.
Palmer, Friend. *Early Days in Detroit*. Detroit: Hunt and June, 1906.
Pietrusza, David. *Judge and Jury: The Life and Times of Judge Kenesaw Mountain Landis*. South Bend, IN: Diamond, 1998.
Pomrenke, Jacob, editor. *Scandal on the South Side: The 1919 Chicago White Sox*. Phoenix: Society for American Baseball Research, 2015.
Richter, Francis C., editor. *The Reach Official American League Base Ball Guide for 1906*. Philadelphia: A. J. Reach, 1906.
Ritter, Lawrence. *The Glory of Their Times, the enlarged edition*. New York: William Morrow, 1984.
Seymour, Harold. *Baseball: The Golden Age*. New York: Oxford University Press, 1971.
Spink, Alfred H. *The National Game, 2d ed*. St. Louis: National Game Publishing, 1911.
Webster, Gary. *Tris Speaker and the 1920 Indians: Tragedy to Glory*. Jefferson, NC: McFarland, 2012.
Wood, Gerald C. *Smoky Joe Wood: The Biography of a Baseball Legend*. Lincoln: University of Nebraska Press, 2013.

Newspapers

Appleton (Wisconsin) Post-Crescent
Baltimore Sun
Boston Globe
Boston Herald
Boston Post
Boston Traveler
Brooklyn Eagle
Chicago Evening American
Chicago Herald
Chicago Herald-Examiner
Chicago Tribune
Cleveland Plain Dealer
Daily Oklahoman (Oklahoma City)
Day Book (Chicago)
Dayton Daily News
Dayton Herald
Des Moines Register
Des Moines Tribune
Detroit Free Press
Detroit Times
El Reno Daily Democrat
Grand Forks (ND) Herald
Indianapolis News
Kane (PA) Republican
Logansport (Indiana) Press
Long Beach Independent
Los Angeles Times
Louisville Courier-Journal
Milwaukee Sentinel
Nebraska State Journal (Lincoln)
New York American
New York Daily News
New York Evening World
New York Times
New York Tribune
Ottawa Citizen
Philadelphia Inquirer
Philadelphia North American
Pittsburgh Post-Gazette
Pittsburgh Press
Reading (Pennsylvania) Times
St. Louis Globe-Democrat
St. Louis Post-Dispatch
St. Louis Star and Times
Toledo News-Bee
Washington Evening Star
Washington Post
Washington Times
Wisconsin State Journal

Magazines

Baseball Digest
Baseball Magazine
Baseball Research Journal
The National Pastime

Sport
Sporting Life
The Sporting News
Sports Illustrated

Internet Sites

Baseball History Daily. https://baseballhistorydaily.com
Baseball Reference. http://www.baseball-reference.com
Library of Congress. http://www.loc.gov
National Baseball Hall of Fame and Museum. http://www.baseballhall.org
Project Retrosheet. http://www.retrosheet.org
SABR Baseball Biography Project. http://sabr.org/bioproject
Shoeless Joe Jackson Virtual Hall of Fame. http://www.blackbetsy.com Society for American Baseball Research. SABR. http://www.sabr.org

Index

Acosta, Merito 40
Agnew, Sam 90
Alexander, Grover 30, 88, 122
Algren, Nelson 164
Allerdice, Bruce S. 137
Altrock, Nick 66–67
Arellanes, Frank 17
Armour, Bill 5
Asinof, Eliot 86, 94, 101, 113, 121, 149, 164, 177, 180
Attell, Abe 93, 125, 144, 146, 148
Austin, Jimmy 54
Austrian, Alfred 127, 131, 149, 150

Baker, Frank 26, 37, 73
Baker, Newton D. 75
Ball, Neal 25
Ball, Phil 35
Barry, Jack 37, 60
Bedient, Hugh 25–26, 30
Bell, Ralph 30
Bender, Albert (Chief) 26
Bennett, Harry 170–172
Benton, Rube 63, 65–66, 123–125, 134
Benz, Joe 31–32, 35, 40, 53, 75, 96
Birmingham, Joe 25
Blackburn, Lena 37, 39
Boland, Bernie 168
Borton, Babe 33
Boston gamblers riot 59–61
Brigham, Henry 130
Brown, Mordecai (Three-Finger) 35
Brown, Warren 82
Burns, Bill 92–93, 102, 125–126, 134–135, 144, 146, 148–149, 152–153
Burns, George 62–65

Cadillac, Antoine de la Mothe 4
Callahan, James (Nixey) 27–28, 31–32, 37–38
Cannon, Ray 160, 162
Carney, Gene 135
Carr, Charlie 9–10, 20
Carrigan, Bill 15–16, 22
Cassidy, Daniel 144–147, 162, 167, 180

Chance, Frank 32, 34
Chandler, A.B. 174
Chapman, Ray 42, 118
Chappell, Larry 42
Chase, Hal 22, 32–34, 36, 76–78, 93, 123–124, 144, 146, 165
Chech, Charlie 18
Chesbro, Jack 10, 88
Cicot, Jean (ancestor) 3
Cicotte, Al (grand-nephew) 172–174
Cicotte, Alva (brother) 172
Cicotte, Ambrose (father) 3–4
Cicotte, Archange (mother) 3–4
Cicotte, Eddie: birth 3; career with Boston 14–26; confession 127–128; death 180; employment at Ford 170–172; family 3–4; and Federal League 35–36; friendship with Ring Lardner 30, 100; grand jury testimony 128–130; in 1917 World Series 61–66; in 1919 World Series 96–108; and 1920 collapse 118–120, 137–138; involvement in scandal 87–94; knuckleball 8–9, 12–13, 15–16, 54–56; marriage 6; minor leagues 4–7, 9–12; no-hitter 54; outlaw ball 155–162; pronunciation of name 3, 68, 148; sale to Boston 12; sale to Chicago 26; shine ball 43–45, 57–59, 86; and 30-win bonus 94–95, 112; trial 140–154; and World War I 70, 73, 76
Cicotte, Eddie Junior (son) 176, 179
Cicotte, Edward V. (relative) 3
Cicotte, Francis of Assisi 3
Cicotte, Francis Xavier 3
Cicotte, Rose (daughter) 6, 102
Cicotte, Rose (Freer) (wife) 6, 46, 81, 141, 146, 176–177
Cicotte, Virginia (daughter) 46
Cicotte, Zacharias 3
Cobb, Ty 7–8, 33, 35, 40, 53, 57, 79–80, 117, 166–167, 178
Cochrane, Mickey 171
Collins, Eddie 26, 28, 37–38, 42, 47, 52–54, 58, 64–66, 72–73, 76, 80–84, 90, 92, 96, 98–99, 102, 106, 113–115, 118–120, 137, 139, 147, 163, 167–168, 170, 181
Collins, Jimmy 15

201

202 Index

Collins, John (Shano) 39, 59–60, 62–63, 83, 98, 112–113, 136, 139
Collins, Ray 20, 22, 25
Collyer, Bert 123
Collyer's Eye 111–112, 122
Comiskey, Charles 27, 32, 34–38, 39–43, 46, 51–52, 72, 74–76, 78–79, 81, 84, 87, 91, 93–95, 97, 100–102, 104, 109–111, 113–115, 119, 124, 126–128, 135–136, 138, 141, 145, 152, 154, 162–164, 167, 174, 180
Comiskey, Charles II (grandson) 180
Connolly, Tommy 116
Cooper, Brian E. 87
Costner, Kevin 182
Coumbe, Fritz 88
Crawford, Sam 10, 35, 80
Criger, Lou 16–17
Crowder, Enoch 73–74
Crowe, Robert 143–144, 153
Crusinberry, Jim 60, 81, 86, 105–106, 123, 126

Danforth, Dave 43–44, 56–57, 72, 75–76, 96, 168
Darrow, Clarence 153
Daubert, Jake 96, 98–99, 105
Devlin, Jim 49
Donovan, Patsy 19, 22–23
Douglas, Phil 32
Doyle, Larry 38
Duncan, Pat 99, 101, 103, 106, 174

Edwards, Henry 99
Eight Men Out 86, 94, 101, 113, 121, 149, 164, 177, 180
Eller, Howard (Hod) 77, 96, 105, 107
Emery ball 45
Engle, Clyde 7, 22
Evans, Billy 140
Evans, Frank O. 111–112

Faber, Urban (Red) 35–37, 40, 47, 56, 61, 63, 65–66, 70–72, 75, 80, 82, 86–89, 93, 114–115, 117–119, 121, 136, 138–139, 168, 180–181
Falk, Bibb 138
Falls, Joe 178–179
Farrell, James T. 125
Farrell, J.H. 156
Federal League 35
Felsch, Oscar (Happy) 39, 47–48, 58–59, 63–66, 74, 80–81, 83, 87, 91–92, 99, 101, 105, 107, 112–114, 118–119, 121, 124, 129–130, 133–135, 137, 148, 150, 151, 159, 161–163, 167, 175, 177, 180
Field of Dreams 68, 182
Fisher, Ray 23, 96
Flack, Max 90
Fletcher, Art 65
Fohl, Lee 86, 88
Ford, Henry 170–172
Ford, Henry II 172
Ford Motor Company 76, 170–172

Ford, Russ 45
Foster, Eddie 24
Fournier, Jack 37, 39, 46, 51
Frazee, Harry 59, 78
Frick, Ford 174
Friend, Hugo 146, 148–149, 151–152
Frumberg, A. Morgan 152
Fullerton, Hugh 32, 52, 97, 109–111, 123

gambling and game-fixing 48–50, 76–78
Gandil, Arnold (Chick) 51–52, 59, 63, 65–66, 72, 76, 82, 86–87, 90–93, 99, 101–104, 106, 112–113, 115, 124, 129, 132, 134–135, 144, 145, 145, 147, 148, 149, 153, 156, 163, 165, 167–168, 170, 174–175, 177, 178, 180–181
Gardner, Earle 22
Gehrig, Lou 33
Giamatti, A. Bartlett 170
Gilmore, James 35
Gleason, William (Kid) 28–29, 32, 36, 46, 72, 80–83, 87, 89, 93, 96–97, 99–100, 102, 104–107, 109–110, 112–113, 115–116, 118–120, 126–127, 138, 140, 147, 164, 168, 182
The Glory of Their Times 120
Gorman, George 145–146, 150–151
Grabiner, Harry 42, 110, 113, 127, 131, 136, 164
Graney, Jack 84
Great Baseball Mystery 99
Green, Danny 8
Gregg, Vean 25
Griffith, Clark 25–26, 57
Groh, Heinie 96, 98, 101, 105
Groom, Bob 25, 56

Hall, Charlie 20–21, 25–26
Hamilton, Earl 54
Hartzell, Roy 34
Heath, Spencer 116
Hendicksen, Olaf 26
Hendrix, Claude 122
Herzog, Buck 64–65
Heydler, John 77, 102, 110, 142
Hodge, Shovel 120
Hoie, Bob 81, 164
Holke, Walter 63, 66, 78
Holmes, James (Ducky) 11–12
Honig, Donald 121
Hooper, Harry 18, 30
Hoyne, Maclay 143, 145
Hudnall, George 162
Huff, George 15
Huggins, Miller 116
Hughes, Tom 24
Huhn, Rick 167
Hulbert, William 49
Huston, T.L. 136

Isbell, Frank 8

Jackson, Joe (Shoeless) 25, 41–42, 47–48, 59, 62–63, 65–66, 72–74, 80–81, 83–84, 91–92,

94–96, 98–99, 101, 103–107, 112, 114, 116–119, 128, 131–135, 137, 141, 143, 146–149, 151–152, 156, 158, 161–163, 165, 167, 174, 180–181
Jackson, Joe S. 6
James, Bill 89, 96, 107, 112, 125–126, 147, 167
Jennings, Hugh 28, 73
Johnson, Byron (Ban) 45, 59, 61, 71–72, 74, 75, 78, 84, 90, 102, 110, 115, 124, 127, 141–142, 145–148, 152–153, 166, 172
Johnson, Walter 24–25, 30, 33–35, 53, 58, 73, 94, 104
Jones, Davy 172
Jones, James Earl 182
Jourdan, Ted 113
Judge, Joe 73

Kauff, Benny 62, 64–65
Kelley, Henrietta 102, 108, 110, 131
Kerr, Dickey 82, 87, 89, 92–93, 97, 102–103, 106–107, 112, 114, 117–119, 124, 126, 138–139
Kiefer, Joe 138
Kitson, Frank 8
Klepfer, Ed 42
knuckleball 8–9, 12–13, 15–16, 54–56
Kohout, Martin 33
Koob, Ernie 56
Kopf, Larry 99, 101, 103–104
Krapp, Gene 25
Krause, Harry 23

Lajoie, Napoleon 25, 45
Lake, Fred 16, 17
Lamb, William F. 128, 133, 149
Landis, Kenesaw M. 142–145, 148, 154–156, 159–160, 166–170, 172, 174
Lange, Frank 32
Lardner, Ring 30, 50, 100, 104
Leibold, Harry (Nemo) 83, 92, 108, 112, 121, 138–139, 172
Leidy, George 6–7
Leonard, Hubert (Dutch) 75, 166
Loomis, Fred 123
Lord, Bris 26
Lowdermilk, Grover 87, 89, 96, 99
Lowe, Bobby 172
Luhrs, Victor 99, 104
Luque, Dolf 96
Lynn, Byrd 74, 83, 105, 137, 139
Lyons, Ted 181

Mack, Connie 23, 37–40
Magee, Lee 77–78
Maharg, Billy 92–93, 102, 125–126, 134, 146, 150, 153
Mails, Walter (Duster) 124
Mathewson, Christy 18, 30, 35, 53, 77–78, 88
Mayer, Erskine 96, 169
Mays, Carl 84, 87–88
McAleer, Jimmy 23–24, 26
McCarty, Lew 63
McClellan, Hervey 138–139

McCormick, Barry 60
McDonald, Charles A. 122, 127–128, 131–132, 150
McGraw, John 18, 34–35, 62, 78, 80
McGuire, Jim (Deacon) 15–16
McInnis, John (Stuffy) 37, 45
McIntyre, Matty 8
McLain, Denny 88
McMullin, Fred 45, 60–63, 65, 83, 87, 91–93, 104, 112, 114, 120, 129, 135, 138, 144, 146, 148, 174
McRoy, Robert 23
Meek, David 159–160
Milan, Clyde 24, 52, 73
Miller, Ward 54
Moeller, Danny 24
Moran, Pat 106
Moren, Lew 13
Murnane, Tim 21
Murphy, Eddie 83, 119, 138–139, 168

Nallin, Dick 84
Navin, Frank 11, 23, 146–147
Neale, Earle (Greasy) 99, 103
Niekro, Phil 13
Noyes, Win 169

O'Brien, Buck 23, 25
Oldring, Rube 26
O'Neill, Norris (Tip) 110
O'Neill, Steve 25
Owens, Brick 137

Pape, Larry 18, 25
Payne, George 116
Peckinpaugh, Roger 25, 121
Pegler, Westbrook 175–177
Pelty, Barney 25–26
Perritt, William (Pol) 62, 77
Pershing, John J. 142
Pick, Charlie 45
Pipp, Wally 46, 73, 113
Pomrenke, Jacob 81, 128, 149
Powers, John 35
Pratt, Del 54
Prindiville, Edward 148, 151

Quinn, Jack 19, 75–76, 83–84, 87, 181

Rariden, Bill 63, 65, 78
Rath, Morrie 96, 98, 101, 105, 130, 151, 182
Replogle, Hartley 124, 127–128, 130–133, 143, 149–150
Reuther, Walter 171
Reutlinger, Harry 133, 135
Rice, Grantland 114
Richter, Francis 161
Rigler, Cy 105
Ring, Jimmy 77, 96, 103–104, 106
Risberg, Charles (Swede) 52–53, 62, 65, 74, 80, 87, 91–92, 98–99, 101, 104, 106, 112, 114–116,

118–119, 121, 129, 135, 137, 144, 148, 150, 156, 158–163, 166–168, 170, 176–177, 180
Ritter, Larry 120
Roach, Roxie 22
Robbins, George S. 60
Robertson, Charlie 96
Robertson, Dave 63, 65
Rogell, Billy 179, 182
Rogers, Will 142, 170
Rose, Pete 170
Roth, Andy 5–6
Roth, Bob (Braggo) 39, 42
Rothstein, Arnold 93, 97–98, 103, 107, 146, 148–149, 152, 175
Roush, Edd 35, 96, 99–100, 103, 105
Rowland, Clarence (Pants) 37–38, 40, 45, 51, 54–56, 61–65, 72–73, 80–81, 167, 168
Rucker, George (Nap) 7, 9, 13
Ruether, Walter (Dutch) 96, 98–99, 106
Runyon, Damon 58–59
Ruppert, Jacob 136
Russell, Ewell (Reb) 32, 34, 36, 40, 46–47, 54, 56, 64, 72, 75, 96, 168
Ruth, George (Babe) 33, 43, 46, 59, 79, 84, 87–88, 90, 108, 114, 116–118, 178, 181

Sailer ball 57–58
Sallee, Harry (Slim) 62–63, 96, 100, 107
Sanborn, I.E. 53, 58, 63, 84, 118
Schaefer, Herman (Germany) 24
Schalk, Ray 28–29, 39, 54, 60, 65–67, 72, 76, 79, 83, 87, 92, 100–101, 103, 105, 112, 114, 132, 139, 147–148, 164, 167–168, 170, 174–175, 180, 182
Schmidt, Charley (Boss) 13
Schmitt, Leonard 160
Schultz, Todd 135
Schupp, Ferdie 63
Scott, Jim 32, 34–36, 40, 54, 56, 70, 96
Severeid, Hank 87
Shellenback, Frank 44–45, 82, 84, 96, 115
Sheridan, John B. 54, 56
shine ball 43–45, 57–59, 86
Short, Benedict 147, 151, 167
Sinclair, Harry 35
Sisler, George 54
Smith, Clarence (Kid) 32
Society for American Baseball Research (SABR) 81, 149
Somers, Charles 42
Speaker, Tris 15, 18, 21, 33, 35, 40, 46, 58, 86, 88, 99, 104, 114, 166–167
spitball 4, 6, 8, 10, 16, 115
Stahl, Charles (Chick) 15
Stahl, Jake 18, 24

Stallings, George 33, 34
Stanage, Oscar 169, 172
Stricklett, Elmer 10
Strunk, Amos 45, 138
Sullivan, James (Sport) 49–50, 52, 89–93, 97, 103–104, 106, 120, 144, 146, 165, 172, 174, 182
Summers, Ed 8–9, 12–13, 16

Taft, William Howard 19, 142
Taylor, Charles 14
Taylor, John I. 14–17, 19–23
Terry, Zeb 45–46, 52–53
Tesreau, Jeff 62
Thomas, Forrest (Frosty) 9, 13
Thormahlen, Hank 73
Tinker, Joe 35

Unglaub, Bob 15

Veach, Bobby 38, 172
Veeck, Bill 110, 114, 180
Veeck, William L. 122, 124
Vick, Sammy 87
Vila, Joe 140

Wagle, Henry (Kelly) 157–158
Wagner, Heinie 18, 22
Walsh, Ed 8, 10, 28, 31–32, 48, 53, 88
Walsh, Jimmy 45
Weaver, George (Buck) 28, 30, 35, 39, 45–46, 60–65, 73, 76, 82, 87, 91–92, 98, 101, 110, 112, 114, 118–120, 133–135, 141, 148, 150–152, 156, 159, 162, 165, 168, 170, 174–175, 180–181
White, Guy (Doc) 31, 51
Wilhelm, Hoyt 13
Wilkinson, Roy 89, 96, 99, 107, 118–119, 139, 169
Williams, Claude (Lefty) 45, 47, 56, 58, 65, 73–75, 80–82, 87, 89, 91–93, 95, 97, 100, 102, 104–107, 112, 114, 117–118, 124–125, 132–135, 137, 141, 143, 147–149, 151–152, 158, 161, 168, 174, 180–181
Williams, Rip 21
Wilson, Woodrow 53, 75
Wingo, Ivey 98
Wolfgang, Mellie 32, 40, 53
Wood, Joe 15–17, 20–21, 23, 25, 120, 166, 180–181
Woodruff, Harvey 104–105

Young, Denton (Cy) 15, 17, 49, 88, 182

Zeider, Rollie 33
Zimmermann, Heinie 62, 65–66, 90–91, 124

www.ingramcontent.com/pod-product-compliance
Ingram Content Group UK Ltd.
Pitfield, Milton Keynes, MK11 3LW, UK
UKHW042003140426
5217IPUK00015B/964